Starting Points for Your Internet Exploration

The Web is like thousands of TV channels or 10,000 New York Public Libraries—it includes volumes and volumes of information. You can browse the Web, following links in an intuitive way, or you can search for what interests you. Here is a brief list of good starting places. Each of these documents lists or organizes other documents to make it easy for you to find your way to the documents you find intriguing or useful.

The All-in-One Search Page

http://www.albany.net~wcross/an1srch.html

Magellan: The McKinley Group's Internet directory and search tool

http://www.mckinley.com

GNN's Whole Internet Catalog

http://www.gnn.com/gnn/wic

InfoSeek: A search service

http://www.infoseek.com

Inktomi: A search tool using parallel computing

http://inktomi.berkeley.edu

Lycos: An enormous searchable database

http://www.lycos.com

Open Market's Commercial Sites Index

http://www.directory.com

Yahoo: A subject-oriented list

http://www.yahoo.com

Surfing the Internet with Netscape Navigator 2

Surfing the Internet with Netscape® Navigator 2

Second Edition

Daniel A. Tauber and Brenda Kienan

SYBEX®

San Francisco • Paris • Düsseldorf • Soest

Associate Publisher: Carrie Lavine
Acquisitions Manager: Kristine Plachy
Editor: Pat Coleman
Project Editors: Kris Vanberg-Wolff and Maureen Adams
Technical Editor: Peter Stokes
Chapter Artist: Lucka Zivny
Technical Artist: Lucka Zivny
Desktop Publishing Specialist: Alissa Feinberg
Production Coordinator: Alexa Riggs
Indexer: Ted Laux
Companion Disk Developer: Brenda Kienan
Companion Disk Designer: Asha Dornfest
Cover Designer: Design Site
Cover Illustrator/Photographer: Daniel Ziegler

Disk Warranty

SYBEX warrants the enclosed disk to be free of physical defects for a period of ninety (90) days after purchase. If you discover a defect in the disk during this warranty period, you can obtain a replacement disk at no charge by sending the defective disk, postage prepaid, with proof of purchase to:

> SYBEX Inc.
> Customer Service Department
> 2021 Challenger Drive
> Alameda, CA 94501
> (800) 227-2346
> Fax: (510) 523-2373

After the 90-day period, you can obtain a replacement disk by sending us the defective disk, proof of purchase, and a check or money order for $10, payable to SYBEX.

Disclaimer

SYBEX makes no warranty or representation, either express or implied, with respect to this medium or its contents, its quality, performance, merchantability, or fitness for a particular purpose. In no event will SYBEX, its distributors, or dealers be liable for direct, indirect, special, incidental, or consequential damages arising out of the use of or inability to use the medium or its contents even if advised of the possibility of such damage.

The exclusion of implied warranties is not permitted by some states. Therefore, the above exclusion may not apply to you. This warranty provides you with specific legal rights; there may be other rights that you may have that vary from state to state.

Copy Protection

None of the content on the disk is copy-protected. However, reselling or distributing copies of the contents of the disk without authorization is expressly forbidden.

To L.E.M.—sister, mother, friend
and to her mother and family, with gratitude

Acknowledgments

A book is always a collaborative effort; this one has been especially so. We are indebted to the many people who have helped to make it happen.

Thanks go to Marc Andreessen and the fine people at Netscape for a remarkable product, also to Jon Mittelhauser and Kipp E.B. Hickman, also of Netscape, for their good counsel and the extraordinary promptness of their e-mail answers to our many questions.

At Sybex, our gratitude goes to the editorial team of Pat Coleman, whose lightning swift pen cut swathes through our prose, and Kris Vanberg-Wolff and Maureen Adams, whose stream of e-mail messages spurred us on. Thanks also to the production team of Alissa Feinberg and Alexa Riggs, who made manuscript and screen shots into an actual book; to Lucka Zivny, who transformed our scribbles into the charming line drawings; and to indexer Ted Laux, master of his craft, who compiled references with admirable compulsion.

Special thanks go to technical reviewer Peter Stokes, who has been friend and colleague through two full cycles of career changes already; to Carrie Lavine, who could market sand in the Sahara; to Sybex heroines Barbara Gordon, Chris Meredith, Kristine Plachy, Janet Boone, and Celeste Grinage, who have all kept their humor and grace through "interesting" times; and to Kip Triplett, Bruce Spatz, and Jim Curran for their new energy and general efforts.

Special thanks, too, to Asha Dornfest for revising Chapter 7 and drafting Appendices B and C, also for making the disk a reality and for her general good cheer; and to the multitalented Michael Gross for his writing contributions to the first edition of this book.

Our profound gratitude goes to family and friends for their support and all the understanding they can muster. For the record, we name: Joani and Jessica Buerhle; Sharon Crawford; Jerry Doty; Rion Dugan; Fred Frumberg; Jessica, Martin, and Lori Grant; Carol Heller; Xuan Mai Le, Katri Foster, and Peter Bazner; the whole McArdle family; Amy Miller; Carolyn Miller; Lonnie Moseley; Wynn Moseley and her family; Freeman Ng; Gino Reynoso; Cordell Sloan; Margaret Tauber; Ron and Frances Tauber; John Undercoffer; Mary Undercoffer; the Undercoffer brothers Carl and Eric; Savitha Varadan; and Robert E. Williams III.

Finally, a fond tip-of-the-hat to Dr. R. S. Langer, gentleman and scholar. It was our privilege to know him and to work with him.

Contents at a Glance

Contents

Part Two:
Navigating and Publishing with Netscape
45

Chapter 3
Navigating Netscape

47

Chapter 4

Newsgroups and E-Mail the Netscape Way

81

Chapter 5
Good and Useful Starting Points

101

Chapter 6
Spots on the Web You Won't Want to Miss

127

Chapter 7
Tools and Techniques for Searching and Finding

179

Chapter 8
You Too Can Be a Web Publisher

213

Part Three:
Getting Started with Netscape
259

Chapter 9
Laying the Groundwork for Installing Netscape

261

Chapter 10
Getting Netscape Navigator Going
309

Chapter 11
Getting and Installing Video Viewers and Sound Players
327

Appendix A
Get Smart with SmartMarks
341

Introduction

Everybody wants to get in on the Internet. If you're one of those folks, but you don't want to have to learn Unix and type a lot of obscure commands to get anywhere, read on. This book, written in plain English and filled with how-to know-how, will get you started in no time exploring and using the World Wide Web, the fastest growing portion of the Internet, via Netscape Navigator version 2. Netscape is the highly popular Web browser used by more than 70 percent of all users active on the Web today. It includes security and other features you won't find in any other Web browser.

 Netscape regularly improves and updates the look of its software. The contents of this book reflect the state of Netscape Navigator 2 as of our publication date. Although the functionality we describe should not differ from the way your browser works, some of our screen captures may not match exactly what you see on your screen.

What's New in Version 2

Netscape Navigator version 2 adds scads of new and improved features to an already successful product. Some of these features enhance the layout options available to those who publish on the Web; others add new dimension in the form of Java technology, which allows dynamic on-screen motion and new frontiers in interactive Web page capabilities. With Netscape version 2 you'll get:

◆ Frames, which, like windows within the bigger Netscape viewing window (or somewhat like split-screen TV), allow more than one Web document to be viewed at a time on your screen

◆ New, expanded e-mail and Usenet news capabilities that let you receive messages from others and send them with ease as well as embed graphics and links to Web pages in your messages

◆ More control over document format features such as text color and alignment

◆ Faster display of images and graphics

◆ Exciting, easy-to-use interactivity in the form of new Java *applets* ("small" programs) that will allow the inclusion in Web pages of such innovations as animations, games, drop-down menus, ticker-tape-style news feeds, and even sophisticated applications useful to professionals and research and business teams

This keeps Netscape way ahead of the pack, still setting the standards in the Web browser race toward new technologies.

Is This Book for You?

If you want to start exploring the beautiful, graphical World Wide Web using Netscape, this book is for you.

This book has been written by two Internauts with years of combined experience and professional Internet involvement. It avoids jargon and explains any necessary terms clearly. It's a great place to start for beginners, but that's not all. Because it includes information on publishing on the Internet, on the latest searching tools, and on getting and using special tools to enhance your Web experience, this book is a good follow-up for people already familiar with the Internet.

Getting and installing Netscape involves setting up a connection that is able to "introduce" your Internet service provider to Netscape each and every time you access the Internet using Netscape. Setting up this connection was quite a tricky procedure in days gone by, but don't worry. This book covers connecting via Windows 95, which includes all the software you need to make a Netscape connection through your own Internet service provider. This book also covers making your connection with some other very popular options: Netcom's NetCruiser software and CompuServe's NetLauncher. Using such providers as these gives you the vital connecting software (known as SLIP/PPP) you need.

This book also shows you clearly how to get Netscape from the Internet itself and how to set up a working, reliable connection. You'll be up and running in no time.

 Instructions for setting up a connection and getting Netscape are in Chapters 9 and 10; information on service providers is in Appendix B.

Throughout this book you'll find the Internet addresses of dozens, if not hundreds, of sites that will provide you with additional information on every topic in this book, from getting connected and getting tech support to publishing a bang-up Web page to announcing your Web page. You'll also find the Internet addresses of interesting sites that will get you started and keep you going in your Web travels—these sites cover topics from Art to Education, Personal Finance, Sports, and Travel, with lots of cool and useful stuff in between.

What's on the What's Out There Disk

On the disk that comes with this book you'll find a customized What's Out There home page, containing every Internet address mentioned in this book and then some. Through the What's Out There disk you'll have access to hand-picked sites that are especially useful and intriguing; you'll also have access to literally millions of sites via especially good online directories and search facilities. You can make this convenient page your own start-up home page so you'll see its wide variety of Internet resources as starting-place options every time you start Netscape, or you can just keep it handy for reference when you want a quick route to something of special interest.

 Appendix C shows you how to install and use the companion disk that comes with this book. Instructions for navigating the page are a part of the page itself.

How This Book Is Organized

This book is organized into eleven chapters, beginning, logically enough, with Chapter 1, a brief introduction to the Internet. Chapter 2 goes into more detail about the World Wide Web and how Netscape can get you there. Chapters 3 and 4 tell you in basic terms how to use Netscape to its best advantage, Chapter 5 describes some good launch points for your Web travels, and Chapter 6 describes a variety of useful and intriguing places you might want to visit. With basic navigation skills under your belt, you might want to focus your Web travels; Chapter 7 tells you how to use the new search technologies that are such an important part of maximizing your Internet experience. Chapter 8 follows up by showing how you too can be a Web publisher—it includes a primer on HTML, the mark-up language used to create Web documents, along with tips for successful Web page design and even information on how to publicize your Web page. Chapter 9 shows you how to get connected using various popular options for Internet connectivity and then how to get Netscape from the Internet itself. Chapter 10 follows up by providing step-by-step instructions for setting up Netscape to work with your Internet service. Chapter 11 tells you how to get and use video viewers and sound players—special tools that will further enhance your experience of Netscape and the World Wide Web.

Internet and Web terms are defined throughout the book, but you might want to look something up as you go along; so toward the back of the book you'll find a handy glossary.

You'll also find three appendices: Appendix A describes SmartMarks, a terrific Netscape add-on that helps you to organize your bookmarks (listings of favorite Web sites), automatically monitor changes in Web pages, and search the Internet efficiently; Appendix B is a listing of Internet service providers that will work with Netscape; and Appendix C, as mentioned previously, describes what's on the disk that comes with this book.

● Conventions Used in This Book

Surfing the Internet with Netscape Navigator 2 uses various conventions to help you find the information you need quickly and effortlessly. Tips, Notes, and Warnings, shown here, are placed strategically throughout the book to help you zero in on important information in a snap.

Here you'll find insider tips and shortcuts—information meant to help you use Netscape more adeptly.

Here you'll find reminders, asides, and bits of important information that should be emphasized.

 Here you'll find cautionary information describing trouble spots you may encounter either in using the software or in using the Internet.

A simple kind of shorthand used in this book helps to save space so more crucial matters can be discussed; in this system, directions to "pull down the File menu and choose Save" will appear as "select File ➤ Save," and the phrase "press Enter" appears as "press ↵," for example.

Long but important or interesting digressions are set aside as boxed text, called *sidebars*.

These Are Called "Sidebars"

In boxed text like this you'll find background information and side issues—anything that merits attention but can be skipped in a pinch.

And throughout the book you'll find special What's Out There sidebars telling you exactly where on the World Wide Web you can find out more about whatever's being discussed or where to find the home page being described.

What's Out There

The URL for the home page of interest at the moment will appear in a different font, for example, `http://www.dnai.com/~vox/netscape/nsad.html`.

Let's Get This Show on the Road...

Enough about what's in the book and on the disk—to start your Internet exploration using Netscape, turn to Chapter 1; to find out how to get and install the software, turn to Chapter 9.

If You Need Assistance

For answers to your questions about Netscape, call (800) 320-2099. Make sure you have your credit card handy if you have yet to purchase your copy of Netscape Navigator. You can also get help via e-mail at client@netscape.com.

Technical support for Windows 95 Dial-Up Networking is available at (800) 936-4200 or (206) 635-7000, help with Netcom's NetCruiser is available at (800) 353-6600 or support@ix.netcom.com, and help with CompuServe's NetLauncher is available at (800) 848-8900.

Part One:

The Internet, the World Wide Web, and Netscape

The Big Picture

You'd have to live in a vacuum these days not to have heard of the Internet. Scarcely a day goes by without some mention of it on the nightly news or in the local paper. Internet e-mail addresses are even becoming common in advertisements. Millions of people—inspired by excited talk and armed with spanking new accounts with Internet service providers—are taking to the Internet, with visions of adventures on the Information Superhighway.

Contrary to all the fashionable hype, the first time you attempt to "cruise" the Internet, you may be in for a rude awakening. Until recently, most access to the Internet was via text-based viewers that left a lot to be desired in the realm of aesthetics and ease of use. The Internet was trafficked for a long time only by academicians and almost nerdy computer enthusiasts.

In fact, with your old or low-budget Internet account a prompt that looks like this:

```
%
```

may be all you get, even if you're running the thing under Windows. Your trek into cyberspace may feel more like a bumpy ride on an old bicycle.

● A Netscape View of the Internet

That's why Netscape Navigator is so great: It offers an elegant point-and-click interface to guide you through the Internet's coolest resources, all linked to a growing number of global Internet resources. Netscape Navigator is a *browser*—a program with which you can view graphically intriguing, linked documents all over the world and search and access information in a few quick mouse clicks. You don't have to type cryptic commands or deal with screens filled with plain text; all you have to do is point and click on highlighted words (or pictures) to follow the links between related information in a single, giant web of linked "pages." Figure 1.1 compares a text-based view of the Internet with a Netscape view.

Within the Internet is a special network of linked documents known as the *World Wide Web*. With Netscape (as it's commonly called), you can perform point-and-click online research on the Web or just follow your whims along an intuitive path of discovery. Netscape is available for all popular computers—PCs running Windows, Macintoshes, even Unix workstations. Netscape on any of these machines looks just about the same too. (In this book, we focus mainly on the Windows version, although many of the principles we discuss apply as well to the Unix and Mac versions.) There are some differences between using Netscape on a machine that's networked and a machine that stands alone, though.

To run Netscape on your stand-alone (un-networked) PC, you need a dial-up connection to the Internet via a service provider, and not just any service provider—you need one with specific capabilities. You also need software (known as SLIP or PPP) that provides a connection between Netscape and your Internet service provider. (Don't worry. This is not difficult.)

Windows 95 comes with SLIP/PPP software; if you have Windows 95, making an Internet connection that lets you use Netscape Navigator is easy as pie. You have other options for getting connected too—for example, you can run Netscape with Netcom's NetCruiser software, with CompuServe's Net-Launcher, or with any of several others. Turn to Chapters 8 and 9 to find out how to set up your Internet connection and then get and use Netscape.

```
                                                        (p1 of 18)

  [IMAGE]
                THE PALACE OF FINE ARTS - A BRIEF HISTORY


  _____

    "The Palace was not designed as 'a Valentine for San Francisco.' Maybeck
    visualized its colonnade streaming with people, finding a reward within the
    great doors."


    The task of creating a Palace of Fine Arts for the 1915 Panama-Pacific
    International Exposition fell to the architect Bernard R. Maybeck,
    then fifty years old and known for his innovative ideas. Setting to
    work on this new project, he chose as his theme a Roman rain,
    mutilated and overgrown, in the mood of a Piranesi engraving. But this
    ruin was not to exist solely for itself to show "the mortality of
-- press space for more, use arrow keys to move, '?' for help, 'q' to quit
    Arrow keys: Up and Down to move. Right to follow a link; Left to go back.
    H)elp O)ptions P)rint G)o M)ain screen Q)uit /=search [delete]=history list
```

THE PALACE OF FINE ARTS - a brief history

"The Palace was not designed as 'a Valentine for San Francisco.' Maybeck visualized its colonnade streaming with people, finding a reward within the great doors."

The task of creating a Palace of Fine Arts for the 1915 Panama-Pacific International Exposition fell to the architect Bernard R. Maybeck, then fifty years old and known for his innovative ideas. Setting to work on this new project, he chose as his theme

FIGURE 1.1: Here you can see the difference between the old text-based view of the Internet (above) and the easy-to-use, graphically pleasing Netscape view of the Internet (below).

Let's take a quick look at the Internet first. Then, in the next chapter, we'll investigate how the Web fits into the Internet and just what kinds of stuff you can look at out there.

What's Out There

As we go along, we're going to tell you what you can find using Netscape and where that stuff is located. You'll see notes like this describing an item of interest and giving you the item's URL (its *Uniform Resource Locator*, or address on the Web). Don't worry if you don't understand this URL business yet—you will soon, and then you can look for the stuff we've described.

What the Internet Is All About

So what is this Internet thing we're hearing so much about? At its most basic level, you can think of the Internet as a vast collection of even vaster libraries of information, all available online for you to look at or retrieve and use. At another level, the Internet might be thought of as the computers that store the information and the networks that allow you to access the information on the computers. And finally (lest we forget who made the Internet what it is today), it is a collection of *people*—people who act as resources themselves, willing to share their knowledge with the world. This means, of course, that when you interact with the Internet—particularly when you make yourself a resource by sharing communications and information with others—you become a part of the vast network we call the Internet.

The Internet is a global network of networks. When your stand-alone machine gets connected to the Internet, special software on your machine (obtained from your Internet access provider) "tricks" the Internet into accepting your machine as one of the networks that make up the Internet. Your machine—and you—become literally a part of the Internet.

The idea of the Information Superhighway, popularized in part by the Clinton administration, is a convenient metaphor: information flowing great distances at incredible speeds, with many on-ramps of access and many potential destinations. In the Information Superhighway of the future, we might expect an electronic replacement for the everyday postal system (this has already begun to happen in Germany, we're told) and integration of our TV, phone, and newspapers into online information and entertainment services.

What's Out There

The Electronic Frontier Foundation (EFF) is active in lobbying to ensure that the Information Superhighway of the future includes protections for individual rights. You can find out about the EFF, and what it is up to, at `http://www.eff.org`. Other information about the government's initiative for building the Information Superhighway is available at `http://far.mit.edu/diig.html`.

We're not quite up to that fully integrated superhighway envisioned by futurists yet, but the Internet as it exists today delivers plenty of power. The resources and information you find on the Internet are available for use on the job, as part of personal or professional research, or for just plain fun. No matter how you view the Internet, the idea that individuals as well as corporations can access information around the world has a particular appeal that borders on the irresistible.

The Internet does act much like a highway system. High-speed data paths, called *backbones*, connect the major networks; these actually do function much like an electronic version of the interstate highways. Through lower-speed *links*, local networks tie in to the Internet, much as city streets feed onto highways (see Figure 1.2). The beauty of the Internet system is that not all networks are, or even need to be, directly connected, because the Internet structure is one of *interconnection*. You can in effect hop from network to network to get where you want and what you want.

The highway metaphor begins to break down, however, when you realize that the Internet transcends geography. It's a global system, that's true,

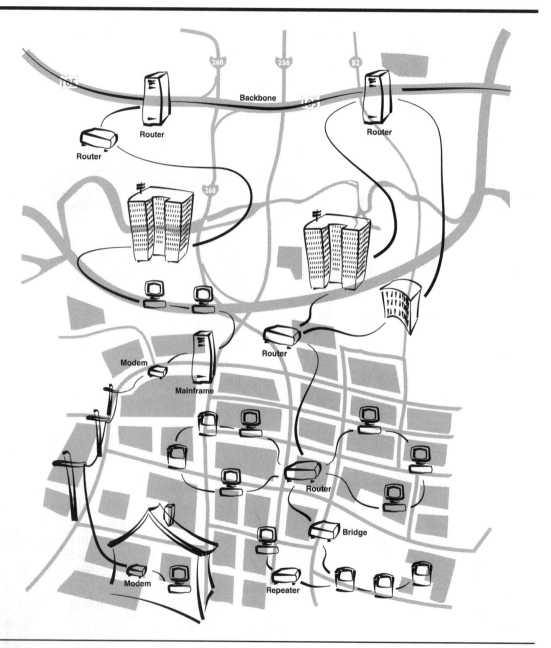

FIGURE 1.2: The Internet can be imagined as a system of highways and roadways, although it has no actual geography.

but when you use the Net, you probably won't be very conscious that the material you're viewing on your screen at one moment is actually located on a machine in Switzerland and that what you see the next moment is actually on a machine in Japan. Perhaps a more accurate metaphor for the Internet would be having a global remote control at your fingertips, able to switch to just about any topic (channel if you prefer) of your choosing. And now, with user-friendly tools such as Netscape, access is no longer limited to scholars and hackers.

Where It All Began

To understand how the Internet came into being, you'd have to go back 30 years or so, to the Cold War era. The think-tank military planners of that age were concerned not only with surviving a nuclear war, but also with communicating in its aftermath if one should occur. They envisioned a control network, linking bases and command posts from state to state, that would remain operational despite direct attacks. With this in mind, the U.S. Defense Department's Advanced Research Projects Agency began work on a computer network called ARPAnet during the 1960s.

The principles of the network were simple. It had to operate from the outset as if it were "unreliable"—to adjust up-front for the possibility of downed communication links. Control, therefore, would be decentralized to further minimize any single point of failure. Data would be split up and sent on the network in individual Internet Protocol (IP) *packets*. (A packet can be thought of as similar to an envelope.) Each packet of data would carry within it the address of its destination and could reach its endpoint by the most efficient route. If part of the network became unavailable, the packets would still get to their destinations via an alternate route and would be reassembled with their full content intact.

Though at first this may sound inefficient, it put the burden of communicating on the computers themselves, rather than on the communications network. That was the foremost issue on the minds of the planners: that the system did not rely on a central *server* (a machine on the network that holds or processes data for the other machines on the network). This proposal linked the computers together as *peers* instead, giving each computer equal status on the network and allowing for different types of computers to communicate, de-emphasizing the communications infrastructure.

Thus, even if large pieces of the network were destroyed, the data itself could still reach its destination because it was not concerned with *how* to get there. So it was that the Department of Defense commissioned the initial implementation of ARPAnet in 1969.

 Perhaps you work in a business where a lot of machines are cabled together as a LAN (local area network). Each of these networks is like a smaller version of the Internet, in that a bunch of machines are linked together; but they are not necessarily linked to other networks via phone lines. LANs also usually have a central server—a machine that holds data and processes communications between the linked machines, which is unlike the Internet in that if your LAN server goes down, your network goes down.

Throughout the '70s and early '80s, the ARPAnet continued to grow, and more developments occurred to spur interest in networking and the Internet. Other services and big networks came into being (such as Usenet and BITnet), and e-mail began to gain wide use as a communications tool. Local area networks (LANs) became increasingly common in business and academic use, until users no longer wanted to connect just select computers to the Internet but entire local networks (which might mean all the computers in the organization).

Today the original Internet, the ARPAnet, is no more, having been replaced in 1986 by a new backbone, the National Science Foundation (NSFnet) network. NSFnet forever changed the scope of the Internet in that it permitted more than just a few lucky people in the military, academia, and large corporations to conduct research and access supercomputer centers. (See Figure 1.3.) With the good, however, came the bad as well. More people using the Internet meant more network traffic, which meant slower response, which meant better connectivity solutions would have to be implemented. Which brings us to where we are today, with demand increasing exponentially as more and more people want to connect to the Internet and discover the online riches of the '90s. (See Figure 1.4.)

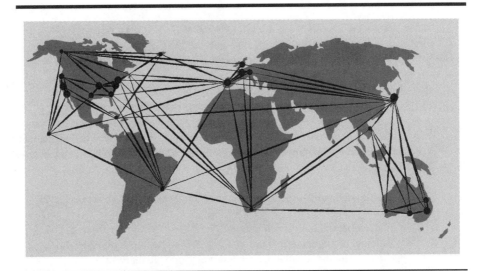

FIGURE 1.3: The Internet is a global resource, with servers on every continent.

The Burning Questions of Control, Funding, and Use

As odd as it may sound, no one person has overall authority for running the Internet. Despite this—or perhaps because of it—the Internet runs just fine. A group called the Internet Society (ISOC), composed of volunteers, directs the Internet. ISOC appoints a subcouncil, the Internet Architecture Board (IAB), and the members of this board work out issues of standards, network resources, network addresses, and the like. Another volunteer group, the Internet Engineering Task Force (IETF), tackles the more day-to-day issues of Internet operations. These Internet caretakers, if you will, have proven quite ably that success does not have to depend on your typical top-down management approach.

Likewise, the Internet's funding system may seem odd. A common misconception is that the Internet, by its very nature, is free, but this is certainly not the case. It costs a pretty penny to maintain a machine that can serve up stuff on the Internet, and someone has to pay those costs. Individual groups and institutions—such as the federal government (via the National Science Foundation), which runs NSFnet—do indeed pay to provide the information

Annual rate of growth for World Wide Web traffic: 341, 634% (1st year)

◆

Annual rate of growth for Gopher traffic: 997%

◆

Number of countries reachable by electronic mail: 159 (approx.)
Number of countries not reachable by electronic mail: 77 (approx.)

◆

Average time, in minutes, during business hours, between registration of new domains: 2
Percentage increase in number of registered domains from October 1994 to January 1995:
28

◆

Estimated number of U.S newspapers offering interactive access: 3,200

◆

Number of attendees at Internet World, April 1995: more than 20,000
Number of attendees at Internet World, December 1994: more than 10,000
Number of attendees at Internet World, January 1992: 272

◆

Date after which more than half the registered networks were commercial: August 1991

◆

Number of financial service firms with registered domains in early 1995: 398
Percentage increases in the number of financial service firms with registered domains
during 1994: 197

◆

Number of on-line coffeehouses in San Francisco: 18
Cost for four minutes of Internet time at those coffeehouses: $0.25

◆

Estimated number of Usenet sites, worldwide: 260,000
Estimated number of readers of the Usenet group
rec.humor.funny: 480,000

◆

At current growth rates, estimated time at which everyone on earth will be on the
Internet: 2004

◆

Amount of time it takes for Supreme Court decisions to become available on the
Internet: less than one day

FIGURE 1.4: These Internet statistics (courtesy of Win Treese) tell an amazing story.

they serve on the Internet. At the other end, new users quickly find out that connecting to the Internet through a service provider (such as Netcom, CRL, or PSI) requires a monthly usage fee; and because it is necessary to connect through a phone line, telephone charges may also be involved. Meanwhile, in the middle, the service providers pay for leasing high-speed communication lines; they also pay to access the Commercial Internet Exchange, and they may even pay to access a regional Internet provider such as BARRNet. As you can see, the Internet is by no means free, although it is a great value.

What You Can Do with the Internet

Once you are connected to the Internet, you can:

◆ Send messages to friends and associates all over the world with *e-mail* (This usually does not involve long-distance charges to you or the recipient; all you're charged for is the call to your Internet service provider, and, if that's a local number, it's a local call.)

◆ Exchange ideas with other people in a public forum with *Usenet newsgroups*. (Note that unlike e-mail, which is more or less private, newsgroups are public. Everyone on the newsgroup can read what you post there.)

◆ Copy files from and to computers on the Internet with *FTP*. Many giant software archives, such as the CICA Windows archive, hold literally gigabytes of files you can retrieve.

◆ Connect to other computers on the Internet with *Telnet*. (In order to connect to another computer, you need permission to use the computer.)

◆ Traverse and search directories of information with *Gopher*.

◆ View documents, browse, search for data, and traverse other resources on the Internet via the *World Wide Web*.

Many of these tools are used (either visibly or behind the scenes) in the course of using Netscape, so we'll talk about each one as it arises in later chapters.

The Internet As Medium

The Internet itself is just a medium. There's plenty of room to develop services to be used to make the most of the Internet, just as happened when the phone system was devised for simple communication and then many products and services were developed to take advantage of its potential (ranging from voicemail, pagers, and automated banking, to the 911 system and, in fact, the Internet).

What's Out There

You can send and receive e-mail messages with Netscape, and you can even embed in your message any Web page you are currently viewing. The Internet itself provides a number of resources you can use via Netscape for finding people's e-mail addresses. At gopher://gopher.tc.umn.edu/11/Phone%20Books/other you can search for people that have recently posted to Usenet newsgroups. At gopher://gopher.tc.umn.edu/11/Phone%20Books are links to many other databases of e-mail addresses.

The Internet's fundamental openness has been responsible for bringing forth a number of tools for use by the masses. A great example of this is, of course, Netscape. In the next chapter, we'll look at how you can access the best of the Internet—the World Wide Web—via Netscape.

Best of the Internet: The World Wide Web via Netscape

Before we leap head first into using Netscape, an appreciation of the World Wide Web is in order. Let's take a quick look at the Web. Then we'll glance at a typical Netscape session, and, still in this chapter, we'll talk more about what Netscape can do.

How the Web Came to Be

The World Wide Web (a.k.a. WWW, W3, or simply, *the Web*) was originally developed to help physicists at Conseil Européen pour la Recherche Nucleaire (CERN), which is the European particle physics laboratory in Geneva, Switzerland. CERN is one of the world's largest scientific labs, composed of two organizations straddling the Swiss-French border—the European Laboratory for High Energy Physics in Switzerland, and the Organisation Européen pour la Recherche Nucleaire in France. The physicists there needed a way to exchange data and research materials quickly with other scientists.

The Web technology developed at CERN by Tim Berners-Lee enabled collaboration among members of research teams scattered all over the globe. How? Through a system that allows for *hypertext* links between documents on different computers.

Unlike regular documents, with static information on every page, *hypertext* documents have links built in so that readers can jump to more information about a topic by (typically) simply clicking on the word or picture identifying the item. That's why they call it hypertext—it's not just text, it's *hyper*text. (The term *hypertext* was coined by computer iconoclast Ted Nelson.) Hypertext is what makes Netscape—and many multimedia tools—possible. The term *hypermedia* is sometimes used to refer to hypertext with the addition of other data formats. In addition to text, Netscape supports graphics and, equipped with the proper external programs, can support sound and video as well.

Before going to CERN, Berners-Lee had worked on document production and text processing and had developed for his own use a hypertext system—Enquire—in 1980. (According to some reports, he wasn't aware of the notion of hypertext at the time, but hypertext has been around since the Xanadu project in the 1960s.)

In 1992, the Web grew beyond the confines of the CERN's research community, and now its use and growth increase exponentially. This was all part of the plan in a sense—the Web was meant to allow for open access—but it's hard to imagine that anyone could have expected the phenomenon that's occurred. Activity on the server at CERN doubles every four months, which is twice the rate of Internet expansion.

Protocols, HTTP, and Hypertext: What It All Means

The Web's rapid expansion can be attributed in part to its extensive use of hypertext, held together by the HyperText Transfer Protocol (HTTP). A *protocol* is an agreed-upon system for passing information back and forth that allows the transaction to be efficient (HTTP is a *network protocol*, which means it's a protocol for use with networks).

Here's how this goes: If you (the *client*) go into a fast-food place, the counterperson (the *server*) says, "May I help you?" You answer something like, "I'll have a Big Burger with cheese, fries, and a cola." Then he or she verifies

On "Mosaic" and Netscape

Maybe you're a bit confused about all the different "Mosaics" and how Netscape fits into the Mosaic picture. The short version of this story is that Netscape is Mosaic-like, but it's not Mosaic… Well, not exactly.

The first version of Mosaic, which was developed by Marc Andreessen and a team of programmers at the National Center for Supercomputing Applications (NCSA), was X Mosaic for Unix workstations. Since then, versions of NCSA Mosaic have become available for Windows-based PCs and the Macintosh. NCSA Mosaic was, for a time, distributed freely via the Net itself. Anyone could download and use the software without charge.

In mid-1994, NCSA began to license the rights to version 1.*x* of the software to other (often commercial) organizations. These organizations are allowed, by virtue of their licensing agreements with NCSA, to enhance the software. They can then *distribute* the enhanced software (called a *distribution*), and they can license others to distribute the software along with whatever enhancements they've included in their distribution. All distributions of Mosaic have the word *Mosaic* in their names.

In their wisdom, the folks at Netscape (Marc Andreessen again, along with some other very smart people) created and marketed a *new* Web browser— one that was faster and more reliable than Mosaic. They also made the new browser *secure*. (They wanted you to be able to conduct economic transactions, or in other words *buy* things, over the Internet without fear of someone stealing and using your credit card number.) The result of this venture, Netscape took the World Wide Web by storm and was soon named by *Wired* magazine as one of its favorite products.

Throughout this book, we're concentrating on the Web browser called Netscape, though most of the principles and many of the features we discuss are true across all platforms and distributions of Mosaic as well.

your order by repeating it, tells you the cost, and concludes the transaction by trading food for cash. Basically, when you walk into any fast-food place, you'll follow that same pattern and so will the person who takes your order. That's because you both know the *protocol*. The fast-food protocol is part of what makes it "fast food."

In just that way, HTTP, which is the protocol that was developed as part of the Web project, enables the kinds of network conversations that need to occur quickly between computers so that leaps can be made from one document to another. You can use other protocols to do the same things HTTP does (Netscape is *open-ended*, meaning that it's designed to support other network protocols as well as HTTP), but HTTP is terrifically efficient at what it does.

Information from Around the Globe

The Web, as we've mentioned, is a network of global proportions. To ensure the continued success of the Web, the W3 Organization, headed jointly by CERN and by MIT's Laboratory for Computer Science (LCS), acts as its formal policy body and guiding light. The relationship between CERN and MIT/LCS was formalized in June 1994 when both organizations announced an "international initiative for a universal framework for the information Web." The goal of the W3 Organization is to further the development and standardization of the World Wide Web and to make the global network easier to use for research, commerce, and future applications.

Web servers are located in many countries around the world, providing information on any topic you might imagine; a typical session using the Web might lead you through several continents. For example, research in the field of psychology may start at Yale and end up at a research hospital in Brussels, all within a few mouse-clicks that lead you along a series of hypertext links from a file at one location to another somewhere else.

The caveat here is that links are forged by the people who publish the information, and they may not make the same kinds of connections you would. That's why it's important to keep an open mind as you adventure around in the Web— just as you would when browsing in a library. You never know what you'll stumble across while you're looking for something else; conversely, you might have to do a bit of looking around to find exactly what you're seeking.

Who Makes This Information Available

Much of the information published on the Web exists thanks to the interest (and kindness) of the academic and research community; almost all information about the Web (and the Internet) is available through the work of that community. Files are stored on computers in research centers, hospitals, universities, and so on.

Increasingly, the Web is a forum for commercial use. Given that the telephone system did not fully develop for personal use until it was seen by commerce as a tool for business, we see commercial use of the Web as a positive development. So far, most commercial users of the Web have adhered to the Internet philosophy in that they give to the Internet as well as use it.

What's Out There

You can retrieve information about creating and publicizing your Web documents from http://www.pcweek.ziff.com/~eamonn/crash_course.html.

Anyone can become a Web publisher, as you'll see in Chapter 7. The Web software was developed at CERN on a NeXT computer, but has since been ported to many different platforms, including Macs, machines running Microsoft Windows, and others running versions of Unix and Linux.

Web servers can be set up for strictly in-house purposes too. For example, a large organization with massive amounts of internal documentation might publish its data for technical support staff using the HTTP service. This makes it possible to expand the idea of *in-house* to mean not just "in the building" but "company-wide." Just as members of a research team can use the Web to collaborate without having to be in the same location, so can members of a company's workgroup.

What Types of Information Exist

Internet directories like Yahoo, which began as the project of two university graduate students, cover specific topics ranging from the academic to the entertaining.

What's Out There

You can access Yahoo at: `http://www.yahoo.com`.

The Web has quickly moved beyond the world of academia and research, however with more and more commercial applications appearing all the time. Large hardware and software vendors often publish price lists, monthly sales figures, and technical support information—for example, Dell Computer's Web service includes a "Solve Your Own Problem" section.

What's Out There

A growing number of high-tech companies are making information available on the Web. Some familiar names—Microsoft, Novell, and Sybex—all maintain a presence on the Web. You can access these companies' home pages at:

```
http://www.microsoft.com
http://www.novell.com
http://www.sybex.com
```

Other nonacademic, consumer-oriented Web servers (see Figure 2.1) include Crayola, which provides colorful background on the making of crayons *and* the removal of crayon-based stains. Time Warner publishes news of all sorts, ranging from the hard-hitting daily stuff to more entertaining fare, at its Pathfinder site (again, you can see this in Figure 2.1). You can tour Graceland via the Web, finding photos of the "King" and listening to sound clips of Elvis music, and you can even order a pizza using a Web order form. (This last is a pilot project so far; the pizza will be delivered only

FIGURE 2.1: Many companies see the Web as a way to put their messages in front of a wide audience. The top home page was set up by Crayola for crayon enthusiasts; the bottom one was set up by Time Warner to provide information to new fans.

if you live in Santa Cruz, California. Solamente in California, eh?) We'll show you how to explore these and many other places in Chapter 5.

What's Out There

We accessed Crayola and Pathfinder with the following URLs:

```
http://www.crayola.com/crayola/
http://www.pathfinder.com
```

The Role of the Browser

So far we've talked mainly about the structure and content of the Web, describing some of the information and links that make up the Web. So how does one jump into this Web and start cruising? You need a tool called a *browser*.

Now at the risk of sounding like the nerds we said you don't have to be, a browser, in technical terms, is a client process running on your computer that accesses a server process—in the case of the Web, the HTTP service—over the network. This is what's being discussed when people describe the Web as being based on client-server technology.

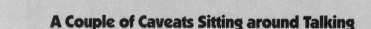

A Couple of Caveats Sitting around Talking

Remember that the Web is ever-changing by its very nature. In this book, we attempt to guide you toward a lot of home pages that seem stable. Some others are just so interesting or unusual we can't pass them up, though. If you don't find a site we've described, it may be that it has gone the way of all things. Not to worry; something even more remarkable will probably crop up elsewhere. Another thing is that in the growing, ever-expanding Web, many of the servers you encounter may not be complete—their links may be "under construction." You'll usually see a warning if that's the case, along with an admonition to wear a hardhat.

More simply put, the browser establishes contact with the server, reads the files—hypertext documents—made available on the HTTP server, and displays that stuff on your computer.

The document displayed by the browser is a hypertext document that contains references (or *pointers*) to other documents, which are very likely on other HTTP servers. These pointers are also called *links*. When you select a link from a hypertext page, the browser sends the request back to the new server, which then displays on your machine yet another document full of links.

In the same way you and a waiter at a restaurant have a client-server relationship when you ask for and receive water, a browser and the Web have a client-server relationship. The browser sends requests over the network to the Web server, which then provides a screenful of information back to your computer.

Before Web browsers such as Netscape were developed, all of this had to be accomplished using text-based browsers—the basic difference between them and browsers such as Netscape is just like the difference between PC programs written for DOS and those written for Windows. (DOS is text-based, so using DOS requires you to type in commands to see and use text-filled screens; Windows, like Netscape, is graphical, so all you have to do is point and click on menu items and icons to see and use more graphically presented screens.) Figure 1.1 in Chapter 1 shows two views of the same information—one viewed with a text-based browser, the other with Netscape.

How Netscape Fits In

Netscape Navigator (often called just *Netscape*), one of the "new generation" of Web browsers, is a lot like the original and still famous Web browser called Mosaic but with considerable improvements. In fact, some of the key programmers who worked on the original Mosaic were behind the creation of Netscape.

Mosaic was developed by the Software Development Group (SDG) at the National Center for Supercomputing Applications (NCSA) at the University of Illinois at Urbana-Champaign. In early 1993, their research for developing an easy-to-use way to access the Internet led them to explore the World Wide Web and use of the HyperText Markup Language (HTML). HTML was being used for marking up documents on the Web—it's HTML

that is used to *make* the document; browsers such as Mosaic and Netscape simply allow you to look at it easily.

HTML, a mark-up language with which text can be made to look like a page, is the coding scheme used in hypertext documents that both handles the text formatting on screen and makes it possible to create *links* to other documents, graphics, sound, and movies. Figure 2.2 shows a Netscape document and the HTML coding that was used to create the document.

Remember, though, that Netscape is not just a way to look at visually appealing documents on the Internet. It also provides search capabilities within a hypertext document through links. We'll get into this more and more as we go along....

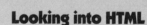

Looking into HTML

If you want to see what HTML looks like, while viewing a document in Netscape, you can select View ➤ by Document Source from Netscape's menu bar. A window will open showing the HTML for that document. You can't change the HTML you see, but you can copy pieces of it or even the whole thing to your Windows Clipboard (highlight what you want and press Ctrl-C) or you can save it as a text file to your local machine (see Chapter 3). Click on OK when you're done, and your view will once more be the document as it appears in Netscape.

Using Netscape to Access World Wide Web Information

Netscape lets you browse the information available on the Web just as you might browse the shelves of a large library. In fact, Netscape makes it so you can easily and quickly browse *entire rooms* of shelves, and the Web makes available literally thousands of "rooms" in "libraries" as expansive as, say, the New York Public Library. Using Netscape, you can skim material quickly, or you can stop and delve into topics as deeply as you wish. Let's take a quick look at a Netscape session in action.

```
<HEADER>
<TITLE>access -- Summer 1994 issue</TITLE>
</HEADER>
<H1> Contents</H1>
<BODY>
<IMG Src="Cover94.2.gif">
<P>
<H4>Cover: Virtual environments for investigating
    science and engineering projects, one of NCSA's
    major technology directions, is the subject of this
    issue. Symbols from science and fine art represent
    the melding of these two knowledge bases that are
    needed in the creation of interactive, immersive
    technologies.
    <br>
    Cover produced on a Macintosh IIci using Adobe
    Photoshop, Adobe Dimensions, Aldus FreeHand, and a
    UMAX UC630 scanner. (Concept and illustration, John
    Havlik; concept and research, Fran Bond)</h4>
<P>
<H3><A HREF="http://www.ncsa.uiuc.edu/General/NCSAContacts.html">Contac
<H3> <A HREF="EdNote.html"><IMG SRC="../Icons/EdNote.gif">
    Editor's Note: Virtually experiencing science</H3></A>

<UL>
<LI> <A HREF = "VEToolset.html"> A virtual environments toolset driven by scien
<LI> <A HREF = "VROOMScientists.html"> VROOM Scientists on VR</A>
```

Cover: Virtual environments for investigating science and engineering projects, one of NCSA's major technology directions, is the subject of this issue. Symbols from science and fine art represent the melding of these two knowledge bases that are needed in the creation of interactive, immersive technologies.
Cover produced on a Macintosh IIci using Adobe Photoshop, Adobe Dimensions, Aldus FreeHand, and a UMAX UC630 scanner. (Concept and illustration, John Havlik; concept and research, Fran Bond)

Contacts Directory

 Editor's Note: Virtually experiencing science

◆ A virtual environments toolset driven by science
◆ VROOM Scientists on VR

FIGURE 2.2:   Here you can see the HTML coding (above) that makes this document (below) look the way it does.

A Typical Netscape Session

In our sample session, let's look for information about the Rolling Stones.

 This is a sample session; it's here to give you an idea of how things go. We'll talk in more detail in later chapters about how to accomplish various things using Netscape.

To start Netscape, we first start our Internet connection, then double-click on the Netscape Navigator icon on the desktop. (We'll go over starting the software again in detail in Chapter 3.) The Welcome to Netscape page (see Figure 2.3) appears on screen. From here we can traverse the Web by clicking on links, which appear on the home page as pictures and as underlined words in blue.

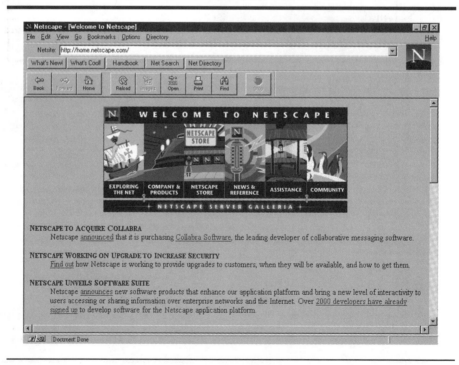

FIGURE 2.3: The Welcome to Netscape page will be your first view of the Internet via Netscape Navigator

Chapters 8 and 9 provide detailed directions for getting connected, then installing and setting up Netscape.

Let's say in an earlier session we found the NCSA Mosaic home page. There we clicked on What's New, and we got the NCSA Mosaic What's New document. Near the top of this document we found a link (appearing as a word in blue) that said something like <u>search back documents</u>, which led us to the CUI W3 Catalog, which is actually stored on a machine at CERN, in Switzerland. The CUI W3 Catalog is a catalog of announcements of new services and information available on the Web. Its URL was shown at the top of the screen while we were viewing the catalog; we stored the URL as a bookmark (more on this in Chapter 3) so we could find it easily again when we wanted to.

What's Out There

The CUI W3 Catalog is not the only catalog of resources on the Web, but it is quite useful and may be a good place to start your search. You can access it at `http://cuiwww.unige.ch/w3catalog`.

To open the CUI W3 Catalog without retracing all the steps we went through when we discovered the catalog, we select File ➤ Open Location. The Open Location dialog box appears.

From our previous session, we know the URL; now we can type this into the URL text box, then press ↵. After a few seconds, the document is transferred from Switzerland and displayed on screen. You can see it shown in Figure 2.4.

To go on with our research on the Rolling Stones, we type into the space next to the Submit button a term to search for, in our case *Rolling Stones*. Then we click on the Submit button to activate the search. It may take a minute to search the database (it's a *big* database). Once the search is done, the results appear on screen.

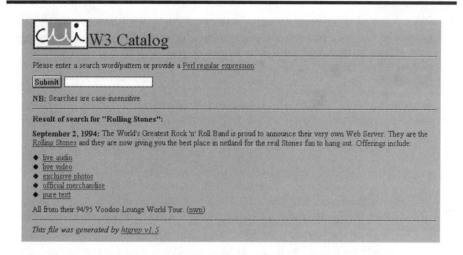

FIGURE 2.4: Searching the CUI W3 Catalog for the term <u>Rolling Stones</u> finds this entry about the Rolling Stones Web server.

The first entry we see starts, "The World's Greatest Rock 'n' Roll Band is proud to announce their very own Web server," and goes on to say that the Rolling Stones now have a Web server with information about their Voodoo Lounge tour. In that description, the phrase <u>Rolling Stones</u> is in blue—it's a link to the server's home page. We click on the link to access the Rolling Stones Web server, and the Rolling Stones home page appears. You can see it in Figure 2.5.

The Rolling Stones home page is our entry point to scads of information about the Voodoo Lounge tour (and perhaps by the time you read this, even more). Here we can click on links to view backstage snapshots, video clips of performances, a schedule of performance dates, and a catalog of stuff to buy.

With our curiosity about the Stones satisfied, we can exit the program directly from wherever we happen to be by selecting File ➤ Exit from Netscape's menu bar.

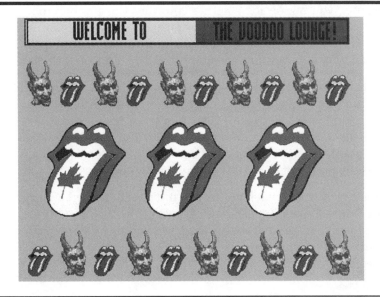

FIGURE 2.5: The Rolling Stones home page looks pretty much like you might expect it to look.

Netscape Is Fast

If you worked along with this session, you probably found that Netscape displayed the pages on your machine in a jiffy. The graphics included in each page trailed the text, appearing just a moment later, however. If your access to the Web is via modem on a stand-alone PC and not from a network, you'll find that there's always *some* delay in transferring images to your screen. This is because there can be an awful lot of data involved in transferring graphics, and your 9600, 14,400, or even 28,800 bps modem acts as a bottleneck through which the data must squeeze. Many Web browsers halt all their other operations while they make you wait for images to appear. Netscape was designed specifically to get around this issue: Instead of waiting 'til the graphics appear, Netscape goes ahead and shows you the text on the page and allows you to start working with it. You can click on links in the text, for example, and move on to the next page of interest to you, before the graphics in the original page have appeared.

Further, you can decide whether you want the graphics to appear at all. Netscape, like other Web browsers, usually shows you both the text and the graphics in a given Web page. But if you find the graphics bogging you down, you can turn the graphics off and see only the text.

To toggle off the graphics, making it so you'll see only text, select Options ➤ Auto Load Images from Netscape's menu bar. After you do this, the Web pages you view will include little markers where the graphics go. If you're viewing a page with graphics toggled off and you decide you want to see the graphics after all, just click on the Images icon on Netscape's toolbar and the page will be reloaded, this time with its graphics.

To toggle graphics back on, so you'll see them loaded a moment after the text for each page appears, select Options ➤ Auto Load Images again from the menu bar. (Note that this is a *toggle* situation, so you can go back and forth in your choice to include or exclude images again and again using the exact same process.)

How Data Travels

Usually you can't install Netscape on your Windows computer and expect it simply to work. You have to go through a little rigmarole to get things going. The interface mechanism between the client—Netscape—and the Web server (the machine dishing up the information you want to view) depends on the Internet protocol known as TCP/IP (Transmission Control Protocol/Internet Protocol). TCP/IP creates *packets* (see Figure 2.6)—which are like electronic envelopes to carry data on a network—and then places the packets on the network. It also makes it possible, of course, to receive packets.

The Domain Name System and Packets

There is a system responsible for administering and keeping track of domains, and (believe it or not) it's called the Domain Name System (DNS for short). DNS is a distributed system that administers names by allowing different groups control over subsets of names. In this system, there can

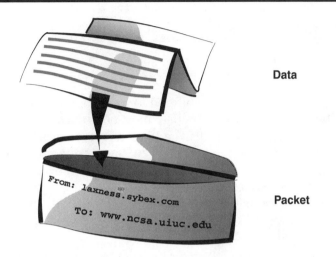

Data

Packet

From: laxness.sybex.com
To: www.ncsa.uiuc.edu

FIGURE 2.6:   Data (e-mail, documents, video, whatever) travels across the Internet in Packets.

be many levels or domains, but the top-level domains are generally standardized, making it easy for mail to be routed.

In addition to the more familiar "English" names, all machines on the Internet have an Internet address in the form of four numbers separated by decimals; this is because, while a user might change the "English" address, an address is needed that will never change. This numeric address is organized in a system commonly called *dotted decimal notation*. An example of a host computer's address would be 130.19.252.21. These numeric addresses work fine for machines communicating with one another, but most people find them cumbersome to use and tricky to remember. To help people out, host computers were given names, such as *ruby* or *topaz*, making it easier to remember and to facilitate connecting.

However, other factors came into play, such as making sure that each machine on the Internet had a unique name, registering the names in a centrally managed file, and distributing the file to everyone on the Internet. This system worked adequately when the Internet was still small, but as it grew in size, so did the size of the file keeping track of all the host names.

E-Mail Addressing

Electronic mail, or e-mail, is the established form of communication on the Internet. In fact, typically this is where most of us encounter the Internet for the first time. A friend tells you his Internet e-mail address at work is kmfez@schwartz.com and asks for your e-mail address, and you begin exchanging messages that magically pop up in your on-screen e-mail in-basket. Users around the country—for that matter, around the world—readily grasp e-mail as a quick, convenient means for conducting research or just for staying in touch (and for doing so without the expense associated with a long-distance phone call).

How does e-mail work? It's actually a lot like the postal service. E-mail uses addressing and a "store and forward" mechanism. This means that there is a standard way of addressing, and the mail is routed from one place to another until ultimately it appears at its destination. Along the way, if necessary, a machine can store the mail until it knows how to forward it.

Of course, there is a little more than that to sending e-mail on its way, but not much. The address in your e-mail header, much like the address on a postal letter, contains all the information necessary to deliver the message to the recipient. In the world of the Internet, a person's e-mail address is made up of two parts: a user name and a computer name, indicating where the user's ID is located. In the example kmfez@schwartz.com, kmfez is the user portion of the address, and schwartz.com is the name of the location (actually a host machine). The last part of the location's name, .com, is known as the *high-level domain*—in this case .com tells you that it is a *com*mercial organization. If .edu appeared instead, you'd know it was an *edu*cational organization.

An address can actually contain many domains, which you see separated by periods, like this: joke.on.you.com. If multiple domains appear in an address, they move in hierarchy from right to left. As you read to the left, the domains get smaller in scope.

The common standard American domains are as follows:

com	Commercial business, company, or organization
edu	Educational institution (university, etc.)
gov	Nonmilitary government site
mil	Military site
net	Any host associated with network administration, such as a gateway
org	Private organization (nonacademic, nongovernmental, and noncommercial)

These domains are referred to as *descriptive* domains. In addition, each country also has its own top-level domain, commonly called a *geographical* domain. Here in the United States, we are in the us domain. Other examples of countries represented with domains include:

au	Australia
ca	Canada
fr	France

Just as you need not know the internal workings of the U.S. Postal Service to use the system and get your mail, you don't need to know all about TCP/IP to use Netscape. But it does help to have some understanding.

TCP/IP is not part of Netscape; it's part of your local network if you're on one. If you're not on a local network, though—if, for example, you're using your stand-alone machine at home or at work—you can still use Netscape. In that case, you have to have special network drivers loaded (not to worry, Windows 95 includes them). These drivers make things go back and forth over the phone connection using the protocol Netscape understands. We'll talk more about this in Chapter 8.

 If you're using a PC on a LAN that's already connected to the Internet, you're probably already set up with the TCP/IP software you need to run Netscape, and you can just use your company's connection. Your Network Administrator can clue you in to the details of running TCP/IP-based software such as Netscape.

What Netscape Recognizes

Netscape has many big selling points, one of which is that it provides one-stop shopping for the Web by handling a variety of *data types*. Data types are just that—types of data. Having standard types of data makes it possible for one machine (indeed, a program) to recognize and use data that was created on another machine (and maybe even in another program). The data types recognized by Netscape include:

- ◆ HTML
- ◆ Graphics
- ◆ Sound
- ◆ Video

The data type that the Web was designed around is HTML, the type the Hyper-Text Transfer Protocol we've talked so much about was designed to transfer.

HTTP servers, the servers that make up the World Wide Web, serve hypertext documents (coded with HTML, as we've discussed). These documents are not just what you view; these HTML documents actually guide you through the Web when you're cruising.

When you view hypertext documents using a line-mode browser (see Figure 1.1 in Chapter 1), you'll see the links displayed as item numbers or as reverse-video, depending upon your display. When you view hypertext documents using Netscape, you'll see the links displayed as text that's either underlined or in a different color than the main text in the document.

Clicking on the underlined or colored text pops you to the next link, which may be another hypertext document or a graphic, or even a sound or video file.

Netscape's Use of Viewers and Players

For those data types that it can't handle directly, Netscape uses external viewers and players. (In this context, a *viewer* or *player* is software that might specialize in displaying a graphic or playing a sound, a movie, or both.) Viewers and players are independent applications developed for viewing, opening, or accessing a particular type of information.

You can configure Netscape to work with specific viewers or players. For example, you might configure video files to be played by Apple's Quick-Time player. (See Chapter 10 for more information on getting and using external viewers and players.)

Netscape Navigator version 2 includes a very credible sound player that will make it possible for you to listen to most sound files if you have a sound card.

How Viewers and Players Work

Briefly, here's how viewers and players work: Netscape looks at the first part (the *header*) of the file; the header tells Netscape what it needs to know to deal with the file appropriately. Text files are displayed on screen, in the very attractive way Netscape displays them. Compressed files, such as graphics, are uncompressed and then displayed. But when Netscape encounters a sound or video file, the program "knows" it needs help, and it launches the appropriate viewer to "play" the file—if you have the viewer on your machine, you won't see much evidence of this; you'll just hear the sound or see the movie on screen.

Many viewers and players are available in the public domain from many Internet sources (including anonymous FTP servers and the Web) and for all types of files. NCSA, for example, makes it clear that it neither maintains nor formally distributes the viewers and players needed to work with the various files that Web browsers can access, but when NCSA learns of one that can be freely distributed, it files a copy of it on a server in Illinois. (Remember that public domain programs are supported [if at all] only by their authors and not by the sites where you got them. If you have questions about how to use any given viewer or player, you must go to its author to get help.)

WARNING With the help of viewers and players, you can play video and sound clips with Netscape, but you should avoid doing so if you have a modem connection (as opposed to a LAN connection) to the Internet. Most sound and video files are multi-megabytes in size. As a rough estimate, each megabyte takes about 15 minutes to transfer with a 14.4K bps modem (that is, on a good day with prevailing winds). It might take literally hours to access a single, relatively short video clip.

Let's talk for a minute about those types of data Netscape most commonly needs a viewer or player to work with. (We'll go into more detail about how to use this stuff starting in Chapter 10.)

Graphics Usually when you encounter graphics while using Netscape, they'll be one of two kinds: those that appear in the document (called "in-line" graphics) and those that require you click on something in order to view them.

Netscape can work with many common types of graphic images, for example, GIF, TIFF, and JPEG. You will only need an external graphics viewer if you come upon a graphics file that Netscape does not support. Because most graphics on the Web are in the GIF and JPEG formats, this is unlikely.

You don't really need to concern yourself with what the names of these various file formats mean unless you plan to publish your own documents. Most of the time, all you'll be doing is looking at things; sometimes the graphic you'll see in your Netscape document window is a link to another document or to a larger, compressed image. Clicking on the picture will begin the process of bringing the other file over the network.

Sound Netscape comes with a perfectly good sound player. Windows audio files (WAV) and Basic audio (AU) files will be recognized as linked data. Remember that sound files can be very large and take a long time to transfer over a slow connection.

Video Netscape can be configured to work with viewers for QuickTime movies (MOV), Microsoft video (AVI), and movie files compressed using the MPEG compression standard. Again, remember that many video files you'll come across as you begin to work with Netscape are, in the words of Tiny Elvis, "huge."

Netscape As a Consistent Interface to Other Internet Resources

In addition to providing a nice graphical user interface to linked multimedia information, Netscape provides a consistent interface to other information types available on the Internet. In fact, some of the links in the hypertext documents on the Web will take you to information on FTP servers, Gopher servers, or WAIS servers. (Read on for the gory details.) You can also read newsgroups and post messages to them from Netscape, and now with version 2, you can even send and receive e-mail.

Let's take a quick look at the kinds of resources that make up the Web and that you can access using Netscape.

FTP: For Transferring Files

We've talked about viewing files; actually obtaining them is a different matter. To transfer a file from one machine (a server, for example) to another (yours, for example), you need FTP (File Transfer Protocol). FTP is one of the means by which you move files around the Internet. Both a communications protocol and an application, it is the application that is of most interest to many people, as we use FTP to obtain files (once we've located them, of course) from all kinds of Internet sources. This kind of file transfer most often works in what is known as *anonymous FTP* mode.

FTP itself only lets you see a list of the files on a computer, whereas something like Netscape lets you see more—the files, the contents of the files, even graphics, sounds, movies, and so on. Still, FTP should not be overlooked for what it has accomplished and still does, namely, allowing users to bring home files, information, and data that otherwise would be left for browsing only.

After retrieving the file, you may need to perform some additional steps if the file has been compressed to save space. This involves using a utility to uncompress, or unzip, the file to make it usable. There are many compression formats in use, so you may find yourself cursing sometimes rather than jumping for joy when you uncover just the file you are looking for but are unable to unzip it.

Wanderers, Spiders, and Robots—Oh My!

In June 1993, there were about 130 Web servers on the Internet. Six months later, there were more than 200. One year after that, the number hit 2,000. So how do you find what you need in this ever-expanding haystack? Wouldn't it be great to know what's out on the Web, and where?

You can find out, by consulting World Wide Web creatures known as *wanderers*, *spiders*, or *robots*. An assortment of Web robots have been developed since the beginnings of the WWW; these programs travel through the Web and find HTTP files—the files that make up the content of the Web. With names the likes of Arachnophobia, W4, Webfoot Robot, JumpStation Robot, Repository-Based Software Engineering Project Spider, WebCrawler, WebLinker, and World Wide Web Worm, you may not see their useful purposes when you first encounter them.

Some robots, such as W4, were designed strictly to track growth on the Web. The statistics cited at the beginning of this piece were gathered by W4; the W4 page of the Web keeps these figures posted and updated.

The more interesting and useful Web crawlers are those that dump the information they gather into a place that's readable by the rest of us browsers. The World Wide Web Worm is one such robot. The information is collected into an indexed database that Web users can search.

The Repository Based Software Engineering Project Spider creates an Oracle database by searching through links within the Web to find HTML files. The data that's extracted is then siphoned off into a WAIS index, which can be searched.

Check out Chapter 6 for information about accessing search tools that use Web crawler terchnology.

Netscape presents FTP directories as a graphical menu using icons similar to those used by the Windows Explorer. Directories are represented by a folder icon; text files are displayed as the familiar sheet-of-paper-with-its-top-corner-folded-down. These items all appear as links—they are underlined so that you can click on them to move to the place in question.

What's Out There

You can retrieve a table listing available compression software at:
`ftp://ftp.cso.uiuc.edu/pub/doc/pcnet/compression`.

Another advantage of Netscape, over say a regular FTP session, is that Netscape reads the file type, so it can display a text file on screen when you click on the link. A regular FTP session involves copying the file to your workstation and then opening it later using a text editor.

Likewise, Netscape will deal with sound, image, and video files that appear as links (in the FTP list) as it does in other contexts, displaying the text, picture, or movie, or playing the sound when you click on the link.

 Netscape may have to be properly configured with the appropriate external player and viewer applications in order to play sounds or movies and display pictures. Also, once Netscape plays the sound or movie, it's gone. You'll learn how to save the images, sounds, and videos in Chapter 3.

Gopher: For Searching and Finding

When you use a URL in Netscape that begins with `gopher:`, your copy of Netscape is talking to a Gopher server. Originally developed at the University of Minnesota as a front-end to Telnet and FTP, Gopher has since caught on as one of the more important information retrieval tools on the Internet.

When you access Gopher information with Netscape, you are presented with a series of menu choices, much like the directory structure one sees in the Microsoft Windows Explorer. By double-clicking on icons, you can traverse the directory structure a level at a time until you come to an item. The great thing about Gopher is that you don't have to know what the item is or even where it is (unlike FTP). If the item is a file to download, Gopher invokes an FTP session. If the item is a link to another computer, Gopher invokes a Telnet session so you can use that computer. If it is something to be displayed—a graphic, a text document, and so on—it will do so on your screen, provided you have the

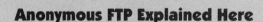

Anonymous FTP Explained Here

Anonymous FTP permits users to access remote systems without actually having user accounts on the systems. In effect, it allows for "guests" to visit a remote site, and it permits just enough computer privileges to access the resources provided. The process involves the user starting an FTP connection and logging in to the remote computer as the user "anonymous," with an arbitrary password that, for the purposes of Internet etiquette, should be your e-mail address. The beauty of using Netscape for anonymous FTP is that with Netscape you don't have to go through all the login steps, you don't have to use a text-based FTP program on your machine, and Netscape displays all the stuff on the FTP server in an easy-to-use graphical interface. You can tell when a Web document you are viewing in Netscape comes from an anonymous FTP site because the URL starts with `ftp:`.

proper client software installed on your PC. All this happens without the necessity of your worrying about Internet addressing schemes, domains, host names, and such.

The other aspect that makes Gopher so powerful is that Gopher servers reference, or *point* to, each other. It really doesn't matter where the data is located or where you start accessing Gopher servers because Gopher is able to take you there seamlessly. This is an obvious step up from using FTP, because with FTP you have to know the name of the FTP machine to get anything from it.

The University of Minnesota Gopher server acts as the master Gopher; by registering with the university, administrators can make their Gopher servers available through the master, thus allowing worldwide access to their servers. Note that there is not a Gopher-formatted resource per se; rather, Gopher acts as a helper to collect the Internet resources into a convenient inventory that lets you find items in much the same way you use the subject card catalogs at a library. In fact, with the way the Gopher servers reference one another, all this information almost appears to be on one gigantic computer.

When you use Netscape, Gopher server information is presented as a graphical menu listing of folders and file icons—just like FTP server files. (See Figure 2.7.) Because Gopher data is indexed, however, you can perform a Gopher search. Netscape has a Find menu option; when you select it, a dialog box will pop up to enable you to describe what you're seeking. (This same dialog box appears regardless of what type of indexed data you're searching—it could just as well be hypertext or a WAIS database.)

Gopher Menu

- About Earthquakes
- About NCEER
- About the NCEER Gopher Server
- Comprehensive listing of professional meetings
- Connect to NCEER ftp
- Connect to other Gophers
- Federal, State and Local Programs
- NCEER Information Service Resources
- Other Earthquake related ftp's
- QUAKELINE Database
- Veronica Searches (search Items in gopherspace)
- Who to contact for help
- NCEER Earthquake Engineering Highway Project

FIGURE 2.7: When you use Netscape to access a Gopher server, you will see folder and file icons much like those that appear in Windows Explorer.

Usenet Newsgroups: All the News You'd Ever Want

The first stop for new Internet browsers after e-mail typically used to be network news (also known as *newsgroups*), although with the advent of graphical tools such as Netscape, this may no longer be the case.

Network news is the great question and answer, ask-and-you-shall-receive-a-reply oracle of this century. It is like e-mail in that you are reading and possibly replying to messages, but unlike it in that you are able to partake of a broader scope of *public* conversations and discussions, with as little or as much participation as you want. You don't even have to take part—you

can just stand back and watch if you'd prefer. There are literally thousands of discussion groups on nearly every subject imaginable; you can join in or just cruise through them as you like.

Network news occurs in a format a lot like that of a private BBS system or a CompuServe forum. Because it is organized into *newsgroups*, it is very easy to work your way through the major headings and then through the newsgroups themselves. You need a *newsreader*, a piece of software that organizes and sorts the newsgroups—a number are available for all the major platforms. You can even download them free from the Internet.

Behind the Usenet Scenes

The major (but not the only) source of network news is Usenet, which is a free service. Usenet was actually born before the Internet, and much confusion exists as to how the two interact. Usenet is not a network like the Internet, there are no Usenet computers per se, and Usenet doesn't even need the Internet.. Rather, what drives Usenet is akin to an agreement set up between those who want to distribute and those who want to read newsgroiups. Network administrators arrange with other administrators to transfer newsgroups back and forth, which usually occurs via the Internet, but only because that's convenient. The site that provides your site with new is called a *news feed*. Some newsgroups end up being transferred by some computers, others by other computers, and so on.

Netscape provides a very capable newsreader. You can subscribe (and unsubscribe) to your favorite newsgroups, post your own articles, and read articles. We'll go over all this in detail in Chapter 3.

E-Mail: For Fast Communications

As mentioned, most people's Internet experience starts with e-mail, the lightning-fast medium for communicating with other individuals or even (via mailing lists) with groups. In the past, some Web browsers allowed you to send e-mail, but they didn't let you receive it. Why's that? Well, basically receiving requires a place for the mail to sit until you retrieve it (a mail box) and a way for you to read it (a mail reader) once you've got it. ...Receiving's more complicated than sending. Netscape version 2 introduces full e-mail capability to the Web browser world—now you can both send and receive e-mail with Netscape.

 A really cool aspect of this is that Netscape's mail reader has lots of new power—it lets you view mail that includes graphics, fancy font effects, and color changes. See Chapter 3 for more on how to use Netscape's new e-mail features

We talked a lot about e-mail in earlier sections of this chapter—take a look at *How Data Travels* and *E-Mail Addressing* to find out how e-mail makes its way around the Internet world.

The Human Side of Hypermedia

The Web is hypermedia-based, which is why the Web is called the Web: The notion of interconnections and multiple branching points, no beginning and no end, is implicit in the Web. The structure of the information is neither hierarchical nor linear. The Web and its hypertext underpinnings offer a rich environment for exploring tangential or directly related information because the hypertext paradigm works the way people do when they're on the road to discovery.

For example, if you were a kid in the '60s or '70s working on a book report about Native American cultures, your process might have looked like this: You began by reading the encyclopedia article on *Indians* (this, remember, is before Native Americans were referred to as such) when you came to a passage describing the dislocation of the Hopi people to a reservation near what is called today Apache Junction, Arizona.

Having never been near Arizona, you decided to find out about its climate, terrain, flora and fauna. Putting the *I* volume aside on the floor, you grabbed the *A* volume and dipped into *Arizona*. Then you wondered,

"What's it like today?" You called the Apache Junction Chamber of Commerce and asked for recent industrial and employment statistics. Later that day, curious about the status of any national reparations made to the Hopi in Arizona, you made a trip to your local library and had a chat with the reference librarian, who in turn brought you copies of various federal government policy statements.

Thus, the kind of discovery process supported by hypertext—and the Web—is really modeled after the way people tend to work when they're learning new things. Following our example using other tools on the Internet, such as Gopher, would be like doing the research for your childhood book report by starting each search for a distinct bit of information from the table of contents of a single book. It's easy to see why the hypertext paradigm and the Web have really taken off. In a hypertext document, if you want more information about something, you can just click on its link and there you are: The linked item could be a document on a server 7,500 miles away. If you were writing that book report today, you might travel all over the world, via the Web, without ever leaving your computer.

Moving Along...

With all this backstory in place, you're ready now to hit the highway. Starting with the next chapter, we're going to dig into how you do what you do with Netscape and the Web. Let's hit the road.

Part Two:

Navigating and Publishing with Netscape

Navigating Netscape

Let's get working with Netscape. In this chapter, you'll learn how to start the program, how to open and save Web documents, how to create Internet shortcuts, and how to switch between documents and other hypermedia (sound and video, for example) via *hot links*.

 This chapter assumes you already have an Internet connection and have installed Netscape on your PC. For information on making your Internet connection work and on getting and installing Netscape, see Chapters 9 and 10.

● Launching Netscape

Launching Netscape is easy. If you followed the instructions for getting the software and setting it up in Chapters 9 and 10, you'll have a Netscape icon on your desktop, and you'll have a new item in your Programs menu named Netscape. To start Netscape, follow these steps:

1. Start your Internet connection. How you do this depends on the sort of Internet service you have—see Chapter 9 for details about connecting to the Internet.

2. Now start up Netscape. You can do this in one of two ways:

◆ Double-click on the desktop's Netscape Navigator icon.

Netscape
Navigator

or

◆ From the Windows Start menu, select Programs ➤ Netscape to display the Netscape window. Then double-click on the Netscape Navigator icon.

SLIP and PPP: The Netscape Connection

Before you can start using Netscape, you must start the connection software that you use to access the Internet. This may seem a bit more complicated than starting many other programs, but it's really no big deal.

Here's how it works: You start your connection software—it can be Windows 95 Dial-Up Networking, CompuServe NetLauncher, or whatever you choose—which then connects your computer to the Internet. This software "introduces" Netscape to the Internet—it is a vital link in your Internet connection. (At one time, this could be accomplished only through special SLIP/PPP software, but nowadays there are new and different technologies, included with Windows 95, for example, that accomplish the same purpose.) Your connection software and your provider will then do a little dance together, passing back and forth the TCP/IP packets that make it possible for you to run Netscape (which is on your machine). Voilà—the Internet accepts your machine as a little network hooked into the bigger, more exciting network called the Internet, and you're on your way!

You can also start Netscape by double-clicking on any Windows 95 Internet shortcut. Internet shortcuts appear as Netscape icons and can be located on the desktop, in folders, or even in other documents. For information on Internet shortcuts, see <u>Using Internet Shortcuts to Web Documents</u>, later in this chapter.

If all goes well (and it surely will), the Netscape window will open, and the Netscape icon in the window's upper-right corner will become animated.

This tells you that Netscape is transferring data, which will appear in a second in the form of a Web page. Whenever Netscape is "working" (downloading a document, searching, and so on), the Netscape icon is animated. It stops when the action has been completed.

What's Out There

You can find out all about Windows 95 Dial-Up Networking at `http://athos.rutgers.edu/LCSR-Computing/win95.html`.

When you start Netscape, you'll see the Welcome to Netscape home page, with its slick, colorful graphics. You can change this start-up home page to something else if you like; we'll tell you how to do that later, in Chapter 5.

The *home page* is where you begin, where Netscape first lands you on your Internet voyage. Think of it as one of many ports of entry into the Web. The Web, you'll recall, doesn't just go from here to there—it's literally a *web*. It doesn't really matter where you start, because everything's interconnected.

You can return to the start-up home page (the one you see when you start a Netscape session) at any time simply by clicking on the Home icon on the Netscape tool bar.

If you followed the steps earlier in this chapter and have Netscape running now, try clicking on the Home icon. This brief exercise will test your Internet connection. The Netscape icon should become animated, and you should see the start-up home page displayed again on your screen.

What's Out There

By default, the start-up home page is the Welcome to Netscape home page. If you change the start-up home page and want to find the Welcome to Netscape home page again, you can use its URL, which is `http://home.netscape.com`.

Home, Home on the Home Page

The start-up home page—any home page, for that matter—may be anywhere on the Web, or it may be on your own machine. Home pages provide a lot of information and change frequently; so you may not want to zip by a Web site's start-up home page. Instead, take the time to review it when it pops up.

You are not limited to seeing the Welcome to Netscape home page at start-up—you can make it so that Netscape won't load a home page on start-up (see Chapter 5), or you can use the What's Out There page that comes with this book, or you can store and start up with one of any number of home pages that you find on the Internet. You can even create your own home page. (Refer to Chapter 8 for instructions on how to do so.)

What You See: The Netscape Interface

Let's look at the parts of the Netscape window. The interface shows the *document view window*. Figure 3.1 shows you what's what.

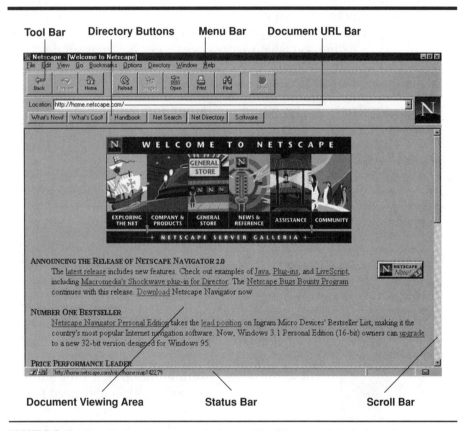

Tool Bar   Directory Buttons   Menu Bar   Document URL Bar

Document Viewing Area   Status Bar   Scroll Bar

FIGURE 3.1: Here's the Netscape window with all its parts labeled so that you can see what's what.

Via the Options menu, you can display or hide the tool bar, the status bar, the location bar, and the directory buttons.

Title Bar In the title bar you can see the name of the page you are currently viewing.

Menu Bar The menu bar in Netscape is similar to menu bars in other Windows applications: It provides you with drop-down menus. When you move the mouse to the menu and click on a selection, choices appear.

Tool Bar The tool bar performs some common actions. It's like other Windows tool bars in that all you have to do is click on the icon for the specified action to occur. If you point at a tool for a few seconds, a *ToolTip* will appear, telling you what the tool does. The ToolTip is simply a text box that displays the name of the tool to which you are pointing. Let's quickly go over the Netscape tool bar icons.

The Tool	Its Name	What You Do with It
Back	Back	Jump back to the previous page or document in your History list (that is, the page you were viewing just prior to the current page).
Forward	Forward	Jump forward to the next page or document in your History list. (If you're on the last item in the History list, this icon is *dimmed*— it looks grayed out.)
Home	Home	Return to the start-up home page.
Reload	Reload	Refresh the currently loaded document. (You may need to do this if, for instance, you have a temporary communications problem with the Web server you're connected to and the page you want to see is incompletely displayed.)

The Tool	Its Name	What You Do with It
Images	Images	Load images into the page you are currently viewing. This icon is dimmed when Netscape is set to load images automatically (that's the default setting).
Open	Open	Open a document via its URL.
Print	Print	Print the current document.
Find	Find	Locate specified text in the current document.
Stop	Stop	Cancel the process of loading an incoming document.

Location Bar Here you'll see the URL (the Uniform Resource Locator) of the current document. We'll get to a discussion of URLs a little later in this chapter.

Directory Buttons Below the location bar is a row of buttons; clicking on any of these buttons affords you fast access to some useful Web pages about Netscape.

Document Viewing Area This is the main portion of the screen—it's where you'll see what you came to the Web to see.

Status Bar The status bar is at the bottom of the screen. As you move the cursor about the document viewing area and come across links, the cursor changes into the shape of a hand with one finger pointing, and the status bar displays the URL for the link. When a document is being transferred to your machine, you'll see numbers in the status bar indicating the progress of the transfer.

◆ The key at the left end of the status bar indicates whether a document is secure.

◆ The "fractured" key indicates an insecure document—one that is transmitted between your local computer and the Web server without encryption. Or, in other words, a clever third-party with serious hacking skills can view it when it's transmitted.

 Security is a topic of great concern to many users who want to protect their personal information—such as credit card numbers and bank records—from theft. Netscape has encryption and security features that make it the preferred Web client for accessing all types of commercial Web servers. Check out A Few Quick Words on Security for more on Netscape's security features.

Scroll Bars These are just like regular Windows scroll bars: They appear on the side of the viewing area, and possibly at the bottom, when the document is too big to fit in the window. Click on the scroll bars to bring into view whatever's off the screen.

Opening Your First Document

You actually opened your first document when you started Netscape and the home page appeared. But let's dig around a little further and see what else we can open.

What's Out There

The Netscape Handbook, online documentation for Netscape, is at `http://home.netscape.com/eng/mozilla/2.0/handbook`.

Following Hot Links

As we've said before, hypertext is nonlinear. (That means you don't have to follow a straight path from point A to point Z, but rather you can skip around from one place to another to another, back to the first, round to a fourth, and so on.) Hypertext has links—*hot links*, they're often called—to other sources of information. You follow these links through a document, or from document to document, or perhaps from server to server, in any way you like as you navigate the Web. (You can think of hypertext as both the text and the links—it's the navigational means by which you traverse the Web.)

How can you tell what is hypertext in a document? Typically, the text on your screen appears highlighted in blue and is underlined, or an image appears with an added border of color. These qualities all indicate hypertext.

Moving around the World Wide Web via Netscape is a snap, thanks to hyperlinks. It's as easy as a mouse click on the hyperlink—each hyperlink points to another document, image, sound, and so on, and when you click, you jump right to whatever's represented by the item on which you clicked.

If we slowed the whole business down and showed you its underpinnings, you'd see that when you click on a hyperlink, Netscape does one of these things:

- ◆ Gets and displays the document that the link specifies
- ◆ Goes to another location in the current document
- ◆ Gets a file, such as an image or a sound file, and through the use of an external viewer or player (another piece of software on your PC) displays the image or plays the sound
- ◆ Gives you access to another Internet service, such as Gopher, FTP, Telnet, and so on

If you still have the Welcome to Netscape home page open, click on a few links. You'll soon see why they call it the Web. Try jumping back and forth a couple of times too by clicking on those tools in the tool bar. When you've had enough, simply click on the Home icon to get back to your start-up home page.

 When you move back to a document you've already seen, the color of the link changes. This is Netscape's way of letting you know you've been to that place before.

A Few Quick Words on Security

Keeping the data that passes across the Internet safe and secure is an issue that bigwigs in both business and government are discussing now and one that will soon become relevant even to the casual user.

You've probably noticed a lot of talk in newspapers and magazines and on TV about commercial ventures on the Web—merchants setting up shop and taking your credit card order and banks offering home services through their sites. You can even use the Web to buy and sell stock. If this data (your credit card number, your bank balance and access codes, or your stock portfolio) is not *safe*, it can be read by some eavesdropper lurking in an electronic shadow. Well, you can surely see the concern!

Fortunately, the designers of Netscape had this issue in mind when they developed the software. Netscape is the first Web browser to allow secured transactions to take place (between your computer running Netscape and a Web server running Netscape's Netsite Commerce server). In practical terms, this means that when you, running Netscape at home, connect to a home page on a special server that was purchased from Netscape Communications, the data sent back and forth can be secure from prying "eyes."

By now you've probably noticed the gold skeleton key icon in the lower-left corner of the Netscape window. Usually, the key appears "fractured" and displayed on a gray background. This indicates that the document you are currently viewing is *insecure*, meaning that a third party sufficiently motivated and equipped can look in on the data being sent back and forth and do with it what he or she will.

If, however, you are connected to a *secure* page—one where such eavesdropping is not possible because the data is "encrypted" before it is transferred and "unencrypted" upon arrival—the key will appear unfractured and on a blue background. (In addition, a dialog box will appear both when you connect to and when you disconnect from that page, telling you of the secure status of the transmission.)

You can find out more about security by selecting Help ➤ On Security from the Netscape menu bar. To get a directory of sites using Netsite Commerce servers, select Directory ➤ Netscape Galleria from the menu bar. To find out more about the security of the current document on screen, select View ➤ By Document Info from Netscape's menu bar.

What's Out There

Take a look at On Internet Security for the lowdown on Netscape's security features. The URL is
`http://home.netscape.com/info/security-doc.html`.

Opening a Document Using Its URL

Sometimes you're going to want to go straight to the document—you know where it is, you just want to see it without starting on a home page and skipping through a lot of hot links. Maybe your pal just sent you the URL for the Exploratorium, a really wonderful interactive science museum in San Francisco.

To open a document using its URL follow these steps:

1. From the menu bar, select File ➤ Open Location or press Ctrl+L.

2. In the Open Location dialog box (see Figure 3.2), type the URL of interest (in our example, `http://www.exploratorium.edu`).

3. Click on Open, and Netscape will find the document for this URL and display it on your screen. (See Figure 3.3.)

You can jump quickly to a document by typing its URL directly into Netscape's location bar—that is, if you have the location bar displayed.

The Web is *very* BIG. And it changes all the time. From time to time you might have difficulty locating or accessing a document. The original may have been removed by its owner, the machine that holds the document may be unavailable or overworked when you try to access it, or the network path between your machine and the server might be down. If Netscape has been trying for a while to access a document without success, it will display a dialog box saying it just plain cannot locate the document (usually it will say "Unable to locate host"). You can go back to the document that was on screen before you tried making the jump by clicking on OK.

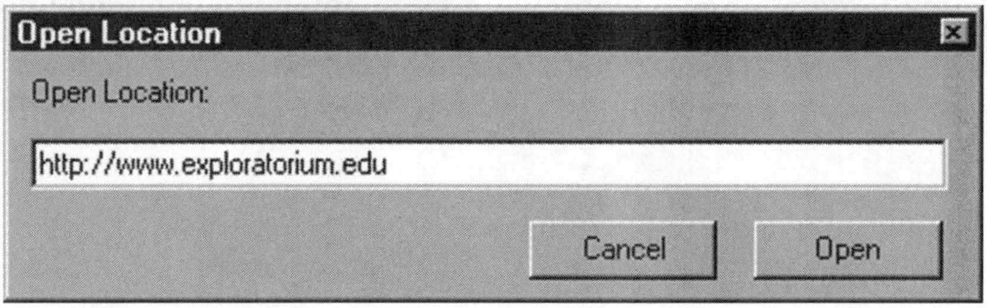

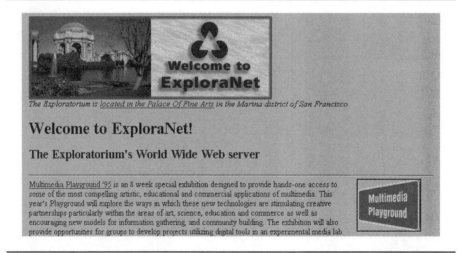

FIGURE 3.2: The Open Location dialog box

FIGURE 3.3: Here's the Exploratorium's home page. We found it using the URL a friend gave us.

Changing the Size and Color of Displayed Text

If you've been working along with this chapter, you'll notice that text appears on your screen in different sizes. Usually, the text that makes up the substance of the page—the "body text"—is about the size you'd expect,

URLs Explained Here

Remember that talk about e-mail addresses back in Chapter 2? There's a standard addressing scheme with which Netscape and the Web work too. It's called the Uniform Resource Locator (URL). The URL pinpoints the locations of documents and other information on the Web so that Netscape and other browsers can find the stuff. The structure of a URL may seem complicated at first, but it's really straightforward.

The components of the URL are:

◆ The type of resource

◆ The name of the machine containing the file (the document or information) to be transferred

◆ The full "path" that locates the file among the directories and subdirectories on the machine

For example, in the URL

```
http://home.netscape.com/home/welcome.html
```

the resource type and transfer protocol are `http:` (which, as you know, is HyperText Transfer Protocol); the double slashes separate the protocol from the rest; the name of the computer is `home.netscape.com`; and the path and filename of the item on the computer is `/home/welcome.html`.

To you, all this navigation and addressing will be transparent most of the time; Netscape uses the URL embedded in the HTML document to locate the document via hyperlinks behind the scenes.

You will sometimes type into a text box the URLs of pages you want Netscape to find and deliver to you. (See *Opening a Document Using Its URL*.) One thing you should keep in mind then is that, unlike e-mail addresses, URLs are *case-sensitive*—capitalization matters! This is because lots of Web servers are Unix machines; in Unix, filenames in uppercase letters are not considered the same as filenames in lowercase letters. All the punctuation marks you see in some URLs are significant too—one misplaced hypen, period, or tilde (~) will trip up the whole works. So if you're typing in a complex URL, look at it closely as you type.

Java Jolts Netscape

The hot word on the Net in '95 was *Java*. Java is a new technology developed by Sun Microsystems that brings a zing of interactivity to the Web, and it's arguably the most revolutionary new feature in Netscape version 2. As a user, you'll get the benefits of Java without any trouble—Java is actually a programming language that allows Web site developers to write smooth little programs called *applets* that are downloaded automatically to your computer along with the Web pages that contain and use them. What these programs can do is almost limitless (although Java includes strict security features that ensure Java programs can do no harm to your computer). The most obvious examples of Java applets may appear in the forms of animated characters jumping around your screen or ticker-tape style news feeds. As of this writing, C|Net Central's Web site (`http://www.cnet.com`) uses Java to display a ticker tape. Java also can be used to create interactive games—even games that are actually part of a Web page.

Some other examples are less glamorous or gimmicky but highly promising. Drop-down menus can become a part of standard Web pages, for example, as can icons that will change in informative ways as your pointer moves over them. The Java Telemed Prototype page is a particularly intriguing, extraordinary example of what the not-too-distant future holds—it's a prototype for a remote medical system in which doctors can see and navigate around in three-dimensional X rays (see Figure 3.4). You can examine the Java Telemed Prototype at `http://www.acl.lanl.gov/~rdaniel/classesJDK/PickTest2.html`.

Because Java is a full-featured programming language that gives developers tools to work with both Netscape and the Web, Java technology enables as-yet-unimagined possibilities. As of this writing, the technolgy in Netscape is so brand new that developers are just getting rolling. The year 1996 is bound to bring a wealth of developments in this area.

You can find out more about Java technology at the Web site maintained by the creators of Java, Sun Microsystems (`http://java.sun.com`). More at the Gamelan site at `http://www.gamelan.com`. Here you'll also find a collection of Java applets that you can download and add to your own Web pages without much trouble at all.

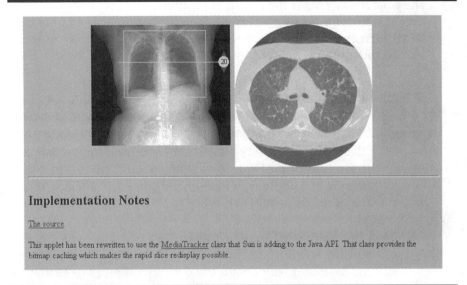

Implementation Notes

The source.

This applet has been rewritten to use the MediaTracker class that Sun is adding to the Java API. That class provides the bitmap caching which makes the rapid slice redisplay possible.

FIGURE 3.4: In addition to the cute and glamorous, Java technology enables extraordinarily practical uses such as this prototype of a three-dimensional X-ray that medical teams can navigate and examine.

while the title of the page is larger. (For a more complete discussion of the composition and elements of Web pages, see Chapter 8.)

Changing Fonts and Type Sizes

You might find that while Netscape displays body text clearly and sensibly enough, the titles on a page are too large. When a single, short title crowds out the body text, you have to scroll around a lot to read anything. You can change the font and size of displayed text in Netscape.

Here's how you do it:

1. From Netscape's menu bar, select Options ➤ General Preferences. The Preferences dialog box will appear.

2. From the tabs along the top of the dialog box, select the Fonts tab. The Preferences dialog box will be updated to reflect your choice.

3. Now, in the Fonts and Encoding area, you can make settings for either a proportional or a fixed font.

The *proportional* font is the one used for most of the text—body, head, and lists. The *fixed* font is the one used for preformatted text (a rarely used HTML element). Because the fixed font is so seldom used, we're going to stick to the proportional font in our discussion.

Leave the Preferences dialog box's "encoding" set to Latin1. Latin1 is the proper setting for English and most European languages. Note too that while other choices are apparent in this dialog box, they aren't really available to you unless you have a version of Windows that's been localized to a specific language or country. Leave this stuff alone unless you know what to do with it.

4. Click on one of the Choose Font buttons, which are along the right of the Fonts and Encoding area. Each of the buttons will display the Choose Base Font window for the corresponding font—either for the proportional or fixed font. The Choose Base Font window will appear.

5. From the Font List in this window, select a font. (The fonts that appear on this list are those that are installed on your system. If you've installed lots of fonts, they'll appear here. Otherwise, you'll see the fairly standard set of fonts that comes with Windows.)

6. Now select a font size, if you like, from the Size list. As a practical matter, the size you choose should probably be between 10 and 12 points.

You can now repeat Steps 4 through 6 for the other font.

Note that the Choose Base Font window's sample area changes to reflect your choice of font and size.

The changes you make will take effect as soon as you close the Preferences dialog box (which you can do, of course, by clicking on OK).

You might wonder as you go along, How does changing one font size change the style of more than one kind of text on a single page? Good question. Basically, Netscape displays different sizes of text (the title, headings, body text, and so on) in comparison to one "measure"—the basic font size. Netscape will display the title so-and-so many times larger than this base measure, and so forth. It is the base measure that you are changing in the procedure we just described.

Changing Colors

In Netscape, you have the option of changing the *color* of text. Imagine that! To do so, follow these steps:

1. From Netscape's menu bar, select Options ➤ General Preferences. The Preferences dialog box will appear.

2. From the list of tabs along the top of the dialog box, click on the Colors tab. The Preferences dialog box will be updated to reflect your choice.

You can choose whether you want the selections you are about to make to override any existing settings in the documents you'll be viewing. For example, you might want all the text other than links in all the documents you view to be purple, even if the document's designer made the text black. Or you might want the document designer's wishes to outweigh your own.

3. To make your upcoming color choices override any other settings, select the checkbox Always Use My Colors, Overriding Document.

or

To allow the settings that exist in a given document to override the color choices you are about to make, deselect the checkbox Always Use My Colors, Overriding Document.

4. Now click on the Choose Color button for the element whose color you want to specify. Your choices are:

◆ Links

◆ Followed Links

◆ Text

◆ Background

The Color dialog box will appear.

5. In this dialog box, you can select any of a number of predefined colors by clicking on one in the Basic Colors area.

or

You can define a custom color by clicking on the Define Custom Colors button. In that case, the window will expand to include a wide range of colors. Click in the box wherever a color you like appears. Click on the Add to Custom Colors button. The color you have specified will appear in the Custom Colors part of the Color dialog box. Click on it to make it your selected color.

6. Click on OK to close the Color dialog box. The Preferences dialog box will reappear.

7. In addition to controlling the color in which text appears, you can also control the color of the background—what appears behind the text. To change the background, either

◆ Click on the Choose Color button next to Background and choose a color as you did above, or

◆ Click on the Browse button and select a graphics file to use as the background. When you choose to use a graphics file instead of a solid color as the background, the graphics file is tiled to fit the window, no matter the window size.

8. When you are done specifying Netscape's colors, click on OK. The Preferences dialog box will close, and you will once again see the Netscape window.

The changes you've made will take place immediately. If you don't like the results, you can always go back and repeat the whole color-changing process, selecting something new and different.

 You can also always go back to the original, default color scheme. Simply deselect any custom colors you've indicated, and be sure you've clicked on the Default button next to Background.

Saving Stuff to Your Local Machine

Let's say you've been skipping around the Internet and looking at a lot of stuff and you found something really nifty you want to hold on to.

Saving takes up valuable disk space. This means you don't want to save everything. You do want to save things you want to keep for reference or access quickly in the future. For an alternative to saving, see the section Using Internet Shortcuts to Web Documents, later in this chapter.

You can save a document to your local hard drive in three ways. We'll get to those in a second; first, a word or two on naming files in general and hypertext files in particular.

Naming the Files

Some of the documents you'll want to save don't conform to the Windows 95 filenaming conventions. With Windows 95, a filename cannot include a number of special characters:

\ / : * ? " <> |

But filenames you find on the Web may include all types of characters that Windows 95 does not recognize. This is because the files you find on the Net are often created and stored on Unix machines, and their names follow the Unix filenaming system. But you're using Netscape—a *Windows* product—and that means Windows is really doing the saving. If you don't change the filename when you save the file to disk, an error message will appear saying you can't save the file. If this happens, go back and change the filename using Windows 95 conventions.

Saving Stuff You Can See

To save the page you are viewing at the moment to your hard disk:

1. From the menu bar, select File ➤ Save As. The Save As dialog box will appear (see Figure 3.5). This is much like a Save As dialog box you'd see in any other Windows application.

So What If You Have a Different Browser?

One line of thinking goes that Web documents should be viewable by any person with any Web browser; so pages should be thoughtfully designed to take into account the failings of browsers other than Netscape. Another line goes that one should exploit all the wonderful features Netscape has to offer, including fancy things such as special colors and the use of columns, frames, and tables even though people using Web browsers other than Netscape might not be able to view that stuff as it was intended to appear. You can sometimes see the evidence of this "debate" on the Web in the form of messages that say something like "Use Netscape for best viewing" or "Netscape not required." Let's take a look at what all this talk is about.

Netscape, since its nascent moment, has always pushed the envelope of what a Web browser can do. Netscape 1.0 supported HTML version 1.0 and some of the proposed HTML+ extensions; at the time, all other Web browsers were offering only HTML version 0.9. Netscape 1.1 supported the newly proposed HTML 3.0 standard. When Netscape introduced Netscape 2.0, it became the first commercial browser to support Java, Sun Microsystems' extension to the Web that allows adding more interactive and animated functionality to Web pages.

What does all this advanced thinking mean to you? Well, by using all the advanced HTML and Java features that Netscape supports, Web page authors can create state-of-the-art, visually sophisticated documents. For example, the background of a document can be a pattern instead of a solid color. A document can include small animation windows that are automatically updated and even fancy formatted tables, multicolumn lists, and drop-down menus. See *Java Jolts Netscape* earlier in this chapter for more about that extraordinary technology.

The only drawback in using these amazing features is that Web browsers other than Netscape cannot (yet) display them on screen correctly. A document designed to take full advantage of Netscape's advanced features can look disappointingly different when viewed with some other Web browser. But you have Netscape, so you'll be just fine, right?

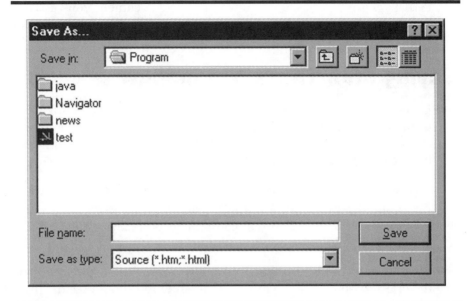

FIGURE 3.5: The Save As dialog box

2. In the File Name text box, type a filename. You needn't type an extension because the program will automatically assign either HTM or HTML—the extensions for hypertext files. (If you want to be sure the program is assigning one of those extensions, just take a look at the bottom of the dialog box, where the Save as type drop-down list appears.)

3. Pull down the Save in list by clicking on its down arrow. From the list, select the drive to which you want to save the file. Below the Save in drop-down list, the contents of the drive you selected will appear as a list of folders and icons.

4. In that list, double-click on the directory into which you want to save the file.

 If you want to place the file in a subdirectory (within a directory), first double-click on the directory that contains that subdirectory so that you can see it. For sub-subdirectories, repeat this process as needed until you find the target subdirectory.

5. Click on the Save As dialog box's Save button.

Perhaps this is obvious, but you won't see the document you've saved on screen when you save it. You'll know it's been saved when you check the Directory list and see the filename there.

Saving Stuff That's Not in View

Let's say the page you are viewing at the moment includes a link to something (maybe to a sound or to an image) that you want to save to disk to check out later. You can save the stuff at the other end of the link without first having to travel that link. Just follow these steps:

1. Pointing to the link that goes to the stuff you want to save, click the right mouse button. A menu will appear.

2. Now follow Steps 2 through 5 in the section (*Saving Stuff You Can See*) that precedes this one.

To verify that the save was successful, you can use the Explorer to look in the directory to which you just saved the file. You should see the file listed.

Viewing Documents You've Saved

You can view a document you've saved to your local hard drive by selecting File ➤ Open File from Netscape's menu bar. The File Open dialog box will appear; again this is a standard Windows dialog box. Select and open the HTM file of interest by double-clicking on it. By the way, saving a file and then viewing it this way is a lot faster than accessing and viewing it when it's somewhere else in the world; the drawback is that if the owner of the document has made changes to it, you won't know about them. A really cool aspect of this, though, is that when you view a document that's been saved to your local machine, *the links have been saved with it,* and you can simply click on those links and start up your Web travels again.

Using the rightmost button on your mouse, click once on any item (text, a link, anything) in the Web page you're viewing. A menu will appear offering you options pertaining to that item.

Using Internet Shortcuts to Web Documents

As an alternative to saving Web documents to your local machine, you can create Internet *shortcuts*. These shortcuts are a Windows feature; they look just like files on your local machine—appearing as icons on your desktop, files in folders, or the like, but instead of *being* a document (like a word-processed document, for example) they *point* to documents on the Web. Internet shortcuts offer you the advantage of having direct access to Web documents whatever else you happen to be doing on your computer. You can embed an Internet shortcut in any application that takes advantage of current OLE technology (that means most Windows 95 applications) or on your desktop; so it'll be there for your convenience when you want it.

The big advantage to having and using an Internet shortcut, as opposed to saving the actual Web document on your machine, is that the shortcut takes you to the Web document of interest as it exists "live" on the Net. When you save and view a document, on the other hand, you'll be viewing the document as it existed when you saved it—you may not be seeing the most current version. Shortcuts also conserve disk space—a shortcut takes up only a few bytes of disk space regardless of the size of the original document, while saving a whole document may take up tens of thousands of bytes.

The drawback to shortcuts (it isn't much of a drawback) is that you must be connected to the Internet to view documents with them. (They're *shortcuts* to documents on the Web, not the documents themselves, remember.) This means that the best use of shortcuts is for getting to Web documents you need to see "live." If you want to save a document you don't expect to last long on the Web, or if you don't want to pay for connect time to view a document, you may want to save the document instead of using a shortcut to get to it.

Creating an Internet Shortcut

You can create an Internet shortcut to the document you are currently viewing in Netscape by following a few simple steps.

Creating an Internet Shortcut on Your Desktop

Creating an Internet shortcut on your desktop is an end in and of itself and is the means to creating one in a Windows application. Here's how to do it.

1. With Netscape running and the Web page of interest in view, point your mouse any place on the Web document that is not a graphic or a link. (White space is a good choice.)

2. Click the right mouse button. A menu will appear.

3. From the menu, select Internet shortcut. The Create Internet Shortcut dialog box will appear.

4. In the dialog box's description text box, type a description of the Web page of interest to help you identify it in the future. Leave everything else alone.

5. Click on the OK button.

You won't see any immmediate difference on screen, but the next time you minimize or close Netscape, you'll see your new Internet shortcut appearing as an icon on your desktop. It'll look like the classic Netscape icon you're so used to seeing, with the name of the Web document under the icon.

You can also create an Internet shortcut by clicking on a hypertext word or phrase (or any other link) in a Web document and then dragging that link from Netscape's window to the desktop. When you release the mouse button after this clicking and dragging procedure, an Internet shortcut will appear where you placed it.

Placing a Shortcut in a Windows Program

Having created an Internet shortcut for the Web document of interest on the desktop as described in the section before this one, you can now pick up the shortcut there and place it in a Windows application. It's easy.

1. Follow the procedure for placing an Internet shortcut on your desktop, as described in *Creating an Internet Shortcut on Your Desktop*.

2. Open the Windows application *and the document* (or spreadsheet, or whatever) where you want the shortcut to conveniently be at your disposal.

3. Resize or otherwise position the application's window (containing the document into which you want to place the shortcut) so that you can see both it and the shortcut that appears on your desktop.

4. Click on the Internet shortcut of interest and drag it to the document in the application's window, dropping it where you want it to appear.

5. Save the document as you would if you'd made any other changes to it, using the familiar File ➤ Save or Save As features you know so well.

In the future, when you open that Windows application document (whether it's a word-processed document, a spreadsheet document, or whatever), and you then double-click on the Internet shortcut you've created, Netscape will start and load the URL, taking you automatically to the Web page of interest.

If you have an e-mail program that uses OLE technology—the Windows 95 Inbox, for example—you can drop one of these shortcuts into an e-mail message, and when the recipient of your message clicks on the shortcut (assuming he or she has Netscape), Netscape will do its thing, and the Web page of interest will appear.

Activating an Internet Shortcut

Any time you see an Internet shortcut, you can double-click on it, and Netscape will launch itself and display the page to which the shortcut points.

Jumping Back and Forth While Viewing a Document

The Back and Forward icons on the tool bar provide a convenient way to jump back and forth among the hot links you've followed.

This is because Netscape tracks the documents you visit in a History list. The Back and Forward icons actually let you travel through the History

list. If you have Netscape running, try clicking on the Back icon to jump backward along the links you just followed, and then try clicking on Forward to jump forward.

There is an end to this—if you jump back to the first document you viewed in a session, or forward to the last one, you reach the end of history. The Back or Forward icon, depending on which end of history you reach, will be grayed out. (You can, as always, create more history—click on another hypertext link to explore further.)

At the bottom of many documents, you'll find a hot word that says something like <u>Go Back</u>, which, if you click on it, will quickly jump you back to the last document you viewed. It's usually quicker, however, to click on the Back icon on the tool bar to go back.

You Can Get There from Here in a Snap: Bookmarks

A big part of managing your Netscape tour of the Web is tracking what you found and liked. One way you can revisit what's worthy is to save files to disk, a process we described earlier in this chapter. But you don't always want the stuff on your disk—it takes up valuable space. When you stumble across something on the Web that you want easy access to in the future, you should mark it with a *bookmark*. In the menu bar you'll find a drop-down menu devoted entirely to bookmarks. Let's take a look at it.

Appendix A describes Netscape's great new add-on, Smart-Marks, which you can download and use with Netscape Navigator. SmartMarks lets you categorize bookmarks even more comprehensively than the original bookmarks feature. You can even arrange to be notified automatically when specified pages change. SmartMarks also includes easy-to-use access to many of the popular searching resources on the Internet, such as Yahoo and Lycos.

Bookmarking Documents

When you're viewing a page or a document that you like so much you want to view it again later, select Bookmarks ➤ Add Bookmark from the menu bar. The name for whatever page you're so taken with will appear immediately on your Bookmark list, which is at the bottom of the Bookmarks menu, below the Go to Bookmarks option.

Keep in mind that you're not saving the page itself when you create a bookmark—you're saving the page's URL. This means that when you revisit the page you found so interesting, it may have changed. This can be both an advantage, in that you may find even more interesting stuff there next time, and a disadvantage, in that whatever you liked so much the first time might be gone on your next visit.

 The difference (to the user) between an Internet shortcut and a bookmark is that the shortcut can appear on your desktop or in another Windows application document, whereas a bookmark appears only on the Bookmark list in Netscape.

Quickly Jumping to Documents on the Bookmark List

Any time you are using Netscape, regardless of where you are or what you're viewing, you can jump to any page you've bookmarked. Simply pull down the Bookmarks menu and select the name of the page to which you want to jump.

Bookmark Management

After a while, when you've bookmarked a lot of pages, you'll find the list growing to unwieldy proportions. The bookmarks themselves might seem to be in no particular order. (Actually, bookmarks are listed in the order you created them, but that's not very helpful when you're digging through a long list.)

Fortunately, Netscape allows you to impose some order on all this seeming chaos. You can toss out the old and unused stuff if you want, but you can also shift things around so that they make more sense. You can put related pages next to one another on the Bookmark list; you can even group

related pages under folders, which then appear as submenus of the Bookmarks menu.

Rearranging Bookmarks

You can easily rearrange items in your Bookmark list. Let's say we've created three bookmarks: One is the Exploratorium home page, which we saw earlier in this chapter, the second is the Rolling Stones home page from Chapter 2, and the third is the home page from the National Center for Earthquake Engineering Research (NCEER) at SUNY Buffalo.

The first and the third pages might fit nicely together into a *science* category. Here's how to put them next to each other on the Bookmark list:

1. From Netscape's menu bar, select Bookmarks ➤ Go to Bookmarks. The Bookmarks window will appear, as shown in Figure 3.6 (where the three bookmarks are displayed).

You can use the Bookmarks window as a handy way to jump to a document you've marked. Simply double-click on the bookmark for the page to which you want to jump. The page will appear in the Netscape window.

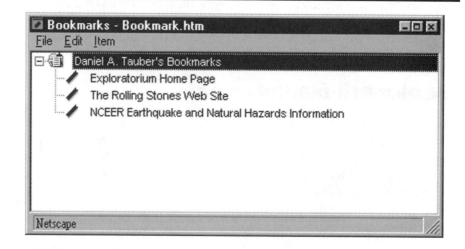

FIGURE 3.6: The Bookmarks window

2. Highlight the bookmark you want to move by clicking on it and then drag (by holding down the mouse button as you move the mouse) it up or down to its final resting place. Once you have moved the mouse pointer to the bookmark's final location, release the mouse button. You'll now see the bookmark in the new location.

That's all there is to it.

Creating Folders

When you've created a long, long list of bookmarks, rearranging them may seem tedious. In the end, it's also a poor solution to your organizational woes—you'll still find yourself searching line by line through the list. Worst yet, you'll end up with a Bookmarks menu too tall for Netscape to display. A better way to deal with the problem is to group bookmarks in *folders*, which will appear on the Bookmark list (that is, on the Bookmarks menu) as submenus. (Bookmarks grouped under a folder will appear as options on these submenus.)

Here's how to create folders:

1. If it's not already open on your screen, open the Bookmarks window by selecting Bookmarks ➤ Go to Bookmarks from the menu bar.

 Netscape conveniently provides useful information about any highlighted bookmark in the Bookmark Properties window. To view the Bookmark Properties window for the highlighted bookmark, select Item ➤ Properties from the Bookmarks menu bar. You'll find the name of the highlighted page, its URL, and the dates when you created the bookmark and when you last visited the page. There's even a text box into which you can type your own description of the bookmarked page.

2. From the Bookmarks menu bar, select Item ➤ Insert Folder. The Bookmark Properties dialog box will appear.

3. In the dialog box's Name text box, give the new folder a descriptive name—one that will help you find this stuff when it appears on the Bookmark list. (We'll call our new folder here *Science*.) Once you have entered a name, click on OK. The dialog box will close, and the Bookmarks window will reappear, with your new folder listed.

4. Highlight and drag the folder to a position above the bookmarks you want to appear in the folder. Following our example from the previous section, we moved the new folder to a location above Exploratorium and NCEER.

5. Now that you've created and named a new folder, you'll have to group bookmarks under it. Highlight and drag a bookmark to the folder. As you move the bookmark over the folder, a highlight will appear over the folder. When this highlight appears, release the mouse button. The bookmark will appear as an item in the folder—the bookmark's title will be indented under the folder's title.

6. Repeat Step 5 for each bookmark you want to place in a folder. When you've finished, close the Bookmarks window by selecting File ➤ Close from the menu bar.

Now if you pull down the Bookmarks menu, the folder you created will appear as a submenu (marked on its right side by an arrow), but the bookmarks you placed in it won't be listed there. Not to worry—simply select the new folder, and the bookmarks grouped in it will appear.

The History Window as Bookmark List

You might think of the History window as a pseudo-Bookmark list. The History window is a log of every move you make in your Netscape session. Each time you launch Netscape, the History window starts empty; then it fills up with a list of your moves as you go along. To see the History window, select Window ➤ History from the menu bar (a highlight appears over the name of the current page). You can then double-click on any page listed here and jump to that item. Thus, you can use the History window as a kind of short-term Bookmark list.

You can use the History window to retrace your steps. This is more convenient than continuously clicking on the Back icon, but it's not *terrifically* convenient. You have to look at all the places you've been, find the one you want, and select it.

A list of the last so many pages you visited appears on Netscape's Go menu, and that provides another route to the past. The actual number of pages displayed on the Go menu depends on the video display on your computer—Netscape displays enough to fill the height of your display.

To add items from the History window to your Bookmark list, highlight the item of interest in the History window, and then click on the Create Bookmark button. The next time you check into your Bookmark list, you'll find a new bookmark there.

Displaying the Bookmark List

Netscape gives you a good deal of control over the way the Bookmark list is displayed on the Bookmarks menu. Once you've created a folder, you can tell Netscape to put any new bookmarks in it. By default, you see, Netscape will put a new bookmark at the top level of the Bookmark list, which means directly on the Bookmark list and not in any folder you've created. To change this and to put any new bookmarks automatically and directly into a folder, first open the Bookmarks window. Then, highlight the folder you want to use, and from the menu bar, select Item ➤ Set to New Bookmarks Folder. It's that simple.

Netscape also allows you to "shrink" the Bookmark list so that when you pull down the Bookmarks menu, only the bookmarks contained in one folder are displayed. This may be useful if you've got a *lot* of folders and you're only going to be using one group of bookmarks in a given Web session. To do this, highlight the folder you want to see on the Bookmarks menu in the Bookmarks window. Now, from the menu bar, select Item ➤ Set to Bookmark Menu Folder. To change the list back and display all bookmarks (and folders) again, highlight the topmost folder in the Bookmarks window, and from the menu bar, select Item ➤ Set to Bookmark Menu Folder.

Removing Items from Your Bookmark List

Out with the old and in with the new! You can remove any bookmark or folder from your Bookmark list, making room for fresher material.

To delete items from your Bookmark list, follow these steps:

1. From the menu bar, select Bookmarks ➤ Go to Bookmarks to open the Bookmarks window.

2. In the window, highlight the bookmark or folder you want to remove.

3. From the Bookmarks window's menu bar, select Edit ➤ Delete.

If you delete a folder from your Bookmark list, any bookmarks under that folder will also vanish.

4. When you've finished removing bookmarks and folders, select File ➤ Close from the Netscape Bookmarks menu bar to return to the Netscape window.

The items you deleted will no longer appear in the Bookmark list (that is, on the Bookmarks drop-down menu).

Netscape includes a great feature that allows you to see which of your bookmarked Web pages have changed since the last time you visited them. To get the latest, highlight the page(s) of interest in the Bookmarks window (or highlight nothing if you want to check all the bookmarked pages), and from the menu bar, select File ➤ What's New. Netscape will venture forth to check the Web pages and report which of them have been modified since your last visit. The title of any page that has changed will appear as usual in the Bookmarks window, but now it'll have a little yellow icon next to it.

● Quitting Netscape

You can quit Netscape any ol' time—even when the Netscape icon (the N) is animated.

To leave Netscape, simply do the following:

1. If the N is animated, click on the Stop button on the tool bar. This will cancel whatever Netscape is trying to do at the moment. (If the N is not animated, skip this step.)

2. To actually quit the program, double-click on the Control button in the upper-left corner of the screen, *or* select File ➤ Exit from the menu bar. The Windows desktop will reappear.

3. Remember, you are still connected to your Internet Service provider, and you must break this connection, using whatever techniques are specifically appropriate. (Check with your Internet service provider to find out about that.)

The Ol' Bookmark-List-Becomes-a-Web-Page Trick

Here's a nifty trick: You can make your Bookmark list into a Web page that links you to all your favorite places. This is possible because Netscape stores your bookmarks in an HTML file that can be viewed and navigated like any other Web page. With Netscape running, follow these steps:

1. From the menu bar, select Bookmarks ➤ Go to Bookmarks. The Bookmarks window will appear.

2. Select File ➤ Save As from the menu bar. The Save As dialog box will appear.

3. In the dialog box, type a filename—something like FAVES.HTM or whatever you like that will remind you that this is your own personal Bookmark List page. Click on the Save button. The Bookmarks window will reappear. From the menu bar, select File ➤ Close to return to the Netscape window.

Now you can open up FAVES.HTM (or whatever you called it) just as you would any other HTML file you've saved to your local machine. The first cool thing is that you'll find you have created a Web page version of your Bookmark list, which you can use as your own home page or pass on to friends and colleagues for their use. The second cool thing you'll find is that all the headings and organization you've done in your Bookmark list will be included in the page. The third cool thing is that any descriptions you've provided for individual items (in the Bookmarks window's Description box) will appear as text describing the links. Yes, we said links. Because, of course, all the items you've bookmarked appear in this page as clickable links to those resources you found so appealing or useful that you just had to bookmark them.

What's Out There

Want to be hip to what's happening on the Net? The latest Net Happenings are the topic at `http://www.mid.net/NET`. And you can get advance information about new versions of Netscape and other Web browsers via the Browser Watch site at `http://www.ski.mskcc.org/browserwatch/`.

Now, with your basic skills in place for navigating the Web via Netscape, let's take a look at how you can communicate with others (via newsgroups and e-mail) the Netscape way.

Newsgroups and E-Mail the Netscape Way

Before the advent of the wonderful World Wide Web and its attending browsers, there was an Internet, and it was already a happening place. Much of what went on via the Internet then took the form of talk—typed talk, to be sure, but talk nonetheless, in the form of newsgroup articles and e-mail. For a long time, many people thought newsgroups *were* the Internet—the whole Internet. Even today, e-mail is one of the most popular features of the Net, and newsgroups are a highly viable forum for discussion on all sorts of topics.

In earlier versions, Netscape provided a competent newsgroup reader and the ability to send e-mail (but not receive it). Among the stellar accomplishments appearing in Netscape Navigator 2 are an improved newsgroup reader and a full-featured e-mail program that lets you send *and receive* e-mail using Netscape. Let's take a look.

Reading and Writing Usenet News with Netscape

Unlike many other Web browsers, Netscape provides you with fully workable access to Usenet. Usenet is a collection of discussion groups, called *newsgroups*, each organized around a specific topic or area of interest. Access to Usenet is through a feature of Netscape called Netscape News. Using Netscape News, you can read and post *articles* (messages) to those newsgroups that interest you.

Before you can start using Usenet with Netscape, you must set up Netscape to work with the way you access the Internet, whether that's via an Internet service provider, an online service such as CompuServe, or whatever. This is a special aspect of installing Netscape. See Chapter 10 for details.

What's Out There

What Is Usenet will tell you all about Usenet newsgroups at the URL `ftp://rtfm.mit.edu/pub/usenet/news.answers/usenet/what-is/part1`.

Starting Netscape News, the Newsgroup Reader

Netscape News is quite easy to start up. Simply follow this single step:

1. From Netscape's menu bar, select Window ➤ Netscape News. The Netscape News window will appear.

That's all there is to it. Now you can start reading and writing Usenet news.

Reading Usenet News for the First Time

At first glance you may find the Netscape News window a bit confusing. Don't worry—we're going to tell you how to use it. The window has a number of sections—each displays different information. A list of Usenet news servers appears in the upper-left side of the window (you told Netscape the name of your Usenet news server when you got Netscape working with your Internet connection). Clicking on any of the news servers (most likely you'll only have one server listed) displays a list of newsgroups located on that server to which you are subscribed. In the upper-right side of the window is a list of articles in the currently selected newsgroup. The actual articles appear in the bottom part of the window.

What's Out There

DejaNews keeps a giant archive of past Usenet news articles that you can search at `http://www.dejanews.com`.

One Way to Get into a Newsgroup

Netscape News lets you *subscribe* to groups you read or participate in regularly. When you subscribe to a newsgroup, its name appears in the Netscape News window, and you can start using the newsgroup by just clicking on its name.

To subscribe to a newsgroup, follow these easy steps:

1. If the Netscape News window is not already open, select Window ➤ Netscape News from Netscape's menu bar. The Netscape News window will appear, looking something like it does in Figure 4.1.

2. From the Netscape News menu bar, select Options ➤ Show All Newsgroups. A dialog box will appear warning you that it may take a while to get the list of all newsgroups.

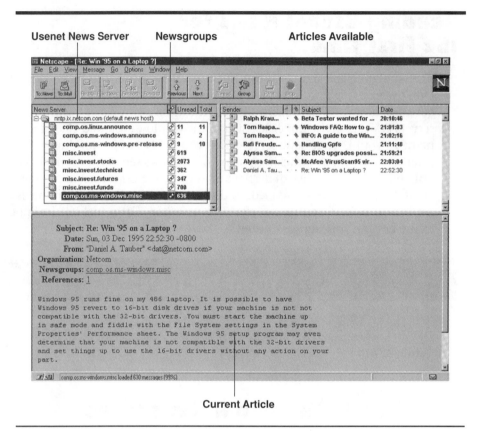

FIGURE 4.1: The Netscape News window gives you access to Usenet news.

3. Click on OK to dismiss the warning dialog box. Netscape News will start downloading the list of newsgroups from the news server to your machine. While the list of newsgroups is downloading, the mouse pointer will be an hourglass. You can follow the downloading progress in the status bar along the bottom of the Netscape News window.

4. When the list of newsgroups has been downloaded to your computer, it will appear in the Netscape News window, listed under the news server. Locate the newsgroup to which you want to subscribe, and select the checkbox that appears to its right.

The newsgroup to which you've subscribed will appear with a checkmark to its right in the list of newsgroups. The two numbers that appear next to it tell you how many articles in that newsgroup you have yet to read and how many articles are available in total. In Figure 4.2, you can see that we've subscribed to a newsgroup called `comp.os.ms-windows.misc`, which is a hotbed of talk about Microsoft Windows.

nntp.ix.netcom.com (default news host)		
comp.os.linux.announce	11	11
comp.os.ms-windows.announce	2	2
comp.os.ms-windows.pre-release	9	10
misc.invest	619	
misc.invest.stocks	2073	
misc.invest.technical	362	
misc.invest.futures	347	
misc.invest.funds	700	

FIGURE 4.2: The newsgroups you subscribe to will be listed in the Netscape News window.

What's Out There

The Great Renaming FAQ contains a fascinating history of Usenet at `http://falcon.jmu.edu/~bumgarles/gr.html`.

Another Way to Get into a Newsgroup

The URLs for newsgroups start with `news:` rather than with `http:`. Knowing this handy fact, you can access a Usenet newsgroup by selecting File ➤ Open Location from Netscape's menu bar and, in the window that appears,

typing the newsgroup's URL (which is just the name of the newsgroup preceded by news:) into the text box and clicking on Open. This is a quick way to get into a newsgroup, but it does not preserve your access to the newsgroup—next time you want to go there, you'll have to repeat this procedure.

Once you've accessed a particular newsgroup using this technique, you can read articles and, using the skills described in the sections that follow (check out Posting a Reply and Posting a New Article), you can write to the newsgroup.

Unsubscribing from Newsgroups

You won't always want to remain a subscriber to a particular newsgroup. Your interests will change; the newsgroup will grow dull. In fact, Netscape automatically subscribes to three newsgroups for you. They provide helpful information for new Usenet users but aren't really necessary once you've become accomplished. After a while, you'll probably want to let them go. Unsubscribing is really easy. Click on the checkbox to the right of the newsgroup name to remove the x. When you do this, the name of the newsgroup will disappear from the list of newsgroups to which you are subscribed. You can always resubscribe if you want to pick up that newsgroup again.

Reading Articles in Subscribed Newsgroups

To read articles once you've subscribed to a newsgroup, click on that newsgroup's name in the Netscape News window. All the "unread" articles in the newsgroup will appear along the right side of the window (see Figure 4.3). To read an article, simply click on it in this list. When you do this, Netscape transfers the contents of the article to your computer and displays it in the bottom part of the window.

Ralph Krau...	· ◆	Beta Tester wanted for ...	20:10:46
Tom Haapa...	· ◆	Windows FAQ: How to g...	21:01:03
Tom Haapa...	· ◆	INFO: A guide to the Win...	21:02:16
Rafi Freude...	· ◆	Handling Gpfs	21:11:48
Alyssa Sam...	· ◆	Re: BIOS upgrades possi...	21:59:21
Alyssa Sam...	· ◆	McAfee VirusScan95 vir...	22:03:04
Daniel A. Tau...	· ·	Re: Win '95 on a Laptop ?	22:52:30

FIGURE 4.3: A few of the unread articles listed for a newsgroup called comp.os.ms-windows.misc (a general discussion group about Microsoft Windows)

Reading Along a Thread

Notice also in Figure 4.3 that articles are listed by authors' names and that some articles appear indented below others. Some less-capable newsgroup readers display articles only in the order they were posted, but Netscape arranges articles by *subject* in the order they were posted. A message that is not indented is the beginning of a discussion on a particular topic. A message that appears indented below another is a later message about the same subject; often it is a reply.

By ordering the messages in this way, Netscape allows you to read all the articles about a subject, one right after the other. Messages grouped by subject in this way are called *threads,* and reading messages this way is called *reading along a thread.* A thread is essentially a string of related articles—they're related in that they are usually responses that follow the original article.

To read along a thread, first open any article you want by clicking on its name. (Because Netscape lists the articles in each thread in the order they were posted, it's probably a good idea to start with an article that begins a thread—in other words, one that is not indented.)

When you're done reading the first article, you can read the next article in the thread—this can be the next contribution to the discussion or a reply to the message you just finished—by clicking on the Next button. If you're in the middle of a thread, you can read the article posted prior to the one you're looking at by clicking on the Previous button. This button

and all the others you need to read newsgroup articles are at the top of the Netscape News window.

Let's quickly go over all the buttons Netscape News provides for reading articles.

The Tool	Its Name	What It Does
To:News	Post new	Posts a new article
Re:News	Post reply	Posts a reply to the article you are currently reading
Re:Both	Post and reply	Posts a reply to the current article and e-mails the reply
To:Mail	New message	Sends an e-mail message
To:Mail	Reply	Sends an e-mail message to the author of the article you are currently reading
Forward	Forward	Forwards the current message to someone else via e-mail
Previous	Previous	Moves to the previous article in the thread you are currently reading
Next	Next	Moves to the next article in the thread you are currently reading
Thread	Mark thread read	Moves to the first article in the next thread, marking the current thread as read

The Tool	Its Name	What It Does
Group	Mark all read	Marks all the articles in the current newsgroup as read
Print	Print	Prints the current article
Stop	Stop	Interrupts the transfer of an article to your computer

Posting a Reply

If you want to post a reply to an article you've read, follow these easy steps:

1. With an article open (presumably the one to which you want to reply), click on the Reply button. A window will appear, as shown in Figure 4.4.

In the window's Subject box, the subject of your post (taken from the original article) will appear. In the Newsgroup box, the newsgroups in which the original article appeared will be listed.

2. If you'd like to include the original message in your reply, click on the Quote button at the top of the window. The original message (the one to which you are posting a reply) will appear in the window. To make it easy for you to see what's what, each line in the original message will be prefixed with the > symbol. You can delete any part (or all) of the original message if you like.

3. Type your reply to the original message in the text box along the bottom of the window, and click on the Send button at the top of the window.

Your reply will be posted automatically to the groups in which the original article appeared.

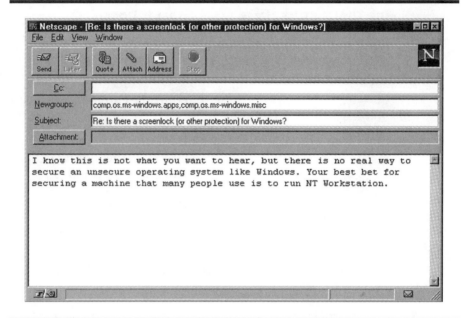

FIGURE 4.4: This window is your door to writing newsgroup replies.

You needn't feel compelled to quote the entire original article in your reply. It's considered good form to delete as much of the original message as necessary 'til you get down to the part that is immediately relevant to your response. Further, you can add or delete newsgroups listed in the Newsgroup text box as you wish. This is a simple matter of typing in the names of any newsgroups you want to add or of highlighting any you want to delete and then wielding your Delete key.

Posting a New Article

You can post new articles to start new threads as well. Simply click on the New icon at the top (or the bottom) of the Netscape News window. The procedure after this point is exactly the same as that for posting a reply, except that the subject of the article is not filled in and there is no text in the Message text box. Refer to the preceding section (*Posting a Reply*) for more information.

Do You Need Help?

For answers to your questions about using Netscape, call (800) 320-2099 or e-mail client@netscape.com. Keep your credit card handy if you haven't paid for Netscape just yet.

Sending and Receiving E-Mail the Netscape Way

Netscape version 2 offers a full-featured e-mail program, Netscape Mail, that allows you to send *and receive* e-mail. This is new to the world of Web browsers and is quite a nifty feature. Heretofore, Web browsers allowed you to send e-mail but not to receive it. That was because receiving e-mail involved much more complicated issues of, for example, storing messages 'til you read them. Netscape has licked this challenge, and now you have the e-mail capability in your Web browser to prove it.

NOTE Before you can use Netscape Mail, you must set up Netscape to use your Internet service provider's POP3 mailbox and SMTP mail server. This is not difficult; turn to Chapter 10 for more information.

Starting Netscape Mail

To start Netscape Mail, take these simple steps:

1. From the Netscape menu bar, select Window ➤ Netscape Mail. The Password Entry dialog box will appear (see Figure 4.5).

2. Type the password assigned to you by your Internet service provider, and click on OK. In a few seconds, the Netscape Mail window will appear. You can see it in Figure 4.6.

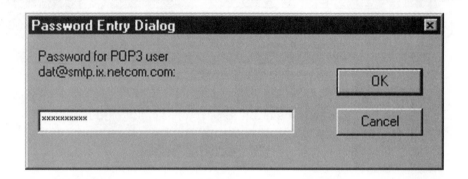

FIGURE 4.5: In the Password Entry dialog box, you must enter your e-mail password.

Incoming Mailbox   Current Mail Message   Mail Messages

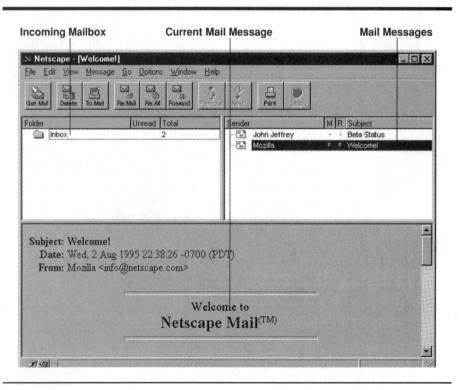

FIGURE 4.6: The Netscape Mail window allows you to read and send e-mail to anyone on the Internet.

With the Netscape Mail window open, you are ready to start getting and sending e-mail.

Reading Your Mail

The Netscape Mail window is divided into several sections, much as the Netscape News window is. Along the upper-left side of the Netscape Mail window you'll see a list of folders—you'll probably have only one listed right now because nothing much has happened yet, and that will be the Inbox. Along the upper-right side of the Netscape Mail window (see Figure 4.6) is a list of messages from the current folder. The current message is displayed in the bottom part of the Netscape Mail window.

The buttons that appear along the top of the Netscape Mail window are shortcuts to many commonly used and popular features.

The Tool	Its Name	What It Does
Get Mail	Get mail	Retrieves mail waiting on the mail server
Delete	Delete	Deletes the highlighted message
To: Mail	New Mail	Creates a new message
Reply	Reply	Replies to the author of the current message
Reply All	Reply All	Replies to all the recipients of the current message
Forward	Forward	Forwards the current message to someone else

The Tool	Its Name	What It Does
⬆ Previous	Previous	Moves to the previous message
⬇ Next	Next	Moves to the next message
🖨 Print	Print	Prints the current message
⬢ Stop	Stop	Stops transmission or whatever activity is occurring

Sending a Message

Sending a message with Netscape Mail is easy. Just follow these steps:

1. From the Netscape Mail menu bar, select Message ➤ New Mail Message. The Message Composition window will appear. It will be empty, but in Figure 4.7 you can see one that contains all the information you'll eventually have entered into it.

2. In the Mail To text box, type the e-mail address of the person to whom you want to send an e-mail message.

You can also get the e-mail address from your Address book; click on the Mail To button to gain access to it. (See Creating Your Very Own Address Book for more details about this handy feature.)

3. Now in the Subject field, type a subject for the message you are about to write.

4. Click in the big text box along the bottom of the window, and start typing your message.

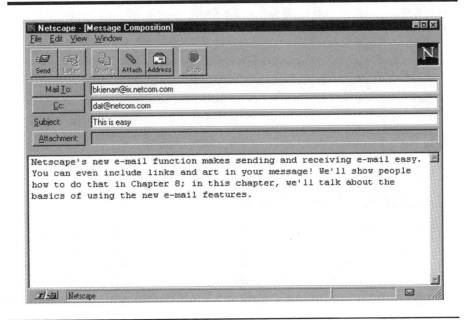

FIGURE 4.7:   In the Message Composition window, you'll enter all the stuff that makes up your e-mail message.

5. When you are done typing your e-mail message and are ready to send it, click on the Send button along the top of the window. Your message will go off in a matter of seconds, and you will be returned to the Netscape Mail window.

What's Out There

Find your favorite star's e-mail address with Martha's Celebrity E-Mail Compilation, at the URL http://www.galstar.com/~bkeller/maddress.html.

Creating Your Very Own Address Book

Netscape provides you with the convenience of keeping an address book in which you can organize and store the e-mail addresses of all the people with whom you correspond. The Address book works and is useful both in Netscape Mail and Netscape News—any time you need to enter an e-mail address in either case you can use your handy Address book. But first you have to get the addresses in there.

One Way to Add People to Your Address Book

Adding new e-mail addresses to your Address book is as simple as most other Netscape tasks. Usually, you'll find you want to add the e-mail address of someone to whom you're replying. To do this, you'll of course start with either an e-mail message or a Usenet article from the person whose e-mail address you want to add to your book appearing on screen.

1. With the e-mail message or Usenet article from the person you want to add to your Address book on screen, right-click your mouse (preferably and most safely in some white space in the message). A menu will appear.

2. From the menu, select Add to Address Book. The Address Book Properties dialog box will appear.

3. This dialog box has in it text boxes where you can type information about the person you are adding to your Address book. In the Nick Name text field, type a nickname for the person. (In the old days we called this a "handle." You can just use the person's given name if you like.) Nicknames must be single words and contain only lowercase letters.

4. In the Description text box you can enter a description or notes about the person whose e-mail address you are adding. For example, you might want to make notes about how you met this person, why he or she is of interest, or what you mean to contact him or her about in the future.

5. You'll find that the Name and E-Mail Address text boxes are already filled out—this is a result of the message from the person being open. Now finish up by clicking on the OK button to add the e-mail address to your Address book. The Address Book Properties dialog box will close.

Next time you open the Address book window you'll see the new e-mail address listed.

Another Way to Add People to Your Address Book

If you know someone's e-mail address and you just want to add it to your Address book without being in mid-reply to a message, follow these steps:

1. From the Netscape menu bar, select Window ➤ Address book. The Address Book window will appear.

2. From the Address Book window's menu bar, select Item ➤ Add User. The Address Book Properties dialog box will appear.

3. This dialog box has in it text boxes where you can type information about the person you are adding to your Address book. In the Nick Name text field, type a nickname ("handle") for the person, or just use the person's given name. Nicknames must be single words and can contain only lowercase letters.

4. In the Description text box you can enter a description or notes about the person whose e-mail address you are adding. For example, you might want to make notes about how you met this person, why he or she is of interest, or what you mean to contact him or her about in the future.

5. In the Name and E-Mail Address text boxes, type the name and e-mail address of the person whose address you're adding to your book.

6. Now click on the OK button to add the e-mail address to your Address book. The Address Book Properties dialog box will close.

Now you'll see the new entry you just created in the Address book window.

Using Your Address Book for Sending Mail

In the section titled *Sending a Message* earlier in this chapter, we told you the basics for sending e-mail, but it can be a more convenient process. Once you've got people listed in your Address book, you can start using it to make sending e-mail easier. To send e-mail to someone who's listed in

the Address book, follow these steps:

1. From the Netscape menu bar, select Window ➤ Address book to open your Address book.

2. In the Address Book window, locate and double-click on the name of the person to whom you want to send mail. The Message Composition window will appear, with your intended recipient's name and e-mail address filled in.

3. Go ahead—write and send your e-mail message as you usually would.

That's all there is to using Netscape's multifunctional, convenient Address book.

Replying to a Message

Replying to a message is very much like writing a new message. Just follow these steps:

1. With the message to which you want to reply on screen, click on either the Reply or the Reply All button. (Remember, the Reply button will address your reply only to the person who sent the message; the Reply All button will address your message to everyone involved—including all the people who were "CCed.") Regardless of which buttons you click, the Message Composition window will appear.

2. In the Message Composition window, you'll see that the Mail To, Cc, and Subject fields are already filled in, based on information that came from the message to which you are replying. You can modify any of these fields if you like, or you can leave them as is.

3. In the text area near the bottom of the window, type your message. You can include the contents of the original message in your reply by clicking on the Quote button.

4. After you type your e-mail message, click on the Send button. In a matter of seconds, your message will be transferred from your computer to your Internet service provider's mail server—it's on its way!—and the Netscape Mail window will reappear on your screen.

Now you know how to send a reply.

You can embed HTML (hypertext, images, and more) into your e-mail messages—effectively making your messages into documents. See Chapter 8 to find out how.

Quitting Netscape Mail

When you're finished reading and replying to your mail, quitting Netscape Mail is a quick, standard procedure you can accomplish in just one step. From the menu bar, select File ➤ Close. The Netscape window will appear.

Now you can practice any of the skills you picked up in this chapter, or if you're done for now, you can quit Netscape altogether.

We're on Our Way!

Now that you know how to use all of Netscape's basic features, including the newsgroup reader and e-mail program, let's turn our attention in Chapter 5 to some great starting points for your Web exploration, and then, in Chapter 6, to lots of way cool places you can visit via Netscape Navigator.

Good and Useful Starting Points

You can jump into the Web from any of what seem like zillions of places. But you won't always want to wander the Web; sometimes you'll want to focus your travels. When you're following links from one document to another, it's easy to forget how you got to that gold mine of resources. You may find it difficult to retrace your steps.

Fortunately, there are some great comprehensive starting points on the Web that can really help get you going. Several really terrific meta-indexes exist, and there are lots of smaller indexes that focus on specific topics. Many Web sites—Netscape's included—provide What's New pages along with the more entertaining What's Hot or What's Cool pages, all listing interesting sites, usually by category. Netscape itself provides several tools that can help you retrace your electronic trail.

● The Big Picture

In Chapter 3 we told you how to start Netscape and navigate. The first time you start Netscape, the Welcome to Netscape page will be the default—the page you see automatically. (Later, you can display a different home page on start-up, if you like.) The Welcome to Netscape page is a perfectly good place to start—we'll look a little more closely at what it has to offer in a second. There are many other good starting places, however. Before we look at these in detail, let's go over some general information about home pages.

Indexes and Directories: An Industry Is Born

What good is a Web index or directory? Well, imagine TV without the benefit of those handy programming guides that come with your Sunday paper, or imagine a really huge library without a card catalog—whether it's in a file cabinet or on a computer. You wouldn't know what's where when or how to find anything.

...That's the Web without indexes and directories. An entire industry of Web indexing has arisen from this need; today there are at least five well-known Web directories, all competing to be the biggest, the best, or both.

Most directories use a Web crawler of some sort to scour the Net for sites, which are then indexed by topic. Yahoo is that type; its main feature is a browsable index. Some directories go further by also offering reviews and rating systems so that you can pick and choose before you spend all your time wandering around online. Magellan is an example of that type; its entries are also searchable, however, offering additional options for finding what you seek quickly and easily. These days, most directories *are* searchable, adding another dimension to their usefulness, and many are beginning to offer editorial content in the form of features such as Best of the Web awards, contests, articles, and informative material such as weather reports and newsfeeds. In this chapter we'll introduce you to the more popular meta-indexes and to some additional tools for tracking where you've been.

What Is a Home Page, Really?

You can look at this in a couple of ways. To you, the user, the home page is a starting point for exploring a single site on the whole World Wide Web. You can think of a home page as a kind of "main menu." This analogy breaks down a bit because the Web is neither hierarchical nor linear and Netscape is by no means menu-driven; but a home page does outline your options—at least the options for moving along the links from this site to other points of interest, as imagined by the publisher of this site. To whomever publishes it, the home page is part advertisement, part directory, and part "reference librarian." Publishers of a Web site's home page have to think through its construction completely to make clear what the page is about and what can be found there.

 Just to clarify things a bit, a <u>Web site</u> may be a single page or a collection of pages. The main page among a number of pages is a <u>home page</u>. A <u>Web server</u>, by the way, is the machine and software that houses the Web site.

In reality, a home page is a hypertext document that has links to other points on the Web. The start-up home page, the one that is automatically loaded each time you launch Netscape, should be one that helps you get going. It may be the default Welcome to Netscape page, some other home page that provides a general starting point, or one that is specialized to your interests. You can even set up Netscape not to access and display a home page, though why you'd want to start out without the benefit of a good start-up home page is beyond us.

Changing Your Start-Up Home Page

For new users and experienced users whose purposes are fairly general, the Welcome to Netscape page or another of those we describe in this chapter might be best. For example, you might find it handy to make your start-up home page the Magellan, a big directory of Internet resources. That'll give you a good launchpad that's more general and comprehensive than the Welcome to Netscape page, which is devoted primarily to Netscape and Netscape users. For those with special interests, a specific home page geared to those interests might be better. Let's say, for example, that you're doing a long-term research project on the subject of language and thought. You know what you want—none of this general stuff. For the duration of your project, you might set your start-up home page to the one published by Stanford University's Linguistics Department. That way, each time you launch Netscape, you'll immediately see the Stanford Linguistics Department's home page, and you can begin your research from that point. When you've finished that project and begin another—this time writing environmental assessment reports for a large government

contractor—you instead use the U.S. Geological Survey's home page as your start-up page.

> To speed Web access, you might want to choose as your start-up home page one residing on a server that's geographically close to you—the closer the better. This is getting easier to do, with the Web's rate of growth. Or perhaps you work for a company that has its own home page. Remember: You can actually get anywhere on the Web from almost anywhere else on the Web, so it makes sense to make your start-up home page as convenient for you as possible. You can even construct your own custom home page using Netscape's nifty bookmark features, as described in Chapter 3, or using HTML, as you'll see in Chapter 8.

To change your start-up home page, you'll use Netscape's Preferences dialog box—this handy dialog box is your entrance way to changing many facets of Netscape's behavior on your machine.

Here are the steps for changing your home page:

1. Start Netscape by clicking on its icon, without bothering to start your Internet connection. (What we're doing here is strictly a local operation.)

2. From the menu bar, choose Options ➤ General Preferences. The Preferences dialog box will appear.

3. From the tabs along the top of the Preferences dialog box, select Appearance.

4. Roughly in the middle of the dialog box, find the Start With option. Next to it are two choices: Blank Page and Home Page Location. Click on Home Page Location to make it active. In the text box below this, you'll find the URL for the home page currently slated for display at start-up (see Figure 5.1).

5. Highlight that URL and type in its place the URL for the home page you want.

6. Click on the OK button. The Preferences dialog box will close, and the Netscape window will reappear.

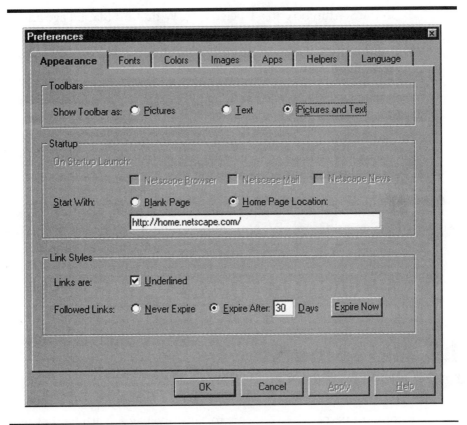

FIGURE 5.1: Enter the URL for the home page you want to appear at start-up. The URL shown here is the default Welcome to Netscape page.

When next you start Netscape, you'll see the home page you just designated as your start-up page rather than the original default start-up home page.

Let's say you have some reason for not wanting to see any home page at all when you launch Netscape. The steps you'll follow to do this are similar to those for changing the start-up home page:

1. With Netscape running (you don't have to be connected to the Internet while you do this), select Options ➤ General Preferences from the menu bar. The Preferences dialog box will appear.

2. From the tabs along the top of the Preferences dialog box, select Appearance.

3. In the Startup box area labeled Start With, find Blank Page and click on its radio button.

4. Now click on the OK button. The Preferences dialog box will close, and the Netscape window will appear.

What could be easier? When you launch Netscape again, you should see absolutely no home page. Instead you'll see an empty document window.

 Even though you've changed your start-up home page or arranged for none to appear at start-up, you can access the Welcome to Netscape page whenever you want. From Netscape's menu bar, select Directory ➤ Netscape's Home. In addition, you can always place a bookmark on the Welcome to Netscape page, as described in Chapter 3.

Now let's look at some good all-purpose home pages, starting with the default start-up home page you've heard so much about.

The Welcome to Netscape Page

The topmost part of the Welcome to Netscape page—with its slick graphics and friendly message—should be familiar to you from Chapter 3 (see Figure 3.1).

If you scroll down the page, you'll see links to information on Netscape products and the company itself, along with more links to instructions on basic Web navigation skills (we've already got that covered in this book).

What's Out There

You can always go home again. The URL for the Welcome to Netscape page is http://home.netscape.com.

This is where you'll find out about and get new versions of the Netscape browser when they're available. Of most interest to us at the moment, however, are the links that lead to exploring other stuff on the Internet. Check them out.

The Netscape What's New Page

Netscape provides a What's New page, which includes (what else?) links to new items on the Web. You can access Netscape's What's New page by clicking on the What's New! directory button or by selecting Directory ➤ What's New! from Netscape's menu bar. The What's New page will appear, showing links for what's new. The length of this listing at any given time depends on how many Web sites have been announced in the current month.

 Many Web sites offer a What's Hot category, a What's Cool category, or both. Through glancing at these, you can see some great Web presentation and content—take a look once in a while just to browse around.

What's Out There

Netscape's What's New page, a great source for what's happening, is easily found at the URL http://home.netscape.com/home/whats-new.html.

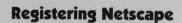

Registering Netscape

The first time you start Netscape, take the time to read the licensing agreement that appears on screen and register the program. It's the honest, right thing to do, and it couldn't be easier. You can check out the licensing agreement and register via links on the Welcome to Netscape page.

The agreement says that Netscape is free for the use of students, faculty members, staff of educational organizations, employees of nonprofit corporations, and *individuals evaluating the program*. If you fall into the last group, you must pay a license fee of $39 once your evaluation period is up.

Filling out the registration form is terrifically simple; really it's just like filling out a paper registration card, except that you're doing it on screen.

Follow links on the Welcome to Netscape page or open the URL
`http://home.netscape.com/misc/quick_purchase` to get to the Netscape Quick Purchase page. Here you can fill out the simple forms to order and pay for a copy of the latest version of Netscape Navigator (a.k.a. "Netscape") or any number of other software products Netscape offers.

What's Way Cool!

Netscape's What's New page doesn't just tell what's new, but also what's truly *outstanding*. Check out the What's Cool! page by clicking on the What's Cool! Directory button or by choosing Directory ➤ What's Cool from Netscape's menu bar. You'll find a page filled with links to outstanding Web pages grouped by month (for the last few months).

The Magellan Internet Directory

The Magellan Internet directory, put forth by The McKinley Group, an Internet publishing company, stands out from the crowd for several reasons:

◆ It is a comprehensive, browsable directory of Internet resources of all types, not just Web pages.

◆ It presents reviews of these sites, written and edited by a knowledgeable staff of real human beings.

◆ It includes one of the best search tools available among Internet directories.

◆ It is international in scope rather than U.S.-centric.

When you access Magellan (see Figure 5.2), you'll be offered the choice to browse or to search. The Search the Magellan button appears first on the

Enter any text you'd like to begin your search. You can use capital or lowercase letters or a combination. **Examples**: "Frank Lloyd Wright houses," "Chinese history," "companies that sell computer software," "culinary schools," "influence of women in Italian politics."

Click on **Help**, above, for more search tips and options... Just browsing? Click on **Browse Categories** below.

New Search | Advanced Search | Add Site | Help | Feedback | About Magellan

BROWSE CATEGORIES

Browse Categories | What's Hot | News | Sports | Weather
About Magellan | McKinley People | McKinley Products | McKinley Jobs

U.S. Licensing information is available. International inquiries are welcome.
Explore advertising opportunities with Magellan.
Find out about exciting job opportunities with The McKinley Group!
Copyright © The McKinley Group, Inc., 1995. All rights reserved.

FIGURE 5.2: Magellan, a comprehensive and accessible Internet directory, is a great launching point for your travels, whether you're browsing or searching.

page as of this writing; look down the page slightly, and you'll find the Browse Categories button. You'll also be offered some extra-value features, such as a What's Hot section that changes frequently and shows you sites that the Magellan editors find especially interesting and buttons that take you straight to News, Sports, and Weather. Whether you search for a topic that interests you or browse the huge, clickable, hierarchical menu of categories and subcategories, you'll wind up with more than a screenful of descriptive reviews (see Figure 5.3), each with a one- to four-star rating and links both to the described site and to a summary of Magellan's findings about the site.

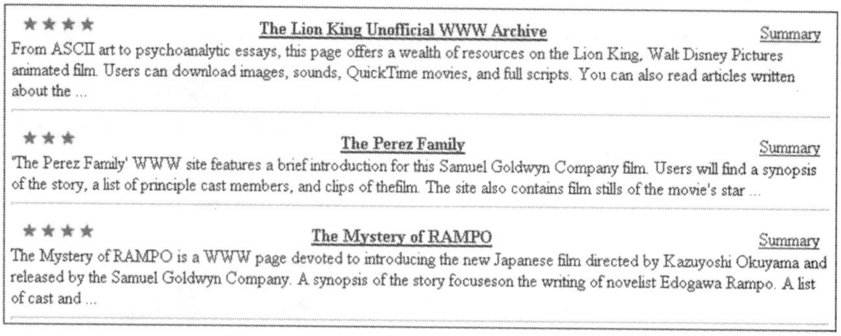

★ ★ ★ ★   <u>The Lion King Unofficial WWW Archive</u>   <u>Summary</u>
From ASCII art to psychoanalytic essays, this page offers a wealth of resources on the Lion King, Walt Disney Pictures animated film. Users can download images, sounds, QuickTime movies, and full scripts. You can also read articles written about the ...

★ ★ ★   <u>The Perez Family</u>   <u>Summary</u>
'The Perez Family' WWW site features a brief introduction for this Samuel Goldwyn Company film. Users will find a synopsis of the story, a list of principle cast members, and clips of thefilm. The site also contains film stills of the movie's star ...

★ ★ ★ ★   <u>The Mystery of RAMPO</u>   <u>Summary</u>
The Mystery of RAMPO is a WWW page devoted to introducing the new Japanese film directed by Kazuyoshi Okuyama and released by the Samuel Goldwyn Company. A synopsis of the story focuseson the writing of novelist Edogawa Rampo. A list of cast and ...

FIGURE 5.3: Magellan offers fully searchable, descriptive reviews of sites and a convenient one- to four-star rating system.

What's Out There

You can embark on worldwide Web exploration from the launching point of the Magellan Internet directory; its URL is at `http://www.mckinley.com`.

If you do use the browsing techniques for approaching Magellan, you'll find a carefully thought through categorization and subcategorization of topics ranging from Arts to Health to Sports to Travel, with everything in between. Clicking on any link on the page will take you to a page of further refined subcategories; click on another, and you'll get a listing of reviewed and rated sites, focused on the selected topic. Take a look at the reviews, and you'll probably find what you seek, without the trouble of browsing the actual sites.

You can add a site you admire or one you've created by clicking on the <u>Add Site</u> link. On the form that appears, you can type the title and URL of the page you want included. You can also enter a description of the page and the category under which you believe the link should go, the keywords that best describe its content, and the audience to whom you think it will appeal. The Magellan editorial team will review your submission, and, if it's of substance or interest, they'll make it part of the big Magellan database.

Magellan Is Searchable

You'll undoubtedly notice the prominent Search feature that appears in Magellan at the top of the home page and again on the review pages. Magellan is fully searchable; in fact, it has one of the best search engines in the business. Internet searches are usually performed in one of several ways: by searching the title of a page, the URL, the keywords associated with the page, or, in the best of cases, the text of the page. Magellan does the most thorough type of search—the full-text search—meaning that it searches the text of the Web page itself. When you search Magellan, you'll get a listing of those sites that most closely match the word or words you typed in the search box.

You may notice that the sites aren't listed alphabetically or in the order of the star rating. That's because they are listed by relevancy—remember, the sites that most closely match your search criteria (the words you typed) are at the top of the list.

You can focus your search again by typing additional search criteria so that you can get quite close to what you seek. Searching is the topic of Chapter 7, and searching is obviously a major feature of Magellan; so turn there for more details.

Yahoo: A Subject-Oriented List

Yahoo, begun at Stanford University by a couple of (presumed) yahoos, has since gone commercial. Yahoo is a hierarchical list of a whopping number of sites on the Web, organized by subject (see Figure 5.4). (The number's growing at a phenomenal rate.)

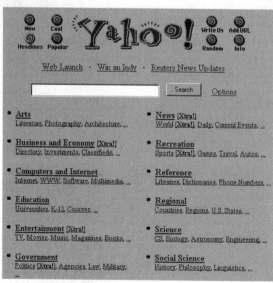

FIGURE 5.4: Click on the <u>Net Directory</u> link (top) in the Netscape home page and then on the <u>Yahoo Directory</u> link to get to Yahoo's subject-oriented list (bottom), and then click around until you find what you seek.

To get to this amazing resource:

1. From the Netscape menu bar, select Directory ➤ Internet Directory or simply click on the <u>Net Directory</u> link. In either case, Netscape's Internet Directory page will appear.

2. Click on the <u>Yahoo Directory</u> link, and you'll soon see a wonder of a page with hundreds of links, each representing a different category of information on the Web.

Another way to get to Yahoo, of course, is simply to:

1. Select File ➤ Open Location from the Netscape menu bar, type the Yahoo URL (`http://www.yahoo.com`) in the Open Location dialog box, and click on Open.

What's Out There

You can mosey on over to Yahoo with the URL `http://www.yahoo.com`.

Some categories we found when we looked were Art, Business and Economy, Computers and Internet, Education, Entertainment, Government, Health, Sports, and so on. (There are plenty more.) Clicking on any link on the Yahoo page will take you to yet another page of links focused on the selected category. Just keep clicking through the links 'til you find what you seek.

If you know of a page that is not in the Yahoo lists, click on the <u>Add</u> link on any Yahoo page. A form will appear into which you can type the URL of the page you want included in Yahoo. The people who run Yahoo will review your submission, and, if they like the page, it will become part of Yahoo's list.

Searching through Yahoo

Searching is the subject of another chapter (that'll be Chapter 7), but let's just pause here for a moment because, like many Internet directories today,

Yahoo is not just clickable—it's searchable. To do a simple search of Yahoo from its home page, follow these steps:

1. At the top of the Yahoo home page, you will find a text box followed by a Search button. In the text box, type one or more words (separated by spaces) that describe what you seek (Yahoo will find only entries that contain all the words you enter in the text box; so be careful about what you enter).

2. Click on the Search button. A page will appear showing a listing of pages (all appearing as links) that contain all the words you set out for the search.

You are not limited to searching Yahoo based on a few simple words. Yahoo also has a search page that gives you much more control over how it locates the information you want. To use this alternative Yahoo searching method:

1. Click on the Options link at the top of any Yahoo page (it's to the right of the Search button). The Yahoo Search page will appear (see Figure 5.5).

2. In the text box, type one or more words (separated by spaces) describing what you seek.

3. Make selections to indicate whether you want:

 ◆ To find pages that include *all* the words you entered or *any* of them

 ◆ To search only URLs, only titles of pages, only descriptions of pages, or any combination of these items

 ◆ The search to be case-sensitive

 ◆ The search to look for whole words or pieces of the words

 ◆ To see the maximum number of documents as the result of your search

4. Click on the Search button. A page will appear showing a listing of pages (all appearing as links) that match the criteria you set out for the search.

To check out the pages that appeared in the listing as the result of your search, simply click on their links. If you click around a while and get away from the page listing the result of your search, you can always go back to that page by selecting Go from the menu bar and then selecting Yahoo Search from the list that appears.

Yahoo Search

Reuters News Headlines | Web Launch

Find all matches containing the *keys* (separated by space)

                         [Search] [Clear]

Find matches in ☑ Title ☑ URL ☑ Comments
☐ Case sensitive matching
Find matches that contain
         ○ At least one of the *keys* (boolean **or**)
         ◉ All *keys* (boolean **and**)
         ○ All *keys* as a single string
Consider *keys* to be
         ◉ Substrings
         ○ Complete words
Limit the number of matches to [100 ▾]

FIGURE 5.5: Yahoo is searchable!

GNN: The Global Network Navigator

The Global Network Navigator (GNN) was at first a project of O'Reilly and Associates, a book publisher. O'Reilly sold its brainchild to America Online some time ago; now GNN operates as a distinct company, producing a Web site that includes strong graphics (which take forever to transfer but look terrific—see Figure 5.6) and that is very long on entertainment value. GNN has a Best of the Net section and a number of intriguing features. Folded into all this is the Whole Internet Catalog, a directory of Internet sites that has been growing since soon after the Web began.

What's Out There

You can circumnavigate the Global Network Navigator starting at the URL
`http://gnn.com`.

Good and Useful Starting Points

FIGURE 5.6: GNN is strong on graphics and entertainment value.

The GNN Whole Internet Catalog is browsable in the extreme—it includes the standard categories from Art to Travel. If you click through them, you'll find listings of subcategories in the areas that interest you. Click some more, and you'll get to the actual sites. At the GNN Whole Internet Catalog home page (`http://www-elc.gnn.com/wic/wics/index.html`), you'll also find buttons for:

New Sites	Those sites that have been added in the preceding week
Top 50	The most popular 50 sites in the catalog
Celebrity Hotlist	A new hotlist every week, devised by the creator or editor of a famous Web site
About WIC Select	An explanation of who does it (The WIC) and how
All Subjects	A more specific clickable index than the one you see on the home page
All Entries	The same type of clickable list, this time showing all the entries in the catalog, in alphabetic order

The Celebrities Hotlist feature is especially fun—here you'll find not only this week's selection (Figure 5.7 shows an example), but also an archive of past lists that is a rich assortment of entertaining and useful sites, hand selected by those who presumably know best.

FIGURE 5.7: The opening lines of the Celebrity Hotlist that appeared the week we wrote this chapter

Of course, you can submit your site to the GNN Whole Internet Catalog; simply click on the Comments button on any page and follow the directions. The GNN team chooses sites on the basis of subject area (they like to populate all areas of interest), taking into consideration design, frequency of updating, and whether the site has a true Web feel. Sites that require the user to pay are generally excluded.

The Mosaic for Microsoft Windows Home Page

The folks at NCSA were the original creators of Mosaic, and they maintain a home page (see Figure 5.8) filled with information about their version of Mosaic for Microsoft Windows. Mosaic, you remember, is the precursor of Netscape and all the other graphical Web browsers.

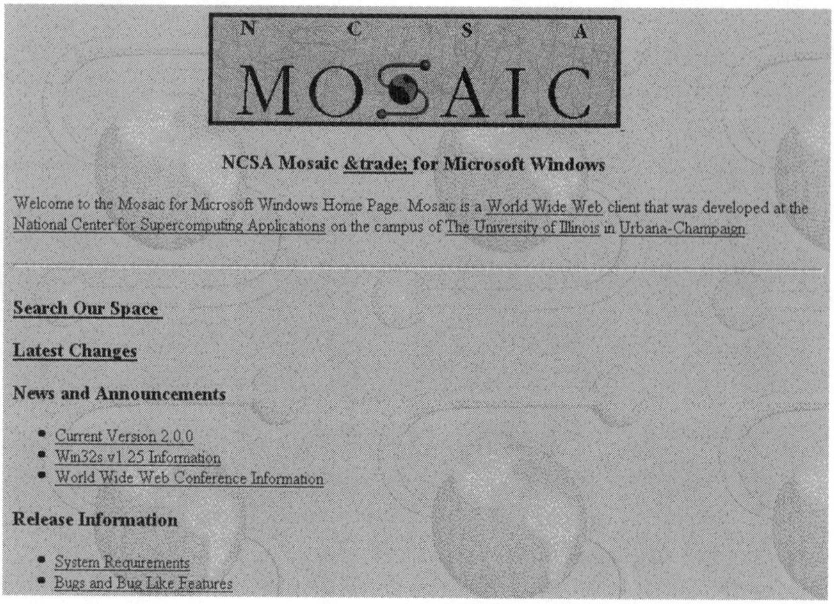

FIGURE 5.8: The NCSA Mosaic for Microsoft Windows home page includes information about the Web, Mosaic, and viewers and players that can enhance your Netscape experience.

This is a good place to visit, in that there are links here to software that you might want to use with Netscape—those external viewers and players discussed in Chapters 2 and 11, for example.

Downloading Viewers and Other Software

When the folks who developed NCSA Mosaic have new versions available, they post an announcement on the Mosaic for Microsoft Windows home page. Likewise, when new viewers and players become available, they post an announcement. In fact, the people at NCSA will tell you about whatever they find that they think you might want, as long as they think it's good. Your option, then, is to take advantage of this opportunity by downloading whatever you think you can use. (See *Mosaic for Microsoft Windows and NCSA Mosaic: A Tale of Two Home Pages.*)

Mosaic for Microsoft Windows and NCSA Mosaic: A Tale of Two Home Pages

The Mosaic for Microsoft Windows home page is different from the NCSA Mosaic home page. If you want information about Mosaic for Windows—the application, new features, bug fixes, and enhancements—look in the Mosaic for Microsoft Windows home page. The NCSA Mosaic home page was the original default home page, covering not only the Windows product, but Mac and Unix products too. When traffic became overwhelming, a split was deemed necessary.

You'll know which home page is which not only by the difference in content, but by the URL. The Mosaic for Microsoft Windows home page, with links to information specific to Mosaic for Windows, has the URL:

```
http://www.ncsa.uiuc.edu/SDG/Software/WinMosaic/HomePage.html
```

The NCSA Mosaic home page—which contains stuff such as general information about the Web, hyperlinks to catalogs, indexes of information that's available by subject—has the following URL:

```
http://www.ncsa.uiuc.edu/SDG/Software/Mosaic/NCSAMosaicHome.html
```

When you're looking over the Mosaic for Microsoft Windows home page and you see an announcement about new software, you'll be told more or less how to get the software. Here are two possible scenarios:

◆ The announcement will say something like "...you can get it here" and will be followed by a blue, underlined word. This indicates that the link is to the software file itself.

◆ The announcement will say something like "...you can get it from X-Y-Z place," and X-Y-Z will be blue and underlined. This indicates that the link is to wherever the software file is located.

In either case, all you have to do is click on the link. If the link is to the software file itself, the Save As dialog box will appear, allowing you to save the file to your local machine. If the link is not directly to the software but rather to its location, some sort of page will appear, probably telling you

about the software; in turn, that page will have a link for you to click on, and when you do, the Save As dialog box will appear.

Saving software files with the Save As dialog box is a very straightforward Windows operation; you probably won't have to (or even want to) rename the files, but you may want to specify the drive and directory you want them to land in.

 Downloading software is a lot like saving files to your local machine, which we described in detail in Chapter 3.

Compressed Files

Often you'll find that the software files you download from the Web are *zipped*—they've been compressed with a utility such as PKZip or Lharc, which you'll know because the filename ends in either ZIP (for PKZip) or LZH (for LHarc). Files are zipped (*compressed, shrunk,* or *compacted*) to make them smaller, so that they can be transmitted more quickly. Compressed files often can be half the size of the original file; some files can be compressed to as little as $^1/_{20}$ their original size. If a file has been compressed, you'll need a companion program to uncompress the file. PKZip/PKUnzip

What's Out There

You'll find a table full of information about available compression software at `ftp://uiarchive.cso.uiuc.edu/doc/pcnet/compression`.

What's Out There

WinZip is a very good Zip/Unzip program for Windows. You can find out all about it—and even download it—from `http://www.winzip.com`.

is available commercially; WinZip is downloadable shareware (which you must pay a fee for if you like it and want to keep using it); and LHarc is downloadable freeware (meaning you can use it without paying for it). Other compression/decompression programs are also available—some emulate or are compatible with their commercially available cousins (WinZip, for example, will compress and uncompress PKZip files).

NCSA's Starting Points for Internet Exploration

NCSA's Starting Points for Internet Exploration is a document that includes links to information about the Web and Mosaic. Near the top of the page is a useful list where links appear for:

◆ Information by Subject

◆ Data Sources by Service

◆ Web Servers Directory

This is a handy all-purpose set of links to services that new Web users may find helpful; let's take a closer look at them one by one.

What's Out There

Jump off from NCSA's Starting Points for Internet Exploration at the URL `http://www.ncsa.uiuc.edu/SDG/Software/Mosaic/StartingPoints/NetworkStartingPoints.html`.

Information by Subject

The Starting Points page has many links to subject-oriented pages of information, enough so that we don't have space to go into detail about all of them, but here's the gist of it.

To get a subject list of available information, select the Information By Subject link. The WWW Virtual Library will appear (see Figure 5.9). You can click on any category in the Virtual Library to see a list of resources for that category. If you have an idea of what topic you want to explore, this is a likely place to start.

For example, if you're interested in geology, click on Earth Science; the Earth Sciences listing will appear. Just as you can do with meta-indexes

What's Out There

The URL for the WWW Virtual Library: Subject Catalogue page is `http://www.w3.org/hypertext/DataSources/bySubject/Overview.html`.

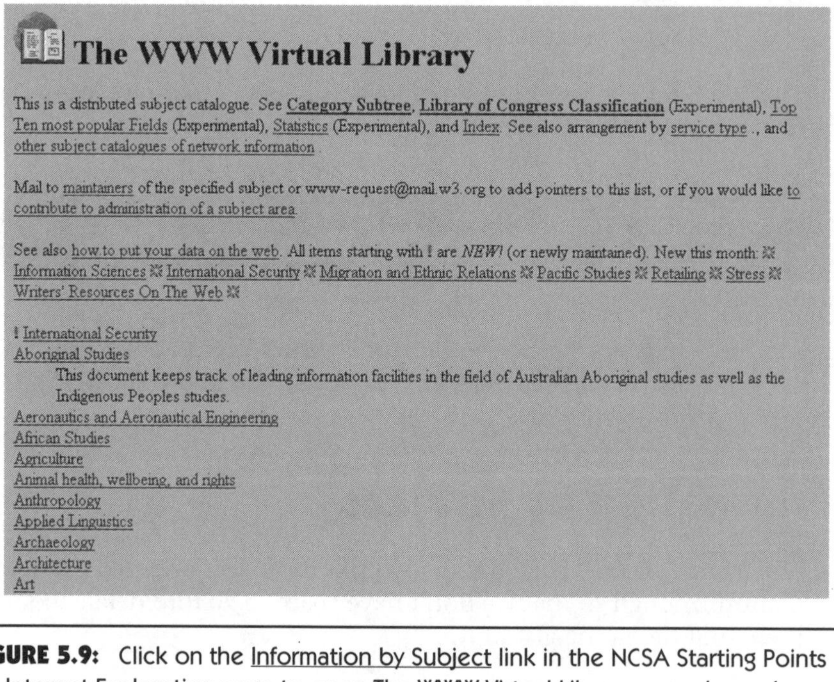

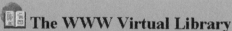

📖 The WWW Virtual Library

This is a distributed subject catalogue. See **Category Subtree**, **Library of Congress Classification** (Experimental), Top Ten most popular Fields (Experimental), Statistics (Experimental), and Index. See also arrangement by service type ., and other subject catalogues of network information.

Mail to maintainers of the specified subject or www-request@mail.w3.org to add pointers to this list, or if you would like to contribute to administration of a subject area.

See also how to put your data on the web. All items starting with ! are *NEW!* (or newly maintained). New this month: ※ Information Sciences ※ International Security ※ Migration and Ethnic Relations ※ Pacific Studies ※ Retailing ※ Stress ※ Writers' Resources On The Web ※

! International Security
Aboriginal Studies
    This document keeps track of leading information facilities in the field of Australian Aboriginal studies as well as the Indigenous Peoples studies.
Aeronautics and Aeronautical Engineering
African Studies
Agriculture
Animal health, wellbeing, and rights
Anthropology
Applied Linguistics
Archaeology
Architecture
Art

FIGURE 5.9: Click on the Information by Subject link in the NCSA Starting Points for Internet Exploration page to open The WWW Virtual Library page shown here.

such as Magellan and Yahoo, you can make further choices from here—for example, you can explore sublistings of earth sciences organizations around the world; delve into pertinent current events; or unearth useful resources, software, and references.

What's Out There

You can dig up the Earth Sciences list with the URL `http://www.geo.ucalgary.ca/VL-EarthSciences.html`.

The United States Geological Survey's home page can be unearthed at `http://www.usgs.gov`.

Data Sources by Service

Another useful way to view all the information on the Web is by service—that is, by FTP, Gopher, and WAIS, in addition to Web sites. If you know *where* you might find what you're looking for—say, if you know it's on an FTP server at UC Santa Barbara—it makes more sense to look for the information organized by the *type of server* rather than by the topic.

From the Starting Points page, you can check out the services listing by clicking on the <u>Data Sources by Service</u> link. A document will appear with hypertext links to additional listings for each service type:

◆ World Wide Web servers

◆ WAIS servers

◆ Network News (Usenet newsgroups)

◆ Gopher servers

◆ Telnet access

What's Out There

You can check out data sources by the type of service they represent via the URL `http://www.w3.org/hypertext/DataSources/ByAccess.html`.

Click on the service type that interests you, and a detailed listing of servers of that type will appear. Click on the specific server you're looking for; a connection will be established to that server, and you can then find what you're seeking. (You started out knowing what and where it was, remember?)

Web Servers Directory

The Web, as we've said, is a *global* network. Unfortunately, many of the meta-indexes are U.S.-centric and include few international sites. Magellan is an exception, but to explore the Web's branches in other countries, you can also use the Internet Directory page's directory of servers. To access it, click on the <u>Web Servers Directory</u> link. The World Wide Web Servers: Summary document will appear. Here you'll find a list of known Web servers around the world, categorized by geographical areas. Each of these areas is further categorized by country.

What's this good for? Well, let's say you're interested in finding out the name of the head of the Computer Science Department at the University of Sydney. This is just the sort of information you're more likely to find on a server in Australia than anywhere else; why not start your search in the right country?

For a more graphical approach than the list offers, click on <u>clickable world map</u>, and you'll get a view like that shown in Figure 5.10.

Open Market's Commercial Sites Index

As the Internet has expanded from its roots as a network of academic and military computers, commercial use has become more and more predominant.

What's Out There

Web servers around the world are listed and even mapped out at the URL `http://www.w3.org/hypertext/DataSources/WWW/Servers.html`.

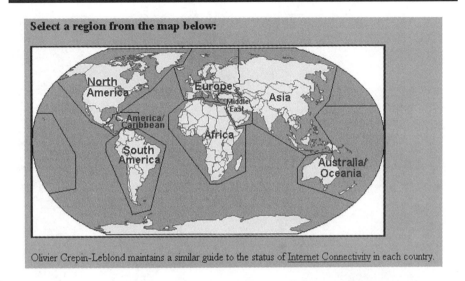

Select a region from the map below:

Olivier Crepin-Leblond maintains a similar guide to the status of Internet Connectivity in each country.

FIGURE 5.10: Click on a continent to start tracking down Web servers located there.

Open Market's Commercial Sites Index page is a helpful resource for investigating commercial use; it has links to and information about businesses that maintain an Internet presence.

More and more products are sold directly on the Internet; you can get information about businesses and the products they offer from Open Market's Commercial Sites Index page, shown in Figure 5.11.

Other Points of Departure

There are literally hundreds (if not thousands) of places from which you can launch your Web explorations, and the list is growing every day.

What's Out There

Make it your business to investigate Open Market's Commercial Sites Index at http://www.directory.net. You can learn more about Open Market from its Web page at http://www.openmarket.com.

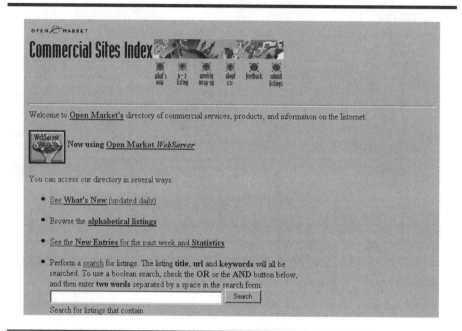

FIGURE 5.11: Open Market's Commercial Sites Index provides links to all sorts of business-related resources.

Individuals such as Scott Yanoff and John December maintain lists that are very worthwhile.

Check out the inside front cover of this book for even more starting places.

Now What?

With Netscape starting-point basics under your belt, let's take a wider look at what's available on the World Wide Web. In Chapter 6, we're going to have a look at some sites so hot they sizzle.

What's Out There

Scott Yanoff's list of Internet resources is easy to find at the URL `http://slacvx.slac.stanford.edu/misc/internet-services.html`. John December's equally interesting list is at the URL `http://www.rpi.edu/Internet/Guides/decemj/text.html`.

6

Spots on the Web You Won't Want to Miss

Along the Infobahn, there are many places you'll want to visit. Here to get you started are some hip, happening, and useful sites we've seen on the Web in our own travels. We've categorized this stuff for your convenience. In this chapter we'll start by introducing you to some Best of the Web sites, and then we'll go into special topics.

Some Real Roadmarkers

Isn't it incredible the way people go for awards shows? We all say we hate the Oscars—they're so biased, so often sentimental, so ickily showy—yet every year millions watch and millions more are influenced by them.

The Web's got its own lineup of "Best of" awards, bestowed upon outstanding Web sites by a variety of authorities and amateurs. These lists can be an interesting browsing experience; let's take a look at some of them just for kicks.

The "Original" Best of the Web

The "original" annual Best of the World Wide Web competition was spawned at the International World Wide Web Conference in Geneva in May 1994.

What's Out There

You can see winners of the Best of the World Wide Web competition through the URL http://wings.buffalo.edu/contest/.

Clnet's Best of the Web

Clnet is an online magazine, a model of the marriage of form and style, that focuses on technology, the Net, and the like. (It's interesting to note that *Clnet* was one of the first sites to use Java technology, in the form of live news feeds in a ticker-tape format on screen.) *Clnet* also broadcasts a national TV show on the same topics.

What's Out There

Clnet's very own view of what's best on the Web can be seen at http://www.cnet.com/Central/Features/Website/.

GNN's Best of the Web

GNN—the Global Network Navigator—gives annual awards to those sites its editorial team thinks best. Awards are given in a number of categories.

What's Out There

GNN shows you what it thinks is best on the Web at the URL http://gnn.com/wic/botn/index.html.

Each category is further divided into amateur and professional sites, and both before and after the actual awards are handed out, all the nominees are listed online, with links to the sites.

Look for the Stars

Another kind of "Best" ranking occurs when some Web directories, such as Point Communications and Magellan, award recognition to a "Top 5%" site (in the case of Point) or to a "Four-Star Site" (in the case of Magellan). A site that wins one of these awards is offered the opportunity to display the award on its home page. When you see the colorful indicators of these awards, you'll know that this site has won a place on another kind of "Best" list.

Arts and Entertainment

The arts are terrifically well represented on the Web—from graffiti to the Louvre, from the blues to *The Tempest*, from architecture to translated Russian poetry to Tinseltown, celebrities, and all sorts of products of the American entertainment dream machine.

Art Crimes: The Writing on the Wall

...Is it art or is it entertainment? Here you'll find hundreds if not thousands of graffiti images from around the world, organized by city.

What's Out There

The handwriting's on the gallery wall at
`http://www.gatech.edu/graf/index/Index.Art_Crimes.html`.

Art on the Net

To get to a true art space—where artists gather, create, and "hang" their work online—go to Art on the Net (a.k.a. Art.Net). Here, you can see a variety of galleries and art styles. One piece from the online gallery is shown in Figure 6.1.

What's Out There

Art on the Net appears at `http://www.art.net`.

Blue Highway

The Blue Highway is all about the blues, from well-crafted profiles of the great blues masters and their lives to images and even WAV sound files you can sample.

What's Out There

Get the blues at the URL `http://www.vivanet.com/~blues/`.

The Electric Postcard

During the writing of this book, one of the most fun moments we had was testing this site. We sent each other charming Web postcards (see Figure 6.2), then we sent them to friends, and then we wished even more of our friends had Web browsers so that we could keep up the good time.

What's Out There

Drop an electric postcard from
`http://postcards.www.media.mit.edu/Postcards/`.

FIGURE 6.1: Art on the Net appears at Art.Net.

FIGURE 6.2: Drop us a postcard, send us a line! You can send electric porstcards.

Elvis Aron Presley Home Page

Die-hard Elvis fans who can't make the real trip to Memphis can tour Graceland from their desktops, thanks to Andrea Berman and David Levine, creators of this Elvis home page, "created to honor Elvis and his cultural and musical legacy...." (This isn't the *only* Elvis page, incidentally. Elvis home pages crop up almost as often as Elvis sightings.)

What's Out There

Elvis is revered at http://sunsite.unc.edu/elvis/elvishom.html.

As always, your machine must have the appropriate sound capabilities (lots o' memory along with a sound card, drivers, and maybe even speakers) to play sound files. Don't try to play sound files if you don't have the stuff to do it. Sound files are enormous, and trying to play them without the proper equipment and software will crash your system.

Games Domain

Games Domain is (simply put) far and away the best resource for lovers of computer games of all kinds. It offers fast access to up-to-date, authoritative information, and it covers FAQs, walk-throughs, and links to other game-related sites. A gamer could spend all his or her days just browsing here, if not for the call of the game....

What's Out There

Your strategy should include a stop by `http://gamesdomain.co.uk/`.

Leonardo

Leonardo, the print publication, is a journal that covers the fusion of art, music, science, and technology. *Leonardo*'s Web site covers the same topics, with an overview of the medium and viewable images and downloadable sound files created by artists and musicians using the arts and technology in innovative ways.

What's Out There

The arts and technology merge in Leonardo's online version at
`http://www-mitpress.mit.edu/Leonardo/home.html`.

Internet Movie Database

For the starstruck or the plain old curious, a searchable, indexed database of movie-related stuff might be just the ticket. Query it by the name of an actor or actress, the title of a film, a genre, or a quote from a movie. You can also get a listing of the Academy Award winners in many key categories, dating all the way from 1920.

What's Out There

The now venerable Movie Browser database is at `http://www.msstate.edu/Movies/`. And if you're interested in film sites, check out a few more: CimemaSpace, at `http://remarque.berkeley.edu:8001/~xcohen/`, is a terrific site for film studies; the Early Motion Pictures site from the Library of Congress at `http://lcweb2.loc.gov/papr/mpixhome.html` is an archive of old films; and Cinemaven, at `http://www.uspan.com/mavin.html/`, is great for reviews of current feature films. Gaze on all that glitters by visiting *Mr. Showbiz* at `http://web3.starwave.com:80/showbiz/`.

The Spot

We loved the Real World on MTV and have to admit a soft spot for that sort of peek-into-the-everyday-life type of entertainment, but even if we were just fans of good stories (which we also are), we would have loved the Spot, shown in Figure 6.3. Here you'll follow the antics of a bunch of actual roommates who take on all that life offers in a group of episodic on-line diaries about their lives in a beach cottage in L.A. known as "The Spot."

What's Out There

You can find out what's up in the lives of a bunch of hip, cool, and groovy housemates at The Spot. Its URL is `http://www.thespot.com/`.

FIGURE 6.3: Stop in at the "spot" every week to stay current; it changes often.

 The Spot was recommended to us by Robert Richardson, author of Sybex's web.guide, a great book of researched and reviewed Web sites, as a truly innovative use of the medium. We couldn't agree more.

People, Entertainment Weekly, and Vibe

Can't get enough of that good-time gossip? Three of the most popular magazines dedicated to entertainment appear in their online incarnations at Time Warner's Pathfinder site.

What's Out There

Blaze a trail to Pathfinder's site at http://pathfinder.com/, and when you get there, simply click on the covers to get to *People*, *Entertainment Weekly*, and *Vibe* online.

Computers and the Net

So maybe you want to upgrade your modem? Find free software to enhance your Internet abilities? Reconfigure and upgrade your entire computer system? All you need to know is where to go for all the technical and product-specific information you'll ever need.

Cryptography, PGP, and Your Privacy

Privacy on the Net has become a major concern in the past couple of years. The Cryptography, PGP, and Your Privacy site will provide you with all the background you'll need to understand these issues. It will also give you a place to get involved in grass-roots electronic activism if you care about privacy.

What's Out There

To find out about privacy issues as they might affect you, pop in on the home page at `http://draco.centerline.com:8080/~franl/crypto.html`.

The Dilbert Zone

Dilbert is the consummate Silicon Valley nerd, whose adventures in techno-employment are undeniably real to those of us who've been in the industry.

What's Out There

The Dilbert Zone is at the URL `http://www.unitedmedia.com/comics/dilbert/`. More industry-inspired comics can be found at another great site, Computer Comics, at `http://zeb.nysaes.cornell.edu/CGI/ctoons.cgi/1-english`.

Falken's Cyberspace Tools

Whether you're using Windows, Unix, or a Mac, you'll find a host of Internet tools that will enable and enhance your Net experience by following the links at this site. Browsers, HTML authoring tools, Web servers, and viewers and players are all featured here, in a neatly arranged system that's organized by operating system.

What's Out There

Find all kinds of cybertools at `http://commline.com/falken/tools.html`.

Linux: A Unix-Like Operating System for Your PC

If you're interested in fiddling around with a Unix clone on your PC (Intel 386, 486, or Pentium), you can find out all about the Linux operating system and its champions at a terrific Web site.

What's Out There

The Linux site serves up background information and how-to documents about Linux and its features at `http://www.linux.org`. Don't leave DOS without it.

For more on Linux, which is a terrific operating system that's no picnic to install but a real delight to use, check out The Complete Linux Kit (Daniel A. Tauber; Sybex, 1995). You'll discover the ins and outs of installing and using Linux, and you'll even get a copy of the software on a convenient CD-ROM.

Sun and Java Technology

Sun, the folks who bring you Java and HotJava, have a happening site where you can find all the latest about these products and everything else Sun wants you to know. Java is a programming language with which you can create truly interactive Web pages that can be viewed using Netscape version 2. The Java site (see Figure 6.4) offers information about how to download the development tool kit for Java and how to write your own Java programs. It also offers sample Java applications.

What's Out There

The Sun will be in your eyes when you visit the Java site at `http://java.sun.com`.

Java(tm): Programming for the Internet

FIGURE 6.4: Check out the Sun site on Java to get the Java development skinny.

Java technology, its appearance in Netscape, and how you as the user will experience it are covered in Chapter 3 of this book.

Xerox PARC PubWeb

The Xerox Palo Alto Research Center (PARC) is well known as the brain trust that created such technical advances as the mouse (the one you're using as you putter on your PC), the graphical user interface, and much,

much more. While you're here, be sure to check out the map viewer, shown in Figure 6.5, which was developed by Steve Putz of PARC.

What's Out There

Pull off the Infobahn and PARC for a while at the URL `http://pubweb.parc.xerox.com/`; if you do, you can check out the way cool map viewer (`http://pubweb.parc.xerox.com/map`).

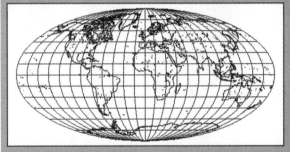

FIGURE 6.5: This map viewer is worth a pit stop.

● Education

The Web started as a tool for research and academia; so plenty of the stuff on it appeals to those in education circles.

AskERIC

ERIC is the Educational Resources Information Center; AskERIC (see Figure 6.6) is a Web site that's packed with resources for education. Find out about conferences, curricula, funding, reference tools, professional organizations—it's pretty much all here.

What's Out There

Learn about AskERIC's fantastic resources for K-12 educators at the URL `http://ericir.syr.edu`.

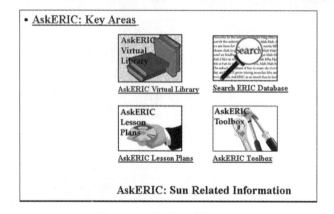

FIGURE 6.6: AskERIC about education.

What's Out There

Web 66, an outstanding source of information for K-12 educators, is at `http://web66.coled.umn.edu/`. MegaMath offers fun math activities for kids (honestly!) at `http://www.c3.lanl.gov/mega-math/index.html`.

EdWeb

A great site that focuses on the use of technology and the Internet as tools in educational reform, this is a wonderful resource for anyone interested in the future of education.

What's Out There

Get into the swing of education's future by visiting EdWeb at the URL `http://edweb.cnidr.org:90.`

Internet for Kids

As a companion to the book *Internet for Kids*, written by a group of innovative educators and published by Sybex, this page introduces kids, parents, and teachers to the Internet through fun activities.

What's Out There

The Internet for Kids page is an easy introduction to the Net; check it out at `http://www.sybex.com/i4kids/.`

Human Languages

With links to just about every human language, including Esperanto (the artificially created universal human language) and even some we've never

What's Out There

Languages are described, discussed, translated, and even pronounced at `http://www.willamette.edu/~jones/Language-Page.html.`

heard of, this site can truly be called comprehensive. Of course, the English section is enormous (as of this writing, most of what's on the Web is in English), with links to dictionaries of olde, medieval, and Shakespearean English among other things. Even Klingon, the alien (not human) language of Star Trek fame, is included in the site, with a pronunciation dictionary that actually speaks!

A Professor's Guilt List for English Lit Majors

From Alcott to Yeats, this site provides a list of all the works of literature a self-respecting English major must have under his or her suspenders. Constructed by an actual professor, this is a great resource for everyone who reads and enjoys English lit.

What's Out There

Read up on great writing by following the list provided by a professor of English Lit at `http://www.next.com/~bong/books/GuiltList.html`.

Stanford University

The Stanford University site has many links that will help those at Stanford, those thinking of going to Stanford, and those who just want Stanford information.

What's Out There

You can look into Stanford and what's happening there via the URL `http://www.stanford.edu/`.

U.S. Geological Survey

The U.S. Geological Survey (USGS) boasts as one of its purposes the publishing of information about the United States' mineral land and water resources, which it has done through traditional means for many a decade. Now the USGS has a Web server. If you live in earthquake country, you'll want to size up the seismic activity stuff—some nifty maps show up-to-date earthquake information (see Figure 6.7).

What's Out There

Unearth the US Geological Survey site at `http://www.usgs.gov`.

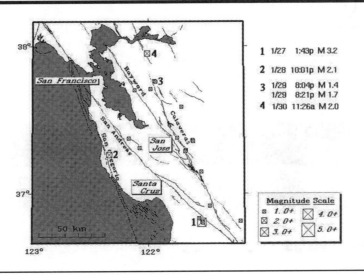

FIGURE 6.7: If you live in earthquake country (or if you're just curious), you'll want to check out the USGS's cool maps.

Many schools from K-12 to universities have their own Web sites, where you can find out about student activities and classes and even take a virtual tour. To find a school that interests you, search the Web using the tools described in Chapter 7.

Food and Beverages

A veritable feast of Internet sites cover food and beverage topics. You can trade recipes with others around the world, find out about nutrition, learn to make medieval food or homebrewed beer, linger for a while at a cybercafe, or investigate restaurants in your city or another. Bon appétit!

Cafe Orbital

The primary site at Cafe Orbital is in French; appropriately so, because this is a virtual French cafe, where you can hobnob with your virtual pals or peruse pages yourself while sipping coffee at your keyboard. There is an easy link to an English translation of the site; so for those of us who lack the French language, there's hope.

What's Out There

Lounge at the Cafe Orbital; its URL is `http://cafe.orbital.fr`.

Epicurious

A Condé Nast publication, *Epicurious* incorporates those two grand dames of food magazines, *Bon Appétit* and *Gourmet*. There's nothing stodgy about

What's Out There

Taste Epicurious for yourself at `http://www.epicurious.com`.

Epicurious. Its graphics are tasty; its content delectable. You can get a look at it in Figure 6.8.

 For a comprehensive listing of food and drink sites as reviewed by a pair of food professionals, look into <u>A Pocket Tour of Food and Drink on the Internet</u> by Ellen Gordon and Peter Stokes (Sybex, 1995).

FIGURE 6.8: Epicurious serves up delicious graphics and delectable feature articles on food and dining.

What's Out There

The URL Minder (`http://www.netmind.com/URL-minder/URL-minder .html`) will track changes in your favorite Web sites and notify you when they occur.

Virtual Vineyards

Virtual Vineyards (see Figure 6.9) is a wine shop run by a very knowledgeable and un-snobby wine expert. Here you can get advice, bone up on wines and vintages, and purchase what strikes your fancy.

What's Out There

Savor the pleasures of Virtual vineyards at `http://www.virtualvin.com`.

FIGURE 6.9: The Virtual Vineyards opening banner

Government and Politics

The Clinton administration showed a strong interest in the Net when it promoted the Information Superhighway. The U.S. and world government have an increasing presence on the Web; a broad range of grassroots activism can also be heard and seen.

George

Billing itself as the first simultaneous paper/Web launch, JFK Jr's political rag is the behind-the-scenes, hip, people-are-politics, Washington-insider's view of American government and its various facets. *George*'s look is shown in Figure 6.10.

What's Out There

That hip focus on the fashionable political scene, *George*, is at the URL `http://www.georgemag.com/`.

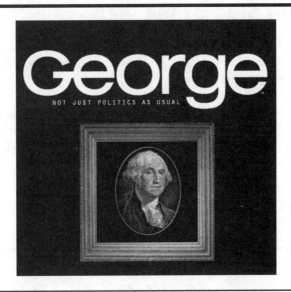

FIGURE 6.10: George bills itself as the first magazine to launch in print and online simultaneously.

Thomas: Congress's Legislative Database

Thomas, the Congressional database service, makes available information about the House and Senate, the e-mail addresses of all members

of Congress, and (especially juicy) the full text of legislation beginning with the 103rd Congress.

What's Out There

Thomas will tell you what's happening in Congress if you stop in at `http://thomas.loc.gov/`.

The Right Side of the Web

On the *right* side of the political coin, you can check out a site (see Figure 6.11) devoted to convincing liberals of the correctness of the ultraconservative viewpoint.

What's Out There

To find out about the more conservative views expressed on the Web, go to the URL `http://www.clark.net/pub/jeffd/`.

FIGURE 6.11: Farther down the page, Reagan's smiling face graces the Right Side of the Web.

Socialist Party USA Cybercenter

On the *left* side of the Web is an informative site about the Socialist viewpoint, where a tongue-in-cheek history of socialism is featured along with the article "How to Be a Socialist."

What's Out There

If you're interested in the political left, you can learn more about socialism at `http://sunsite.unc.edu:80/spc/index.html`.

Supreme Court Decisions

A project of Cornell's Legal Information Institute (LII), the Supreme Court Decisions document provides a searchable database of recent Supreme Court decisions (from 1990 on), indexed by topic.

What's Out There

A searchable database of Supreme Court decisions is available at the URL `http://www.law.cornell.edu/supct/supct.table.html/`.

Health and Wellness

The Web is heaven for information seekers; those who want to find out about health, wellness, disorders, and diseases might look here before trekking off to the public library.

Healthwise

A remarkable site packed with information about health matters, Healthwise features Go Ask Alice, which is itself a terrific resource. Here, you can ask a health-related question anonymously, and the answer of professionals and peers is posted publicly. That means the questions are candid and the answers are informative to all.

What's Out There

You can ask Alice about what ails or interests you at Healthwise. The URL is http://www.columbia.edu/cu/healthwise/.

HyperDoc: The National Library of Medicine

Here's the World-Wide-Web way to look into the National Library of Medicine, part of the U.S. National Institutes of Health in Bethesda, Maryland. The library houses more than 4.5 million books, journals, reports, manuscripts, and audiovisual materials (see Figure 6.12), making it the largest medical library in the world.

What's Out There

Everything you ever wanted to know about Western health and medicine (and perhaps even alternatives) can be learned at the U.S. National Library of Medicine: http://www.nlm.nih.gov/.

FIGURE 6.12: Be sure to stop by the History of Medecine exhibit at the National Library of Medicine.

World Health Organization

Headquartered in Switzerland, the World Health Organization is an international organization dedicated to "the attainment by all peoples of the highest possible level of health."

What's Out There

The World Health Organization provides loads of information on the Web by publishing its newsletters at the URL http://www.who.ch.

News and Weather

The advent of the Web has made a new world for journalism. You'll find a couple of different trends in the look and feel of news on the Net: Some news services, such as the New York Times, deliver a version of their print publication using the Net as a vehicle but not as a new medium. Others, such as CNN Interactive, take advantage of the new possibilities.

CNN Interactive

The news according to CNN Interactive (see Figure 6.13) is definitely *interactive*. You can, for example, read news articles, sports briefs, and movie reviews in the form of text, but you can also actually see and hear brief interviews with key figures and preview films in the form of video and audio clips. For an innovative experience of news on the Web, turn here.

What's Out There

Pick up the daily news at CNN's highly interactive site; the URL is `http://www.cnn.com`.

The New York Times

Here's an example of a news service that seeks to recreate its paper version online (see Figure 6.14). The *New York Times*, in its Internet version, uses Adobe's Acrobat reader (see Chapter 11) to provide the news in a layout that looks essentially like the print version of the paper. You don't have to pay for the Adobe Acrobat software needed to read the online *Times*; it comes with the "paper."

What's Out There

The *New York Times* will arrive on your machine in a form that looks much like the actual paper when you go to `http://nytimesfax.com`.

FIGURE 6.13: CNN on the Web is a truly interactive experience.

Monday November 13, 1995

Internet Edition

Eight pages
© 1995 The New York Times

TimesFax
FROM
The New York Times

FROM THE FRONT PAGE

Budget Battle Rages As U.S. Default Nears

WASHINGTON — Treasury Secretary Robert E. Rubin indicated Sunday that he was preparing to carry out a costly emergency plan to forestall a national default at midweek by juggling the Federal Government's books to pay off investors. With resignation, Mr. Rubin declared, "This is no way to run a country."

Mr. Rubin's comments came as Speaker Newt Gingrich forwarded to President Clinton a bill passed by Congress on Friday to raise the debt ceiling temporarily, a bill that is laden with restrictions on the Treasury's ability to use its small arsenal of weapons to avoid default. Mr. Clinton has vowed to veto the measure, probably on Mon-

Serbs Agree to Return Land to Croatia

ZAGREB, Croatia — Averting a resumption of the war in the Balkans, secessionist Serbs in Croatia signed an agreement Sunday to give up the last slice of Croatian territory under their control.

The agreement, drawn up at the current peace talks in Ohio, calls on the Croatian Serbs to turn over Eastern Slavonia to the Croatian Government during a transition period of one to two years. An international force is to be created, according to the agreement, to insure that the turnover and demilitarization of the area is accomplished on schedule.

"This is a historic signing," said the American Ambassador here, Peter Galbraith. The agreement was signed Sunday afternoon by Mr. Galbraith and the chief United Nations envoy, Thorvald Stoltenberg, along with a senior Croatian official and a Serbian official, in the Serbian-held town of Erdut in eastern Croatia.

The 14-point agreement calls for a 12-month transitional period that can be extended for another year at the request of either party. It gives the United Nations Security Council the mandate to establish a "transitional administration" to govern the region and to "authorize an international force to deploy during the transitional period to maintain peace and security."

By CHRIS HEDGES

FIGURE 6.14: Times Fax is the online version of the venerable New York Times.

The site is actually called *Times Fax*—this is a reference to the condensed version of the *New York Times* that's faxed every day to a world of readers.

Pathfinder

Pathfinder is the big, comprehensive site where Time Warner makes available many of its publications, including *Time, Money, Fortune*, and more

popular-culture oriented rags such as *People*, *Entertainment Weekly*, and *Vibe*, covered earlier in this chapter. At this ground-breaking site, you can communicate with the Time Warner editors and talk to other individuals who share your interests.

What's Out There

Make your way to Time Warner's Pathfinder site at `http://www.pathfinder.com`.

All the News All the Time

The Web, as mentioned, is an extraordinary medium for publishing and reading up-to-date and past news items. Any number of news services and publications already make their content available online; we describe a few in this chapter, but there are so many that you'll probably want to look for your favorites and bookmark them. Here are a few more you can check into:

News Provider	Its URL
AP on trib.com	`http://www.trib.com`
ClariNet	`http://www.clarinet.com`
Financial Times	`http://www.usa.ft.com`
Reuters	`http://www.reuters.com`
Mercury Center Web	`http://www.sjmercury.com`

Some of these services charge a fee; some just ask you to "subscribe" in a quick process that simply tells them who you are. (They generally use this info as a marketing survey.) Some narrow their outline focus to news about business and/or technology. AP is an interesting example of the use of frames, a new feature in Netscape version 2. All are worthwhile.

The Weather Net Index

Whether its general weather trend information, specific prognostications, or storm tracking that interests you, here you'll find links to sites that will get you on your way.

What's Out There

The weather's cleared up for you when you follow links starting at `http://cirrus.sprl.umich.edu/wxnet`.

People Everywhere

The Web is global; so you can find plenty about cultures other than your own. Curious about Russia? Vietnamese business ventures in the U.S.? Indigenous peoples? Women, gays, and "minorities" in the U.S.? It's all here on the Web.

Amnesty International

Amnesty International is an international human rights organization whose site publishes information about how to contact the group and what membership involves.

What's Out There

And to get the latest on human rights developments, turn to Amnesty International at the URL `http://www.organic.com/Non.profits/Amnsty/index.html`.

African/Black Resources

At the African/Black Internet Resources site, you'll find an index with abstracts of literally hundreds of things on the Net having to do with African and Black studies. Another great resource is the African-American Culture and History site, with sections on colonization, abolition, migration, and the WPA, and a major exhibition on the impact of African-American culture on the American identity (see Figure 6.15).

What's Out There

Links to hundreds of African and Black studies sites are at `http://www.sas.upenn.edu/African_Studies/Home_Page/other.html`.

African-American culture and history is exhibited by the Library of Congress at `http://lcweb.loc.gov/exhibits/African.American/intro.html`.

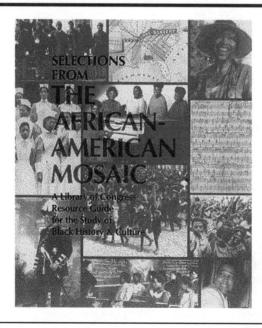

FIGURE 6.15: The Library of Congress' African-American culture exhibit is an especially rich resource.

Gender Issues Directory

This great starting point for the exploration of such issues as the ability of women to break into and succeed in the world of computers and computer science also publishes information on gender studies, women, and feminism in general. There are many links to other sites on the same topics.

What's Out There

Women in computing and other gender-focused topics are discussed at http://cpsr.org/cpsr/gender/gender.html.

Indigenous Peoples' Literature

At this highly informative but somewhat graphically dull site, you'll find guides to Native American languages and a broad range of articles about the current Indigenous Nations of North America.

What's Out There

Native American cultures and languages are the topic at http://kuhttp.cc.ukans.edu/~marc/natlit/natlit.html.

Islamic Architecture in Isfahan

Renowned for its lush, picture-book quality, this site presents a photographic history of Islamic architecture. The text is informative, the photography superb, the layout inviting.

What's Out There

Explore Islamic architecture at http://www.anglia.ac.uk/~rochford/isfahan.html.

Maximov

This complete reference to the Russian government includes contact information for 5,500 members of that government, including the President's Administration, Federal Government, Parliament, and Judiciary, as well as the Administrations and Legislatures of the Russian Federation. Mikhail Gorbachev is quoted as saying that the print version is "An indispensable companion—authoritative and up to date" that he "uses every day." Maximov's home page is shown in Figure 6.16.

What's Out There

A complete guide to the Russian government is available at the URL
`http://www.maximov.com/`.

MAXIMOV'S COMPANION

TO

WHO GOVERNS THE RUSSIAN FEDERATION

A New and **Trusted** Directory of
Political Contact Information for Russia.

FIGURE 6.16: Maximov is known as a complete guide to the Russian government.

The Vietnamese Professionals Society

For information about Vietnamese people the world over (but mainly in the U.S.), this is a great place to start. Like a central meeting hall, this site includes links to other sites, as well as translations of professional journals, listings of meetings, newsletters, Vietnamese software programs, and a wealth of other gems.

What's Out There

Vietnamese people and people interested in the Vietnamese can find out more at `http://www.webcom.com/~hcgvn/`.

Lesbians, Gays, and Bisexuals on the Web

The Society and Culture: Sex site provides paths to a host of lesbian, gay, and bisexual resources, ranging from pages on Domestic Partnership and Same Sex Marriage to the "CyberQueer Lounge."

What's Out There

To find out more about lesbian, gay, and transgender topics, look for the URL `http://www.yahoo.com/Society_and_Culture/Gay_Lesbian_and_Bisexual_Resources/`.

Personal Finance

Money's the name of the game—where to get it, how to maximize it, and what to do with it. (Spend it? Save it?) Here are some sites to consult on these topics.

Consumer Information Center

You'll get all sorts of basic information about personal finance at this site, provided by a U.S. government organization, the Consumer Information

Center. (We thought we were going to find buying advice for retail goods here, but it's much more than that.)

What's Out There

Get the lowdown on all sorts of finance matters at the Consumer Information Center at http://www.gsa.gov/staff/pa/cic/cic.htm.

The Financial Times

That long- and well-known international publication, the *Financial Times*, has gone online, and lucky for us. You'll find top stories on Asia, the Americas, and Europe, along with stock-market indexes presented with a 30-minute delay.

What's Out There

Get financial facts and news at either the *Financial Times* U.S. site at http://www.usa.ft.com or the British site at http://www.ft.com.

Mortgage Calculator

A convenient-to-use mortgage amortization form (see Figure 6.17), created by an individual with an interest in the topic, offers you the opportunity to work out the numbers involved in financing a home.

What's Out There

Work out the numbers for your home financing at the URL http://ibc.wustl.edu/mort.html.

The Mortgage Calculator

Last modified October 11, 1995

Due to popular demand this tells you how much house you can afford

Look here for more calculators, information and links

Why use this form when you get get FREE software for your Mac/PC?

Change these fields as desired: [Calculate Mortgage]

- [100000] Principal Loan Balance
- [7.75] Annual Interest Rate (%) - (Look here or here or here for up to date rates)
  CANADIANS: Add a C (e.g. 7.75C) and I will use a conversion factor to convert your rates to a boring US equivalent to use in my calculations.

- Amortization Length [30] (Years, typically 30 or 15 in US, 25 in Canada)
- **Starting:** Month = [Jan ▼] Year = [1995]
- Show full amortization table? [No ▼]
- [0] Monthly Principal Prepayment Amount

FIGURE 6.17: Figure what your monthly and lifetime mortgage payments will be.

NASDAQ Financial Executive Journal

This quarterly (the *NASDAQ Financial Executive Journal*) is a joint project of Cornell's Legal Information Institute and the NASDAQ Stock Market, which should clue you in to what it covers.

What's Out There

To investigate the *NASDAQ Financial Executive Journal* further, check out the URL http://www.law.cornell.edu/nasdaq/nasdtoc.html.

Wall Street information is at your fingertips at the Wall Street Direct site: http://www.cts.com/~wallst.

Publishing and Literature

To many people, the creation of Web technology is as big a deal as the invention of the printing press. Wide-scale electronic distribution of attractively laid out information is now a reality. Let's look at how a sampling of publishers and information providers (both professional and amateur) are using this new medium.

See the Zines section at the end of this chapter for the scoop on alternative electronic publishing, including a description of a terrific literary zine, Enterzone.

BookWire

Both book lovers and publishing pros will love this comprehensive Web site (see Figure 6.18). Start with the online *Publishers Weekly* bestsellers list and then go on to the links to reviews. More links take you to libraries, publishers, booksellers, news, and even a daily cartoon by Mort Greenberg.

What's Out There

Open up the pages at http://www.bookwire.com/ to find out what's happening in the publishing world. The Pulitzer Prize's background and the current awardees are yours to read at http://www.pulitzer.org/.

Complete Works of William Shakespeare

As browsable, searchable, and cross-referenced as the works themselves, this online collection is the creation of an MIT grad student, Jeremy Hylton. There's even a hypertext glossary built into each of the Bard's works.

What's Out There

The Bard's complete works are set before you at the URL http://the-tech.mit.edu/Shakespeare/works.html.

FIGURE 6.18: BookWire's a terrific starting place for publishing news.

Mississippi Review

Literary reviews—small, carefully edited journals of writing with literary merit—are the gems of contemporary writing, offering newcomers a place to get their breaks and well-known writers a place to publish shorter works. The *Mississippi Review* is a prestigious example of the literary journal.

What's Out There

Contemporary short fiction is showcased for your reading pleasure at `http://sushi.st.usm.edu/~barthelm/index.html`.

Urban Diary

Is it art or is it lit? This hybrid of narrative and collage sometimes looks like typed and scribbled notes on gridlined paper, sometimes like doodles

on a calendar page, sometimes like …well, like someone's underground diary (see Figure 6.19). An obvious plot line never develops, but, hey, that's the nature of postmodern fiction.

What's Out There

A really unusual experience awaits you at `http://gertrude.art .uiuc.edu/ludgate/the/place/urban_diary/intro.html`.

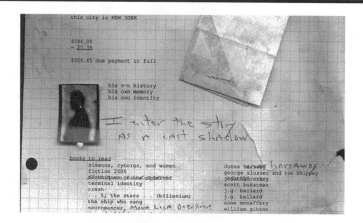

FIGURE 6.19: Is it art or is it lit?

Science and Technology

The Web, and in fact the Internet, started as a research tool, though of course it's grown into much more than that. You can see the effects of these beginnings in the wide range of information on the World Wide Web about everything from nuclear physics to genetic engineering to cancer research to... well, you get the idea. Here's a sampling of some Web servers that are chock full o' fascinating and useful data.

The Exploratorium

Here's a real beauty. The Exploratorium is a hands-on, interactive science museum in San Francisco. To call it a museum, though, is a *bit* misleading—it's a really fun place for the whole family.

What's Out There

The interactive, online Exploratorium experience can be yours through the URL http://www.exploratorium.edu.

MIT Media Lab

Where better to look into computers, science, and technology than at that granddaddy of science and technology academia, the Massachusetts Institute of *Technology*?

What's Out There

You'll get direct access to the MIT Media Lab through the URL http://www.media.mit.edu/.

NASA Information Services via World Wide Web

Voyage here for information about upcoming space shuttle missions, access to the many images made public from the Hubble Space Telescope, and a peak into NASA's strategy for the future. Also very cool, very fresh, is the "live" map of NASA centers around the country (see Figure 6.20) in the NASA Information Services home page.

What's Out There

Space, the final frontier, is yours to explore through the NASA Information Services home page. Its URL is `http://www.nasa.gov/`.

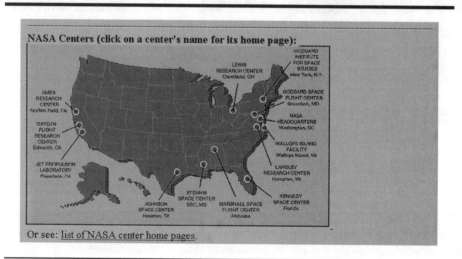

FIGURE 6.20: To find out what's up at any NASA center in the country, simply click on the name of that center in this map.

● Sports

From the major leagues to the minors, to the oh-so-minors and even the fantasy leagues, sports are all over the Net.

Create Your Own Sports Page

Another great gizmo from those fun-loving guys at MIT, this is a long list of sports links from which you can pick and choose those that interest you most and create a customized sports page. You just point and click. What results is a set of links on a page with its own URL.

Remember to place a bookmark on the customized sports page you create. If you don't, you'll never remember its self-generated URL, and you'll have to do the whole business of creating it over again.

What's Out There

Create your very own customized sports page via the URL
`http://tns-www.lcs.mit.edu/cgi-bin/sports/create-form`.

ESPNet Sports Zone

The premiere site for sports information, this one's got real power. College and professional sports are covered big time, with up-to-date scores, feature articles, and player interviews. There's a charge of $4.95 a month for the whole shebang (including the broadcast of basketball games with audio), but there's also plenty here you don't have to pay to view.

What's Out There

Big, better, and busting the mold, ESPNet Sports Zone is at the URL
`http://espnet.sportszone.com`.

Check out the Pathfinder site at `http://pathfinder.com`, and click on the <u>Sports Illustrated</u> link to get to that fountain of sports news.

The 1996 Olympic Games

A timely site devoted to developments in the 1996 Olympics, this site, as of this writing, offers views of the building of the Olympic stadium and village, schedules of events, ticket information, and so on. Presumably it'll keep up with some or all of the actual events as they occur and afterward will provide a history of the events. (See Figure 6.21.)

What's Out There

Keep an eagle eye on developments of the 1996 Olympic games at `http://www.atlanta.olympic.org/`.

GNN Women's Basketball

The GNN Sports Center covers women's basketball, offering scores, schedules, player spotlights, and features. You'll also find an archive of past news, the AP Top 25 poll, and more.

What's Out There

For the hoop-gal news, dribble on over to `http://gnn.com/gnn/meta/sports/basketball/women/index.html`.

FIGURE 6.21: Keep up with Olympic developments at this well-organized site.

Travel

Not only can you travel around the Web—you can use the Web to plot your travels around the world or just around town. The Internet offers all kinds of travel information and services, ranging from stuff about how to get there to what to expect and do once you arrive.

Foreign Languages for Travelers

It's always best to learn a few phrases (such as "Where is the bathroom?") before you travel to a new country.

What's Out There

Expand your foreign language vocabulary at `http://insti.physics`
`.sunysb.edu/~mmartin/languages/languages.html`.

Preview Media

Great vacation information and travel package bargains are available via the Preview Media site (see Figure 6.22). Here you'll find a thoughtful range of insider descriptions and background on locales (we never knew before that Cancun was chosen for development into a resort based on a

computer study). Check out Find-a-Trip, a nifty questionnaire that helps you focus your ideas and select a travel destination.

What's Out There

View vacation wonderlands via the Preview Media travel site at the URL `http://www.vacations.com`. (Note the *s* in *vacations*.)

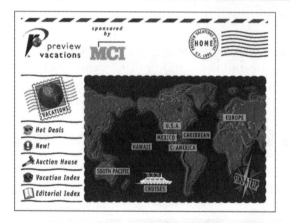

FIGURE 6.22: The postcard-motif graphics are almost as attractive as the deals at Preview Media's travel site.

Rough Guides

Rough Guides appeared first in print, then on TV, and now they're on the Web. In a special deal with Wired Ventures, the folks who bring you *Wired*

What's Out There

Journey via Rough Guides to hip, cool, groovy world travel at `http://www.hotwired.com/rough/`.

and *HotWired*, the very hip, cool, and groovy British travel guides for the masses are available online, with the usual *Wired* flair for the marriage of graphics and content.

World Wide Weirdness

We hardly know what to say about some of this. Anybody can publish a home page, and sometimes you'll run into the strangest, most wigged-out stuff in the world.

Keep in mind that things change on the Web at the whim of the folks who publish there. Pages (and the pages they're linked to) will change and vanish to reflect the times. This is part of the Web's attraction. Don't worry, be happy: You might stumble across one truly amazing thing while you're looking for another.

The Squat

A (very quirky) response to the famous and popular the Spot, which we describe elsewhere in this chapter, the Squat changes the real-life locale to a trailer park in the backwoods of Missouri. There the cast of six acts out lives filled with lazing, guzzling, and just plain lousy living. The Squat's apparent in Figure 6.23.

What's Out There

Look in on the Squat, a "this-is-*real*-life" response to the Spot, at `http://theory.physics.missouri.edu/~georges/Josh/squat/welcome.html`.

Hey, Com'on in!

(If ya can stand the smell)

FIGURE 6.23: The Squat is an even quirkier response to the already quirky Spot.

The Surrealism Server

Time bends across a molten landscape… We aren't even going to tell you what you'll find at the Surrealism server—just that it's weird and wacky and, well, surreal.

What's Out There

It's surreal, and it's at the Surrealism server, which you'll experience at `http://pharmdec.wustl.edu/juju/surr/surrealism.html`.

Zines

Defined by the kind of quirkiness that's so fashionable on the Net and the streets of our cities, zines are all the rage. Anyone can publish an electronic magazine to be distributed via e-mail or the Web; all it takes is a viewpoint you want to make known and a little computer know-how.

In this section, we'll look at a few specific zines—three created by individuals or small groups of friends, and one created by a professional team with high financing. We'll show you where to find out about the proliferation of zines on the Net and where to find out about how to start your own zine.

What's Out There

Several newsgroups are devoted to e-zine and Web zine talk. Make your way via your newsreader to `alt.zines`, `alt.ezines`, and `alt.etext` to check them out.

Enterzone

There are lots of "literary" magazines on the Net and the Web; many of them lean more toward science fiction than real literary fare. *Enterzone* is a hyperzine that breaks the mold, providing a thoughtful selection of not just fiction, poetry, and essays, but also photography, paintings, and even interactive art forms (see Figure 6.24).

What's Out There

Enterzone presents writing and artwork of true merit. Use the URL `http://enterzone.berkeley.edu/enterzone.html` to find *Enterzone*.

geekgrrl

One of the more famous zines, *geekgrrl* conjures images of hip feminists of the '90s speaking up, articulately and engagingly, in print.

What's Out There

Catch up with *geekgrrl* at
`http://www.next.com.au/spyfood/geekgirl/002manga/index.html`.

FIGURE 6.24: Enterzone, a literary showcase

Wired Magazine and HotWired

Dubbed "*Wired* magazine's Rest Stop on the Infobahn," *HotWired* is an online adjunct to the very trendy publication *Wired*. *Wired* was an immediate smash when it was launched in 1993. Devoted to the cybernaut subculture, this rag is high-tech with an attitude. Its progeny, *HotWired*, was launched in late 1994 and was also a smash success. Perhaps unsurprisingly, *HotWired* (see Figure 6.25) is even cooler than its parent. Let's face it: *HotWired is* what *Wired is* *about*.

What's Out There

Get *HotWired* via the Web server for this journal of the cybernaut subculture. The URL is http://www.hotwired.com.

FIGURE 6.25: HotWired, the online progeny of Wired magazine

To access *HotWired*, you'll have to go through the simple hoops of setting up a (cost-free) account. Just follow the on-screen directions the first time you jump in to the *HotWired* world; you'll have your free account in a moment or two, and you won't have to go to any trouble at all next time.

Factsheet Five

Billing itself as "your guide to parallel culture," *Factsheet Five* offers zine reviews, online catalogs, and even journals and articles on electronic publishing issues.

What's Out There

Get *Factsheet Five* at http://www.well.com/conf/f5/f5index2.html.

John Labovitz's E-Zine-List

Listing more than 600 e-zines and Web zines alphabetically and promising new navigational methods, this gem offers a text version of the e-zine list and, perhaps most interestingly, a comprehensive listing of zine-related resources.

What's Out There

John Labovitz's comprehensive list of zines can be seen at the URL `http://www.meer.net/~johnl/e-zine-list/`.

There's also a great e-zine FAQ (Frequently Asked Question list) at `http://www.well.com/conf/f5/ezines.faq`.

Van Der Hoeven's Zine Applet for Java

Java technology, new as of this writing, is bound to open a brave new world of zine publishing. Here's a cutting-edge zine that requires a browser with Java capability to get the full effect.

What's Out There

Jolting Java can be seen in action at this innovative zine via the URL `http://www.fanzine.se/java/jo/zine.html`.

Zine Terminology

There are e-zines, and there are Web zines. What's the diff? Well, an e-zine might be considered by the new elite as the e-mail forerunner of the Web zine, but to the e-zine underground, it's a wider-range medium. (Believe it or not, not everyone has a Web broswer.) The earlier forerunners of e-zines and Web zines might be the fold-and-staple variety of alternative magazines that are (still to this day) photocopied rather than printed. Zines are a low-cost way to publish what you think the world wants or needs to know. In publishing, printing costs are a terrible burden; so the lower you can get your printing costs, the less funding you need to start your own rag. Where else can you get the low-cost/high distribution bang for your buck than on the Net? You too can be a publsiher. (See Chapter 8).

Word

With some stunning graphics and its own quirky viewpoint (one that we don't really share), *Word more or less defines the height of zine culture. It's worth a glance if only for the clever use of art and layout (see Figure 6.26).*

What's Out There

Word has it that *Word*, an online zine with inspiring layout and its own viewpoint, is at http://www.word.com/.

One Thing Leads to Another

Things change. The Web changes all the time—new stuff appears there daily, and part of the wonder of Web exploration is accidentally coming

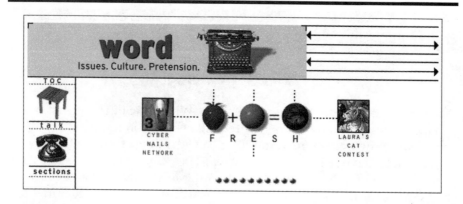

FIGURE 6.26: Visually, <u>Word</u> is striking, though it's probably not going to be the very last word in Web layout for long.

across the unexpected, the unusual, or even the outrageous as you tinker about. After looking through these last two chapters, you should have some ideas about where to get started and the range of stuff that's available. Cruising the Web is your game now—have a grand old time. In the next chapter, we'll look into some great tools for searching and finding whatever you seek on the Web.

Tools and Techniques for Searching and Finding

Okay, so everyone knows the World Wide Web is growing at a mind-boggling rate. Then how does the intrepid Net cruiser find what he or she is looking for among all of what's out there? How does anyone know even where to *begin* a search? As you use the Internet—especially the Web—you may find yourself sucked into a black hole of pointing-and-clicking, following hyperlinks with complete abandon and fascination, yet coming up with little information that's relevant to the project at hand. (That's why they call it *cyberspace*....)

Let's step back for a second and take a look at gathering information in ways that aren't so willy-nilly. The Web is a bona fide research tool, after all—let's find out how it can be used to find information on focused topics. Say, for example, you work in the planning department of a large corporation, and you need to write a business report about the current cause célèbre of corporate America—"reengineering."

Say you want to pepper your report with statistical data—productivity levels in American business over the past ten years, unemployment levels, inflation rates, and so on. You also want to describe the viewpoints of financial, economic, and business experts and address forecasts for the future of business.

The Web is gigantic, webby, and *growing*. (We've said this before.) You just can't expect everything on the Web to be contained in any one place or to be searchable with any one tool. To do your Web research—on our example topic or on any other topic—you'll use a number of tools:

◆ Magellan

◆ Lycos

◆ Inktomi

◆ InfoSeek

◆ The All-in-One Search Page

◆ The CUI W3 Catalog

This chapter's going to introduce you to those useful tools that appear on the Web for searching the Web—in fact, for searching large portions of the Internet—with efficiency and ease.

Netscape offers a free add-on to the Web browser we know and love—SmartMarks. SmartMarks will help you manage the tremendous amount of information you find on the Web; one of its terrific features is that SmartMarks lets you search many of the databases we discuss in this chapter all from one handy Windows-style dialog box. We cover SmartMarks in Appendix A of this book.

About Search Tools

You can use any or all of several search tools on the Web. Each of these gizmos has special strengths and weaknesses—none is perfect, and some are better for some jobs than others. That's why we present an array of options here. You'll get to know and use your own favorites as time goes on.

Just as each Web page you encounter bears the mark of its publisher (in the form of what's included and excluded and how information is presented), each search tool also has been affected by its publishers' knowledge and interest. For example, if you search for material on a specific topic in Yahoo and don't find anything, that doesn't mean your topic is not represented on the Net. Search again, using one of the other tools, and see what comes up there.

When you conduct your search, you'll have to describe the information that you want. In general, you will enter one or more words into a text box on screen. The search *engine* (the program or search tool that actually does the search) you're using will compare this text (called a search *string*) with some part of or all the text associated with all the Web pages this search engine knows. (Most search engines also employ what's called a *Web crawler* to find out in an automated way what's on the Net. That's how they learn of the pages they then "know" about. (See *What Web Crawlers Do*.)

Types of Searches

As mentioned, each search engine focuses on some part of or all the pages; sometimes you'll even be able to specify whether what you are searching for will appear in the Web page's:

◆ Title

◆ URL

◆ Text

◆ All the above

The search engine will sift through the pages it knows of, looking for the text you specified, and it will return a list of all the pages that contain the text you specified. If you specified that the search engine look only in titles, URLs, or text, it will look only *in those parts of* the document(s). Thus, the exact way the search engine matches up what you are searching for with its database is partly controllable by you and partly dependent on the particular search

gizmo you are using. Obviously, the searches that are most often most useful are those that search the text of the page. Even then, some search engines search smaller portions of the text than others do.

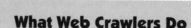

What Web Crawlers Do

At the heart of most Internet search tools is a *Web crawler*, a program that "crawls" around the Web looking at page after page and site after site, bringing the addresses, the titles, and in some cases (descriptive) pieces of the pages' contents into a gigantic searchable database. The speed and efficiency of these Web crawlers is what makes legendary the databases compiled using them. In Chapter 2 you'll find more on Web crawlers in a section titled *Wanderers, Spiders, and Robots*.

When you encounter those text boxes into which you type the stuff you want the search engine to go looking for, it's important to know how much or how little text you are allowed to type and whether the search engine can make some basic distinctions. For example, the smartest search engines "know" enough so that you can type a phrase such as *pigeons for sale* and they will not bother matching the word *for* or will skip over words that include *for*. Other search engines will return everything that matches without much discrimination; so you'd get not just all the sites that include the words *pigeons* and *sale* (the important words in this case) but also *for*mat, *for*tune, be*for*e, and every other instance of the combination of the letters *f*, *o*, and *r*.

This is all pretty basic stuff—very quickly, in fact, search engines are growing more and more sophisticated. All the search gizmos we discuss in this chapter include advanced settings so that you can control how they look for documents and the scope of their searches, and they'll all undoubtedly add features to their already impressive capabilities as time goes on.

There are all kinds of search tools. First we'll look at some of the big names in searching, and then we'll take a look at a terrific all-in-one search page that pulls in lots of options for searching the biggies and the not-so-big. We'll wind up by revisiting an old favorite, the CUI W3

Catalog, with which you can search the archive of NCSA What's New pages.

Along the top of the Netscape window, you'll see two buttons labeled Net Search and Net Directory. (This assumes you haven't turned off the directory buttons via the Options menu.) Clicking on either of these buttons brings you to pages listing, describing, and linking to many of the search tools discussed in this chapter. Prominently featured, in fact, is Yahoo, which we covered in Chapter 5.

Using Logical Operators in More Complicated Searches

To make your searches more specific, you can use *logical operators*—AND and OR, for example—which work kind of like conjunctions in English grammar. The way you actually use logical operators varies a bit from one search tool to another, but the ideas remain the same. In general, if you want to find documents that contain *all* the words in a search string, you can join the words with AND. If you want to find any *one* of the words in a search string, you can join the words with OR.

Here's an example: If you want to find documents that discuss American business, simply entering *American business* as your search string will often result in a list of documents that contain either the word *American* or the word *business*. That would be an awful lot of documents, only a few of which might actually discuss American business per se. If you join the two words with AND, as in *American AND business*, the search tool will look for documents that contain both words, rather than either word. If you joined the words with OR, as in *American OR business*, you'd get all the documents with either word and all the documents with both words. ...Logical, eh?

● Searching with Magellan

Magellan, The McKinley Group's Internet directory, has as its base a search tool that combines a powerful proprietary Web crawler with full-text search capabilities. The Web crawler brings in a huge number of Web sites and documents, which are compiled into a database that includes the URL, the title, and contact information. In the next step, a short review of the site is written by a member of The McKinley Group's editorial team and a rating is applied (one to four stars, indicating the site's relative merit). The rating is based on the site's depth of content, ease of exploration, and Net appeal.

The Magellan search engine finds what best matches the search string you entered and places the most relevant sites—the ones that have the maximum number of matches—at the top of the list it returns. Magellan is a full-text search tool; it searches the URL, the title, and the text.

 You can also browse Magellan's database by traversing a convenient list of categories and subcategories. "Browsing" Magellan, as it's called, is covered in Chapter 5 of this book.

Opening Magellan

The first step in searching with Magellan is to open it in Netscape.

1. From the Netscape menu bar, select File ➤ Open Location The Open Location dialog box will appear.

2. In the dialog box's text box, type the URL for Magellan: `http://www.mckinley.com`.

3. Click on the Open button. The dialog box will close, the Netscape N icon will become animated, and in a few seconds the Magellan home page will appear (see Figure 7.1).

What's Out There

Magellan's home page can be discovered at `http://www.mckinley.com`.

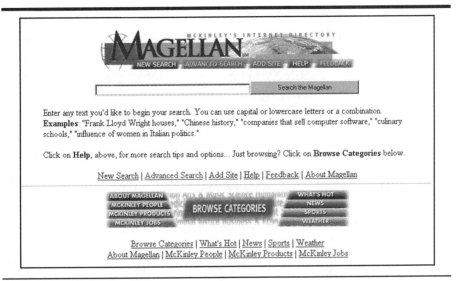

FIGURE 7.1: Magellan is a bang-up search resource that combines a powerful Web crawler and its resulting database with the convenience of reviews and ratings written by a knowledgeable editorial team.

Searching Magellan

With the Magellan home page open, you are ready to start exploring. Take a look at the page; it includes links to other pages that tell you about Magellan and the company behind it.

 A lot of sites and pages are known to Magellan, but not every single one can be. Only those that have been discovered by Magellan's Web crawler will appear in Magellan's database. This is true of all search tools—the Web grows faster than they can catalog it, though Magellan and all the search tools are expanding all the time.

To perform a search using Magellan, follow these steps:

1. In the Search text box of the Magellan home page, type a word or a phrase that describes what you want to find. Magellan works best when you give it a number of words; some examples are on the page itself.

You may have to try a number of variations on the words you use to describe what interests you before you find the exact right resource you need (<u>auto</u>, <u>vehicle</u>, and <u>car</u> will all turn up different pages). Try to be specific, but not too specific. Using the plural <u>books</u>, for example, will omit instances of the singular <u>book</u>.

2. Click on the Search the Magellan button to begin the actual search. The Netscape N icon will become animated. In a few seconds, a new page will appear, listing everything matching your search criteria that was found in the database. (Figure 7.2 shows some of the results of a search for *personal finance*.)

Magellan lists only the first 60 records that meet your criteria, ranking them by relevancy. You can click on More to get any additional records, start again by entering new search criteria and clicking on New Search, or further focus the search in progress.

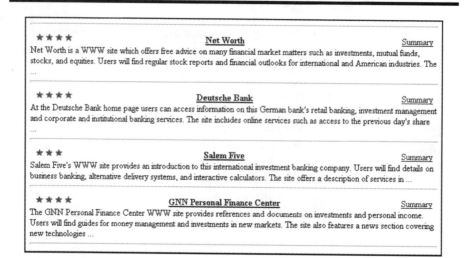

FIGURE 7.2: Here you see some results of searching Magellan for personal finance.

Focusing Your Search

To focus your search further, simply type additional words or phrases in the text box at the top of the Search Results page and click on the Focus Search button. For example, you might want to focus your *personal finance* search by entering *software*; you'd then get a list of sites that relate to personal finance software.

Performing More Complicated Searches with Magellan

You don't have to limit yourself to entering simple text such as we've described as your search criteria. You can use the Advanced Search page to do more sophisticated, complex searches.

To use the Advanced Search page, follow these steps:

1. From the Magellan home page, either click on the words *Advanced Search* in the Magellan graphic at the top of the page, or click on the Advanced Search link at the bottom of the page. Regardless of which you select, a page will appear that has a number of new searching options (see Figure 7.3).

2. In the text box near the top of the page, type a word or a phrase to describe what you want to find, just as you did in the simpler search.

3. You can select either of two types of searches: Regular Search or Concept Search. In a Regular Search, Magellan hunts for the actual words that you enter in the text field; in a Concept Search, Magellan looks for words that you entered and for words that are related to the ones you entered.

To get a lot of very helpful advice about using these search options, click on the Help link in the graphic along the top of the Search the Magellan page and then click on the Advanced Search link.

4. In the Type of Search area of the page, you can control whether all the words, any one of the words, or the exact string you entered in

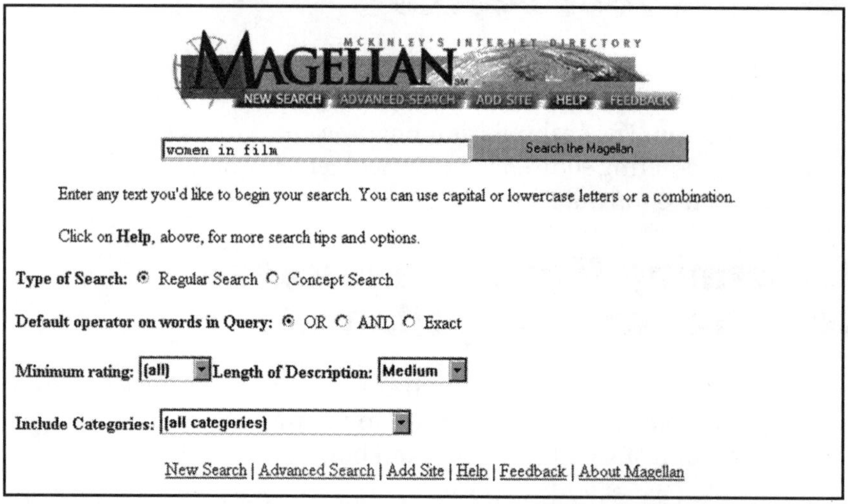

FIGURE 7.3: Click on the Magellan home page's <u>Advanced Search</u> link, and a number of more sophisticated search options will be yours. Here we are searching for <u>women in film</u>.

the text box must appear in an entry for a match to occur. (Remember our talk earlier in this chapter about logical operators?) Specify this by selecting one of the OR, AND, or Exact radio buttons.

5. Now, in the Minimum Rating drop-down list, specify the minimum rating (one to four stars) that you want the sites resulting from your search to have. For example, if you select the three-star option, you'll get only those sites that meet all your other search criteria *and* have been assigned three or more stars by Magellan's editorial team. To display all sites regardless of their rating, select (all).

6. Using the Length of Description drop-down list you can control the length of the site's description as it will appear in the listing you get from your search. Your options are Short, Medium, or Long. Medium is the description length Magellan uses by default (when you are not using the advanced searching options). If you choose Short, you'll get only a single line of text. If you choose Long, you'll get the entire description.

7. Your next option is to limit your search to specific categories. To understand this, just remember that you can browse Magellan as well as search it. The categories the editorial team at The McKinley Group have devised for browsing (ranging from Art to Travel & Tourism) are listed in the Include Categories pull-down list. Simply select what you want. Only pages that are related to the category you've chosen will appear in the list of matching pages that results from your search.

8. Once you've entered the text you want to search for and have filled in any of the other options described in the preceding steps, click on the Search the Magellan button. The famous N will become animated, and in a few seconds a new page will appear, listing everything matching your criteria that Magellan's search engine found in the Magellan database.

The listing that appears will follow Magellan's policy of providing those sites that most closely match your criteria at the top of the list.

If you want all the four-star sites to appear at the top of the list, make that part of your criteria as described in Step 5.

Searching with Lycos

Lycos was developed by a group at Carnegie Mellon University as a tool for cataloging enormous amounts of Internet material. Currently operated by a private company, Lycos has (as of this writing) more than 10 million pages listed in its database. Like other search tools, Lycos is actually composed of two pieces:

◆ A Web crawler that seeks out and catalogs pages on the Web, logging everything it finds into a database

◆ A set of Lycos Web pages with which you can access and search the database

Unlike some others, the Lycos Web crawler records a site's URL and title in the database, *and it records the first 20 lines of the page.*

Opening Lycos

Before you use Lycos, you must open its home page, which is a simple matter. Follow these steps:

1. From the Netscape menu bar, select File ➤ Open Location. The Open Location dialog box will appear.

2. In the dialog box's text box, type the URL for Lycos: `http://www.lycos.com`.

3. Click on the Open button. The dialog box will close, the Netscape N icon will become animated, and in a few seconds the Lycos home page will appear (see Figure 7.4).

What's Out There

You can call on Lycos using the URL `http://www.lycos.com`.

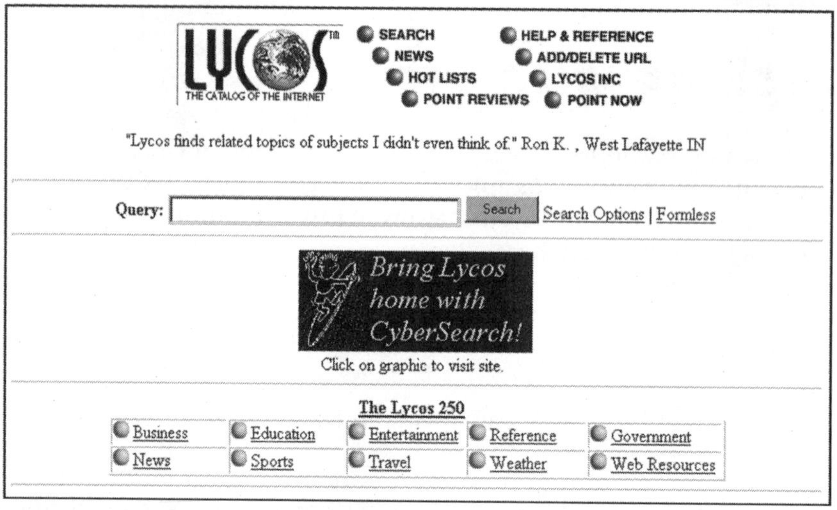

FIGURE 7.4: Lycos is an enormous database with more than 10 million Web pages cataloged in it.

Searching Lycos

Lycos' great strength is that its database is so huge you're bound to find something about your topic listed there. Let's take a look at how to search Lycos.

1. In the Query text box of the Lycos home page, type a word or a phrase that describes what you want to find.

2. Click on the Search button. Lycos will start searching, the Netscape N icon will become animated, and in a few seconds a page will appear with a detailed list describing the stuff Lycos found that matched your criteria.

In this list you'll get the title of each Web page that matched your criteria, along with an outline of the page—the outline is really just a set of keywords that Lycos generated automatically. You'll also get an excerpt of the page (again, generated automatically) showing the beginning of the document. Figure 7.5 shows the results of a search for *Fela Anikulapo Kuti*, a popular Nigerian musician.

Found 523 documents matching at least one search term.
Printing only the first 10 of 185 documents with at least scores of 0.010.

Found 106 matching words (number of documents): fela (41), felafel (33), felag (28), felaktig (33), felaktigt (22), felan (24), felanmalan (41), anikulapo (12), kuti (58), kutina (22), ...

1) Fela Kuti [1.0000, 3 of 3 terms, adj 1.0]

Outline: Fela Kuti

Abstract: Fela Anikulapo Kuti , born in Abeokuta, Nigeria in 1938, is a singer-composer, trumpet, sax and keyboard player, bandleader, and politician. Kuti is one of Africa's most controversial musicians and has continued to fight for the rights of the common man (and woman) despite vilification, harassment, and even imprisonment by the government of Nigeria. Born to Yoruban parents, Kuti was strongly influenced by both parents, his mother being Funmilayo, a leading figure in the nationalist struggle
http://matisse.net/~jal/amnifela.htm (2k)

2) Fela Anikulapo Kuti [0.9268, 3 of 3 terms, adj 1.0]

Abstract: Fela Anikulapo Kuti

http://www.matisse.net/~jal/amnifela.htm (0k)

FIGURE 7.5: Surprisingly, Lycos found a whole bunch of information on the Web about Fela Anikulapo Kuti, a popular but not entirely famous Nigerian musician.

Performing More Complicated Searches with Lycos

The Lycos database is so big that even a search for a little-known topic is likely to turn up scads of pages. You'll often want to perform more focused searches so as to find only the stuff that's most relevant. You can use the Search Options link to do so.

Follow these steps:

1. From the Lycos home page, click on the Search Options link. The Lycos Search Form page will appear, as shown in Figure 7.6.

2. In the Query field of the Lycos Search page, type a word or a phrase that describes what you want to find.

3. Two pull-down lists appear next to the Search Options label. In the first pull-down list, you can specify how many of the words you typed into the box you want to have matched in the search.

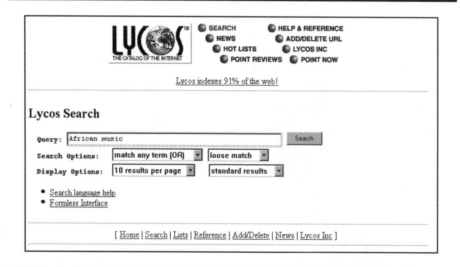

FIGURE 7.6: You'll have great control over your search when you use the Lycos Search page.

The options are:

To Match	Select the Option
All the words	Match all terms (AND)
Any one word	Match any term (OR)
Any *n* number of words (where *n* is replaced by a number from 2 to 7)	Match *n* terms

In the second pull-down list, you specify how closely the search engine must match your criteria. The options are fairly self-explanatory:

◆ Loose match

◆ Fair match

◆ Good match

◆ Close match

◆ Strong match

Selecting loose match will retrieve the most documents; selecting strong match will retrieve the least number of documents.

What's Out There

You can further investigate the search options Lycos presents by looking into `http://www.lycos.com/reference/search-help.html`.

4. Two pull-down lists appear next to the Display Options label. In one of them, you can specify how many of the pages that the search engine finds you want to see. You can choose anywhere from 10 to 40.

Don't worry that you aren't seeing every single page that matches your search criteria. You can simply click on the <u>Next n hits</u> link at the bottom of the page of results to get even more.

In the second pull-down list, you can specify what is to be displayed for each site that matches your search criteria.

If You Select	You'll Get
Summary results	Just the titles of the matching pages
Standard results	The title, the outline, and the excerpt (called an *abstract*)
Detailed results	The title, the outline, and a longer excerpt

5. When you've completed all the settings and your search criteria are fully specified, click on the Search button. The Netscape N icon will become animated. In a few seconds, a page will appear listing the sites that match the criteria you specified.

The Lycos 250

Lycos is a big whopping giant of a database, and it's accessed many, many times a day by a *lot* of people. Wouldn't it be dandy to know which of the sites cataloged by Lycos are most popular—the most sought after sites? The Lycos 250 tells you just that. A browsable list of the 250 most popular entries in the Lycos database, the Lycos 250 is organized into the following convenient categories:

◆ Business

◆ Education

◆ Entertainment

◆ Reference

◆ Government

◆ News

- ◆ Sports
- ◆ Travel
- ◆ Weather
- ◆ Web Resources

To get to this gem of information, follow the steps listed here:

1. On the Lycos home page, click on The Lycos 250 link. The Lycos 250 and Hot Lists page will appear, as shown in Figure 7.7.

The Lycos 250 and Hot Lists

You've seen hot lists before, but you've **never** seen hot lists like this. Because we're not just telling you what **we** think is hot - we're telling you what the **whole Internet community** thinks is hot.

How do we know? Because our Lycos spiders (patent pending) have examined more than 91% of the sites on the net, and for each site visited, kept track of how many **other** sites link to that site. On the Internet, when your site is useful or interesting, other sites link to it, and the more links there are to it, the more people go to it, which reinforces its usefulness and interest, which generates more links, etc.

On the Internet, the number of links to your site **IS** its popularity. And Lycos, by a factor of seven larger than any other catalog, is also the **only** catalog which tracks this popularity.

When time is short and you're looking for the **best** site of a particular type to visit, check the Lycos lists to see what sites the **rest** of the net finds **most** useful.

To start, we present the **Lycos 250**, the 250 most popular sites arranged by subject matter. To fill out some of the categories, we've also added a few sites that aren't in the top 250, but are worthy of note.

- ● Business ● Education ● Entertainment ● Reference
- ● Government ● News ● Sports ● Travel
- ● Weather ● Web Resources

More exciting hot lists will be coming soon, so be sure to come back for more!

[Home | Search | Lists | Reference | Add/Delete | News | Lycos Inc]

FIGURE 7.7: You'll find out which pages in Lycos are most sought after when you check into The Lycos 250 and Hot Lists page.

2. Toward the bottom of The Lycos 250 and Hot Lists page, you'll see links for each of the subject categories. Simply click on one of these links to display the Hot list for that topic (see Figure 7.8).

From the What's Hot! page, you can click on any of the links to go directly to that Web page.

● **Home Pages**

AT&T
Adobe Systems
Apple Computer
Compaq Computer
DEC
FedEx
HaL Computers and Software
Hewlett Packard
IBM
LEGO
LOTUS
Microsoft
Novell
SUN
Silicon Graphics
United Parcel Service

● **Investing**

Experimental Stock Market
   Free value-added service from the MIT Artificial Intelligence lab. Includes stock and mutual fund charts, top stocks
   and more.
Investor Web
   From IPO's to equity investments, a complete analysis

FIGURE 7.8: We clicked on the <u>Business</u> link to see the Business What's Hot! page.

● **Searching with Inktomi**

Inktomi, which debuted in late 1995 amidst great fanfare, is an experimental Web searching tool developed by Eric A. Brewer and Paul Gauthier at the University of California at Berkeley. They developed it is a sample application for *parallel computing*—which just means it runs on more than one computer at a time. This is good, because if one machine fails or slows down, another takes over and keeps the work going. (You may recall that this is the same principle on which the Internet was founded.) What started as the parallel computing experiment of a group of CS (Computer Science) students became a wonderfully useful (and *fast*) tool for finding information on the Web.

Wondering what "Inktomi" means? Well, it's a play on words for one thing—ink-to-me, get it? It's also the name of a mythological spider, according to Native Americans of the Great Plains. This spider was known, apparently, for bringing culture to people and representing the underdog.

Dig around the Inktomi site, and you'll find an interesting paper, *Truth in Document Counting,* that outlines a position on what should and shouldn't be counted when calculating the number of pages or sites a database holds. According to this position, Inktomi, as of this writing (and shortly after its launch), holds 1.3 million documents, and Lycos, according to the same counting methods, actually holds 1.8 million rather than the more than 10 million that Lycos cites.

What's Out There

Inktomi's search qualities are apparent at `http://inktomi.berkeley.edu`.

Opening Inktomi

To use Inktomi, you must of course first open it. Follow these steps:

1. From the Netscape menu bar, select File ➤ Open Location. The Open Location dialog box will appear.

2. In the dialog box's text box, type the URL for Inktomi: `http://inktomi.berkeley.edu`.

3. Click on the Open button. The dialog box will close, the Netscape N icon will become animated, and in a few seconds the Inktomi Web Services page will appear (see Figure 7.9).

The Inktomi Web Services page includes links to information about Inktomi, its sponsors, and the research being conducted by Eric A. Brewer and Paul Gauthier. Check this stuff out at your leisure; it's quite intriguing.

Searching Inktomi

Inktomi is very simple to use. Basically you just type in some text that describes what you want to find and click on the Start Search button. Let's go over the steps in detail, however. Here they are:

1. On the Inktomi Web Services page, click on the <u>Perform a search</u> link to display the Inktomi Search Engine page shown in Figure 7.10.

The <u>Inktomi</u> Search Engine is the first fast web indexer with a large database.

The database is currently 1.3M documents, versus 1.18M for Lycos, 200K for InfoSeek, and 150K for WebCrawler [<u>ways to count URLs</u>].

Inktomi uses parallel computing technology to build a **<u>scalable web server</u>** using commodity workstations; we currently use 4 SparcStation 10s. Inktomi is part of the Network of Workstations (<u>NOW</u>) project at the <u>University of California at Berkeley</u>.

Inktomi was implemented by graduate student <u>Paul Gauthier</u> and Professor <u>Eric Brewer</u>.

- **<u>Perform a search</u>**

- **<u>Add a URL</u>**

- <u>Truth in Document Counting</u>
- <u>More info on our scalable web server research</u>
- <u>Where does the name come from?</u>

FIGURE 7.9: The innovative Inktomi uses parallel computing for a fast, efficient search.

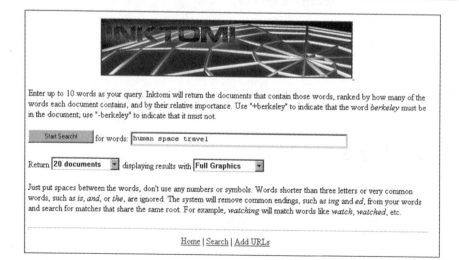

Enter up to 10 words as your query. Inktomi will return the documents that contain those words, ranked by how many of the words each document contains, and by their relative importance. Use "+berkeley" to indicate that the word *berkeley* must be in the document; use "-berkeley" to indicate that it must not.

[Start Search!] for words: [human space travel]

Return [20 documents ▼] displaying results with [Full Graphics ▼]

Just put spaces between the words, don't use any numbers or symbols. Words shorter than three letters or very common words, such as *is, and,* or *the*, are ignored. The system will remove common endings, such as *ing* and *ed*, from your words and search for matches that share the same root. For example, *watching* will match words like *watch, watched*, etc.

<u>Home</u> | <u>Search</u> | <u>Add URLs</u>

FIGURE 7.10: Use the Inktomi Search Engine page to search the impressively compiled Inktomi database. Here we search Inktomi for <u>human space travel</u>.

2. In the text box that appears to the right of the Start Search! button, enter a word or a phrase that describe what you seek. Click on the Start Search! button. The Netscape N icon will become animated as Inktomi searches its database for matching documents, and in a few seconds a new page will appear listing the results (see Figure 7.11).

 The results will be shown in the order of relevancy. In other words, if you type three words as your search criteria, the site that contains the largest number of references to all three of those words will appear first in the list of results.

Inktomi displays only ten documents at a time on its results page. If your search resulted in more than ten matching documents, a [Next 20 hits] link will appear at the bottom of the results page. Clicking on that link will display the next set of matches.

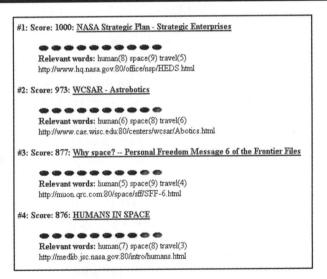

FIGURE 7.11: When you search Inktomi, you'll get a page like this one that lists documents.

Performing More Complicated Searches with Inktomi

Inktomi includes some very easy to use features that let you control which documents it returns. Unlike the other search gizmos and gadgets we discuss in this chapter, Inktomi does not have a separate page for performing advanced searches; instead, all the more advanced features appear on the standard search page. You can create more sophisticated searches using selections from a set of drop-down lists, or you can enter special symbols in the text box when you specify your search criteria. This will give you greater control.

To perform more complex searches with Inktomi, proceed as described here:

1. In the text box where you enter the words that describe what you want to search for, you can add special characters before each word to control its meaning. Here are your options:

Type This	And That Will Mean
	Not prefixing a word with a symbol means that the word may appear or may not appear in the document for the document to be considered a match.
+	Prefixing a word with a + means that the word *must* be in the document for the document to be considered a match.
–	Prefixing a word with a - means that the word must *not* appear in the document for the document to be considered a match.

For example, to search for documents that contain the word *Grateful*, but not *Dead*, type **+Grateful -Dead** as the search criteria.

2. With your search criteria specified, you're ready as rain to move on to the other Inktomi options. In the Return drop-down list, you can specify how many documents Inktomi will return at once. The default setting is 20. You can choose a number from 10 through 100 instead if you like.

The more documents you get at once, the less clicking on the [Next] link at the bottom of the results page you'll have to do. But the more documents you ask for, the longer you'll sit around waiting for them to arrive.

3. In the Displaying Results *with* pull-down list, you can control how much information Inktomi displays about each of the documents that meet your search criteria.

Select	To Get
Full Graphics	A little graphic (an icon) next to the listing for each document; the more blue dots in the graphic, the more relevant to your search the document is.
Text Only	Capital *X*s next to the listing for each document; the more *X*s there are, the more relevant to your search the document is.
Terse Text Only	A number next to the listing for each document; the higher the number, the more relevant to your search the document is.

4. To actually do the search, click on the Start Search! button. The Netscape N icon will become animated, and in a few seconds the results of your search will appear.

Inktomi is a promising new search tool; keep an eye on how its features affect the capabilities of other search tools over time.

● **Searching with InfoSeek**

InfoSeek is yet another combination Web-crawler/database-search tool. InfoSeek differs from others in that the company that brings you InfoSeek allows you to glean *some* results of a search without compensation to them, but charges a fee for full access. For example, you must pay for access to

and searches of Usenet archives, computer industry newspapers and magazines, newspaper newswire services, company profiles, movie reviews, book reviews, video reviews, and so on.

In this section, we'll show you what you can do using the free parts of InfoSeek.

What's Out There

Seek InfoSeek, and you'll find it at http://www.infoseek.com.

Opening InfoSeek

To use InfoSeek, you must first open it. Here's how:

1. From the Netscape menu bar, select File ➤ Open Location. The Open Location dialog box will appear.
2. In the dialog box's text box, type the URL for InfoSeek: http://www.infoseek.com.
3. Click on the Open button. The dialog box will close, the Netscape N icon will become animated, and in a few seconds the InfoSeek home page will appear.

With this page open, you're all set to start searching.

Searching InfoSeek

Searching via InfoSeek is a breeze. Simply follow these steps:

1. In the text box of the InfoSeek home page, type a word or a phrase that describes what you seek.
2. Click on the Search button. The Netscape N icon will become animated, and in a few seconds, the InfoSeek Net Search Results page will appear, showing the results of your search. Figure 7.12 shows an example.

```
Faculty Profiles: MIT Department of Architecture
      Faculty Profiles: Architecture . Stanford Anderson . Head of the Department of Architecture . Professor of History
      and Architecture. . Anderson teaches courses in the history of European and American architecture and urbanism. His
      research ...
      --- [54] http://alberti.mit.edu/arch/fac.html (68K)

Italian Art & Architecture
      "History? When you get to be my age, you don't have to study history: you just gotta have a good memory." . "You
      can't hardly walk ten feet in Italy without bumping smack into art history. Mama's neighbor Steve has been studying
      this for a ...
      --- [54] http://www.eat.com/architecture/index.html (4K)

Risorse italiane in rete
      Indici [Il gopher server Italia] [Il server WWW Italia] [Ciao!Italian Digipages by Cercom - Italiano] [L'edicola
      sull'Italia] [Archivio prime pagine Corriere, Repubblica e Gazzetta, 1989-1995] [Index] [The Webfoot's Guide to
      Italy] [Useful ...
      --- [53] http://italia.hum.utah.edu/doc/risorse.html (41K)

The Italian WWW Virtual Library: Ingegneria
      Ingegneria: Civile . De Architectura - hypermedia on-line architecture, building & construction bookshelf a cura di
      Alfredo M. Ronchi - Dept. ISET Politecnico di Milano. .
      --- [53] http://www.mi.cnr.it/IGST/Ing_Civile.html (1K)
```

FIGURE 7.12: Get a gander at these results of an InfoSeek search for Italian architecture.

InfoSeek displays only 10 matches at first; if your search produced more than these initial 10 matches, you can see the additional ones by clicking on the Next link that appears at the bottom of the page.

Performing More Complicated Searches with InfoSeek

Like Inktomi, InfoSeek does not provide a separate page for advanced searching—instead, you'll conduct more advanced InfoSeek searches simply by entering special characters into the same text box you originally used to do a basic search in InfoSeek.

To perform a more complicated search of InfoSeek, follow these procedures:

1. In the text box where you enter the words that describe what you want to search for, you can add special characters before each word

to control its meaning. Here are your options:

Use This	And That Will Mean
	Entering nothing special with a word means that the word may appear or may not appear in the document for the document to be considered a match.
+	Prefixing a word with a + means that the word *must* be in the document for the document to be considered a match.
−	Prefixing a word with a − means that the word must *not* appear in the document for the document to be considered a match.
[ ]	Surrounding words with square brackets means that the words should appear *near* each other in the document for the document to be considered a match. (InfoSeek considers 2 words within 100 words of each other to be near each other.)
" "	Surrounding words with quotation marks means that the words should appear *next* to each other in the document for the document to be considered a match.
-	Separating words with a dash has the same meaning as surrounding them with quotation marks. The specified words must appear next to each other in a document for the document to be considered a match.

As an example, to search for documents that are about Netscape Navigator, but not about version 2.0, you can type **+"Netscape Navigator" -2.0** in the search box.

2. With the search criteria entered, click on the Search button. The Netscape N icon will become animated, and in a few seconds the results of your search will appear.

The All-in-One Search Page

For a starting point from which to launch a comprehensive search, try the All-in-One Search page. William Cross has composed this page by compiling every search gizmo of merit, ranging from the big whoppers such as Magellan, Lycos, and Inktomi, to smaller, more specialized search tools. This wonderful resource provides you with the opportunity to go to a one-stop location and search a bunch of databases quickly and conveniently.

 William Cross tells us as of this writing that he'll be revamping the All-in-One Search page to take advantage of frames and other Netscape version 2 enhancements. Keep an eye on his site and others for constant improvements, and remember when you run across a site that's changed—that's part of the Web's dynamic beauty!

In the All-in-One Search page, you'll find a link to a French translation of the page; be sure to check out the one in *pig latin* too!

Opening the All-in-One Search Page

To use the All-in-One Search page, you must first open it in Netscape.

1. From the Netscape menu bar, select File ➤ Open Location. The Open Location dialog box will appear.
2. In the dialog box's text box, type the URL:
   `http://www.albany.net/~wcross/all1srch.html`.
3. Click on the Open button. The dialog box will close, the N icon will become animated, and in a few seconds the All-in-One Search page will appear, as shown in Figure 7.13.

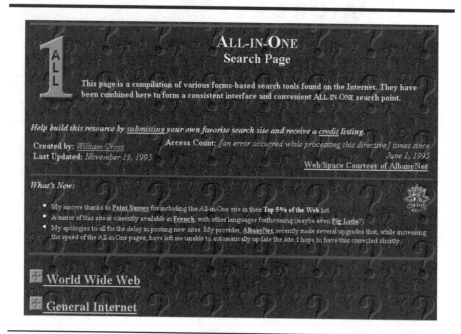

FIGURE 7.13: The All-in-One Search page is a compilation of many search tools—large and small. It is your convenient one-stop way to search the Internet comprehensively.

What's Out There

The All-in-One Search page at `http://www.albany.net/~wcross/ all1srch.html` offers you a single starting point for a comprehensive search of the whole Internet.

Searching with the All-in-One Search Page

Using the All-in-One Search page is very straightforward. *Lots* of search gizmos are included in the page, and, after all, the point of the page is not to have to go from one search tool or area to another. To help you get started, there are categories from which you can choose:

- ◆ World Wide Web
- ◆ General Interest
- ◆ Specialized Interest
- ◆ Software
- ◆ People
- ◆ News/Weather
- ◆ Publications/Literature
- ◆ Technical Reports
- ◆ Documentation
- ◆ Desk Reference
- ◆ Other Interesting Searches/Services

Click on the category that best describes what you seek (Do you know it's a Web page? A technical report?). A page will appear providing you a convenient interface for searching wide and far. For example, if you click on the World Wide Web category, a page like the one shown in Figure 7.14 will appear, and from there you can perform searches of the Web using a variety of tools.

To conduct an actual search via the All-in-One Search page, simply type what you are searching for into the text box below the name of a given search resource and click on the nearby Search button. (There are minor variations on this procedure from one search tool to another, but they're all pretty simple to use and follow the same basic format.) The N icon will become animated, and in a second the results of your search will appear.

The All-in-One Search page provides an interface to other searching resources on the Web; it's not its own search gadget. This means that while the procedures for basic searches you do via this page will vary little, procedures for advanced searches may vary quite a bit. Note too that the results of your search will look quite different depending on which search tool you're using—it's that search tool that is actually returning the results.

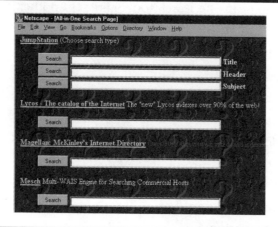

FIGURE 7.14: You can search the World Wide Web via a single page that gives you access to all the big famous search tools and plenty more specialized ones.

All in all, the All-in-One Search page is very intuitive, convenient, and terrifically easy to use. Be sure to add it to your Bookmark list.

Searching the NCSA What's New Archive via the CUI W3 Catalog

We talked earlier in this book about the NCSA What's New document—it lists new services on the Web, and it's updated monthly; so it's always a great starting place for your Web travels. Now what do you suppose happens when the NCSA What's New document is updated? All those handy announcements don't just go away; they're moved (by the Internet's invisible helpers) from the current What's New document into a database. Here's the big news: You can use Netscape to search this archival database.

The archive of What's New pages is kept in a comprehensive database by the people at the Centre Universitaire d'Informatique (CUI), at the University of Geneva in Switzerland. Here you'll find not only the announcements from the NCSA What's New pages, but also items of interest they've gathered from other Web indexes. Searching this database will give you quick entrée to a wide variety of topics and sources of information.

About the Search

Searching the NCSA What's New page archive is a snap. All you have to do is open the CUI W3 Catalog, type some text that describes what interests you, click on a button, and sit back and watch a page of links appear.

Opening the CUI W3 Catalog

To search the What's New page archives, you must first open the CUI W3 Catalog:

1. From the Netscape menu bar, select File ➤ Open Location. The Open Location dialog box will appear.
2. In the dialog box's text box, type the URL for CUI W3 Catalog: `http://cuiwww.unige.ch/w3catalog`.
3. Click on the Open button. The dialog box will close, the Netscape N icon will become animated, and in a few seconds the CUI W3 Catalog page will appear (see Figure 7.15).

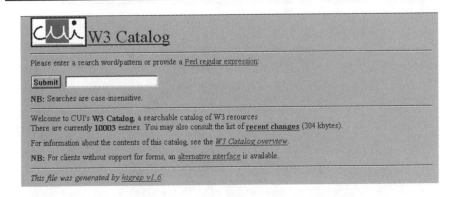

FIGURE 7.15: The CUI W3 page is your path to old (but still valuable) NCSA What's New pages.

What's Out There

You can thumb through the CUI W3 Catalog at the URL `http://cuiwww.unige.ch/w3catalog`.

Performing the Search

With the CUI W3 Catalog page on screen, now is the time to start searching.

1. In the text box near the middle of the page, type a word or a phrase that describes what interests you. (For example, to find information about baseball, type **baseball** in the text box.)

2. Click on the Submit button. This will send the text you typed to the database, where a search will be performed like magic. If the topic of interest is part of any entry in the database, a page containing information (or at least a mention) of that topic will appear. (Figure 7.16 shows what we found when we searched for *baseball*.)

 The CUI W3 Catalog searches many Web resources, not just the NCSA What's New page archives. When you do a search, don't be surprised if you get a page that includes items from other sources in addition to the NCSA What's New pages.

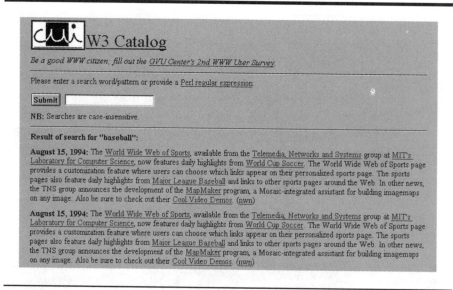

FIGURE 7.16: Searching for baseball came up with these entries, each of which has a link to its actual page.

In the pages you see as a result of your search, you'll find the now familiar blue underlined text that identifies links to other pages. These links behave just like the links in any document—click on a link to go directly to the item it describes.

Performing More Complicated Searches with CUI W3

You aren't limited to searching for simple words such as *baseball* with the W3 Catalog. You can type far more complex strings into the text box to make your search more specific. This is no simple matter, however; it involves entering a combination of text and special symbols, along with having some knowledge of discrete mathematics. The techniques of performing a complex search are beyond the scope of this book, but you can find a how-to discussion on this topic by clicking on the <u>Perl regular expression</u> link on the CUI W3 Catalog page.

Now You Know

Having read this far, you now know everything you need to know to check out what's on the Web. Maybe at this point you'd like to find out how to publish your own Web pages, including how to make your own home page. In the next chapter we'll look at HTML, the great enabler of Web publishing, and how to use it. We'll also explore including HTML in your e-mail messages, effectively making them into Web documents.

8

You Too Can Be a
Web Publisher

By now, having used Netscape to roam the World Wide Web, you've seen the power of hypertext firsthand. You've seen that hypertext acts as both the Web's glue and its strands—binding it together yet hiding the complexities of Internet cruising. HTML (the Hypertext Markup Language) is the *standard* (the agreed-upon system of marking up text to create pages and links) that makes the Web possible. What started out as an experiment has been embraced by the Internet as *the* means of providing information. It will probably come as no surprise that HTML, in the spirit of the Internet, is published and readily available. *Anyone* can use this standard to publish hypertext documents.

Maybe now you want to get into the act. This chapter will tell you how to get started as a Web publisher. There are five basic steps to creating your own Web page:

- ◆ Organizing your concepts and materials
- ◆ *Storyboarding* (sketching out) the page(s) you intend to create
- ◆ Building a prototype
- ◆ Testing the prototype and making adjustments
- ◆ Putting your page on a server

This stuff isn't too difficult—it helps to have a little experience, but, hey, everybody's got to start somewhere. Let's look at how HTML works and how you too can write HTML documents.

 Don't expect to do this on your PC with a dial-up connection to the Internet. To actually publish a document for public viewing on the Web, you'll need access to an HTTP or FTP server. Many Internet service providers provide access to an HTTP or FTP server at little or no additional cost. (We'll go over this in more detail at the end of this chapter.)

What's Out There

A great Beginner's Guide to HTML is available to all at `http://www.ncsa.uiuc.edu/General/Internet/WWW/HTMLPrimer.html`. The Composing Good HTML page is at `http://www.cs.cmu.edu/~tilt/cgh/`.

About HTML: The Hypertext Markup Language

There is plenty to know about HTML and creating and publishing Web documents. Sadly, we'll have to leave the finer points to the bigger books, but let's go over the basics: how to use formatting effects to make your page look attractive; how to make the heads in your documents appear in big, bold letters; how to link your documents to other documents; and how to embed pictures in your document.

The documents you see on the World Wide Web via Netscape look nice, but quite a bit of minor technological magic is going on. In actuality, the files for these documents are stored on a machine somewhere as plain ASCII text files—unlike word processing files, these ASCII text files include no formatting, and they employ no fancy fonts or attributes such as **bold** or *italics*. They are plain as plain can be (see Figure 8.1). All the special effects that you see in a Web document—**bold**, *italic*, <u>links</u> to other documents—are represented in the ASCII text files with special codes that also are made up of plain text characters.

This means, luckily, that you can use any word processor (Word for Windows 95, WordPerfect, whatever) or text editor (DOS Edit, Windows Notepad) to create your HTML documents. We use Microsoft Word for Windows 95 to

---

10 PM
by Brenda Kienan

   How many women lie in darkness in Quakertown, Lansdale, Perkasie; considering their pasts, with the undusted rifle rack hanging over the bed and the green afghan heaped and dragging from the arm of a chair onto the carpet where the kids pulled it down and went on. Through the drawn shades the sound of a thousand crickets and wind sweeping between this trailer and the next. These are the elements of redemption: the wind rising,

---

```
10 PM
by Brenda Kienan

     How many women lie in darkness in Quakertown, Lansdale, Perkasie;
considering their pasts, with the undusted rifle rack hanging over the
bed and the green afghan heaped and dragging from the arm of a chair
onto the carpet where the kids pulled it down and went on. Through the
drawn shades the sound of a thousand crickets and wind sweeping between
```

FIGURE 8.1: The document shown on the top was created in a word-processing program; shown on the bottom is the same document in ASCII format. Notice that all the attributes (bold type) and all the formatting (different font sizes, for example) are lost in the translation.

What's Out There

You'll find loads of resources for creating Web pages at the WWW & HTML Developer's JumpStation—the URL is `http://gnn.com/gnn/netizens/create.html`.

MIT, that wonderland of technology, offers a page called Publishing on the Web and Tech Info at `http://web.mit.edu/publishing.html`.

create our HTML documents; you can use any word processor or text editor you like. The only inflexible condition is that you must save the file as plain ASCII text before Netscape—or any other Web browser—can display it. So be sure your word processor can do that (most can).

Okay, so we just made the big point that you don't need a special HTML editor, yet HTML editors are available. Though unnecessary for writing basic HTML documents, an HTML editor certainly would prove beneficial when you're dealing with hundreds of pages of text. A good HTML editor can help you enter HTML tags and verify that you have all the details correct, making it easier to ensure that your Web documents will be displayed correctly in a Web browser.

What's Out There

A number of freely available programs exist to help you write HTML documents. These can be of great use when you are writing longer documents or complex Web pages. HotDog, a powerful yet friendly HTML editor, is available at `http://www.sausage.com`. Another good editor, WebEdit, is available at `http://www.nesbitt.com`. HoTMetaL PRO for Windows (a favorite) from SoftQuad is available at `http://www.sq.com/products/hotmetal/hmp-org.htm`.

The Elements of Web Page Design

Your Web home page will be accessed by anywhere from dozens to hundreds of thousands of people a day. You'll want it to convey clearly and concisely the message you intend to promote (whether that's your resume, your company's policy on hiring technical professionals, or an account of what's happening at the local soda pop machine). In this section, we'll cover some basic guidelines for successful Web page design, tossing out for your consideration all the big-hitting tips we've picked up in our Internet travels.

Just What Is a Markup Language?

Traditionally, a markup language uses defined sequences of control characters or commands embedded within a document. These commands control what the document looks like when it is output to, say, a printer. When you print the document, the control character sequences or commands format the document, displaying such elements as bold headlines, subheads, bulleted items, and the like. IBM's Document Control Language (DCL) and Microsoft's Rich Text Format (RTF) are two examples of markup languages used by many word-processing programs to create the effects you see on screen and in print.

HTML differs from other markup languages, however, in its overall approach. HTML is unlike typical markup languages in that it is not so much concerned with typefaces and character attributes, but rather with the internal document makeup itself. In a language such as DCL, you use commands to indicate the typeface, font size, and style of the text *in a document*. In HTML, the commands indicate the headings, normal paragraphs, lists, and even links *to other Web pages*.

HTML is derived from the Standard Generalized Markup Language (SGML), which has come into increasingly common usage in word-processing and other programs for creating print documents. HTML follows the SGML paradigm in that it uses *tags* to do its formatting. Tags are pieces of coding that usually, but not always, come in pairs consisting of a start-tag and an end-tag marking off *elements*.

When you create HTML documents, bear in mind that the HTML "standard" is in a state of development, with changes happening to accommodate changes in the World Wide Web and its attending software. If you try something that works one day and not the next, it may be that the standard has changed.

Another minor annoyance is that not all Web browsers support all HTML extensions, or they may support other aspects of the HTML language differently. In fact, some of the HTML tags we illustrate in this book are understood *only* by Netscape. Be this as it may, the basic HTML structure presented in this chapter should work well in most instances.

Get Organized

The best way to get started in the design of your home page is to organize your assets: the existing documents and images you want to work with, for example. Think about the message you want to convey and which types of images or text might be appropriate. (Is it fun and lighthearted or seriously corporate?)

What's Out There

You'll want to find out everything you can about copyright issues; this will come up both when you want to protect your own material and when you want to use something you've "found" on the Net. (That's not always legal.) A U.S. copyright law page published by Cornell University is at `http://www.law.cornell.edu/topics/copyright.html`, and an FAQ (frequently asked question) list published by Ohio State is at `http://www.cis .ohio-state.edu/hypertext/faq/usenet/Copyright-FAQ/top.html`.

Create a Storyboard

With the stuff you want to work with in hand, sit down with paper and pencil (or some nifty drawing software) and plot the thing out. *Storyboard* (sketch) your home page and each page it will link to; include all the elements you're considering (text, images, buttons, hyperlinks), and don't be afraid to make adjustments. If your original concept doesn't flow nicely, can it and start again. *You can't do too much advance planning.*

Build a Prototype and Test It

When you've got your pages planned, go ahead and build a prototype. Then test it, test it, and *test it again*. Ask friends and colleagues to try it out and comment, and do all the fine tuning you can. You want to make your best work public, not some funky work-in-progress.

17 Top Tips for Winning Page Design

You have two seconds to grab your reader's attention. That's common knowledge in advertising and publishing circles. You can't go wrong if you follow these basic tips for designing an attention-getting, successful home page:

◆ Before you start, organize your concepts and materials; create a storyboard that sketches out your ideas and how they'll work.

◆ Make the title precise, catchy, and descriptive.

◆ Keep the page active but loose; don't let it get crowded with images, text, or "doo-dads."

◆ Put the important items at the top of the page; don't assume anyone will ever scroll down.

◆ Balance white space; balance large and small images and blocks of text.

◆ Be sure that anything that looks like a button behaves like a button.

◆ Avoid links that go nowhere; don't create two links with different names that go to the same place.

◆ Make your links descriptive, and use accurate words or images. Avoid the generic: Don't link on "click here."

◆ Use images that contain fewer than 50 colors.

◆ Include thumbnails of larger, downloadable images.

◆ Remember that people will access your page using different browsers (Netscape, various types of Mosaic, Internet Explorer, Lynx) and different platforms (Windows, Macintosh, Unix).

◆ Keep filenames short; make them consistent.

◆ Tell people the sizes of downloadable files if you include them.

◆ Find out if you need permission to use text or images created by someone else.

◆ Establish who's going to be Webmaster and make a link on your page leading to the Webmaster.

◆ Build a prototype and test it thoroughly. Do the fine tuning before you announce your page.

◆ Announce and publicize your page wherever possible.

You can test your prototype without making it public. At the end of this chapter you'll find a section titled <u>Using Netscape to Check Your HTML Document</u> that tells you how.

A Quick Look at Successful Web Page Designs

The best way to get ideas and to explore creating a winning Web page is to study examples. We've been showing you Web pages throughout this book; here we're going to take a look at a few especially well-designed pages, pointing out what makes them so terrific.

Some of the Web pages we show here are a bit out of an amateur Webspinner's range—we're including them anyway, to give you an idea of the possibilities. We haven't shown you the most cutting-edge Web design in this chapter, on the other hand, because we thought you'd like to get more basic ideas about what you can do. For up-to-the-minute views of innovative design, check out the work of terrific Web designers such as Dave Siegel, the folks at Organic, Clement Mok, and Design/Systems. Also look into the "Best of the Web" award givers, and other sites described in Chapter 6.

What's Out There

A great way to explore successful Web page design is to look at the sites of successful Web designers. You may find it useful to keep an eye on what's up with Organic at `http://www.organic.com`, Clement Mok at `http://www.cmdesign.com/cmd.htm`, and Design/Systems of New York at `http://designsys.com`.

Strong Content, Creative Design

The folks at CNN, who brought you the first 24-hour news broadcast, have given their Web site the same hot-off-the-presses appeal (see Figure 8.2). This site demonstrates that it's solid, interesting content, not snappy design effects, that keeps people coming back again and again. Which is not to say that CNN's site lacks design—its clever use of tables, graphics, and heads brings to mind the morning newspaper.

What's Out There

CNN Interactive is yours to explore at http://www.cnn.com.

FIGURE 8.2: CNN Interactive keeps 'em coming back for up-to-the-minute daily news.

A Colorful, Graphical Welcome

Movie Link's showy information resource isn't quite as serious as CNN's, but it's just as complete and timely (see Figure 8.3). Readers can find out

which movies are playing in the city of their choice by clicking on a United States map or by typing the appropriate zip code. This site's modern, playful graphics communicate an effective mixture of technology and entertainment.

What's Out There

Find out where the latest flicks are playing in your neighborhood by looking in on http://www.777film.com.

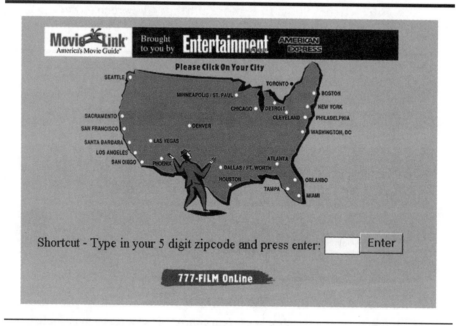

FIGURE 8.3: Movie Link: You'll never need to search that pile of old newspapers for the movie listings again!

Small Graphics and Lots of Buttons

The Rainforest Action Network uses its home page to promote its mission: protecting the world's rainforests. The page shown in Figure 8.4 relies on a mixture of text and colorful custom-made graphics to grab your attention. Plenty of buttons provide an active look and actual interactivity. Each graphic is small, however, so it doesn't take long for this page to load.

What's Out There

Read all about the good work of the Rainforest Action Network; its home page is at `http://www.ran.org/ran`.

FIGURE 8.4: Rainforest Action Network's home page uses small graphics and lots of buttons to catch your eye.

A Stately Symmetry

The Welcome to the White House home page (see Figure 8.5) uses a large image with "hot spots" to lead to more information on other pages. This

page provides no bureaucratic run-around; it's in a simple (perhaps even dignified) symmetrical layout.

What's Out There

Tour the White House interactively by checking in at `http://www.whitehouse.gov`.

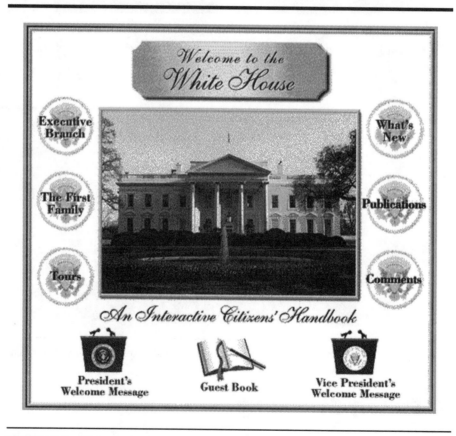

FIGURE 8.5: Welcome to the White House is your entry point to a variety of topics and an electronic tour.

Cool and Cohesive

The Internet Underground Music Archive (see Figure 8.6) presents a slick image by using high-quality graphics and elegant text effects. Notice the use of capital letters and custom-sized ruled lines.

What's Out There

Whether you're a big-time music fan or just a Web wanderer looking for some cool design, check out the Internet Underground Music Archive at `http://www.iuma.com`.

FIGURE 8.6: Take a look (when you get online) at the Internet Underground Music Archive's fun, colorful pages.

An Interactive Classic

One of the most famous and, in our opinions, best examples of Web use is the interactive frog dissection shown in part in Figure 8.7. From the menu in the Frog Dissection home page, you can choose which phases of the dissection you'd like to see; you can follow the entire process one scene at a time in lifelike color. Of course, an added bonus is that millions of people can experience this dissection without killing millions of frogs. This site is a familiar favorite; as of this writing, it's well over a year old—that's ancient in Web years—but its classic design set the tone for the many Web pages that were designed after this beauty. The interactive frog dissection is a classic.

What's Out There

You can experience a brilliantly innovative interactive frog dissection at `http://curry.edschool.virginia.edu/~insttech/frog`.

What's Out There

Dave Siegel is a master Web designer whose site is jam-packed with tips, solid information, examples, and links to other sites you may find helpful in your Web designing adventures. Dave Siegel's home page, at `http://www2.best.com/~dsiegel/home.html`, is in itself an interesting example of good design. Be sure to follow the Web Wonk and Typography links for great advice on Web page design; go to The Nine Act Structure for wonderful information on structuring content, and check out the High Five archive for Dave's hand-picked examples of excellence in Web design and presentation.

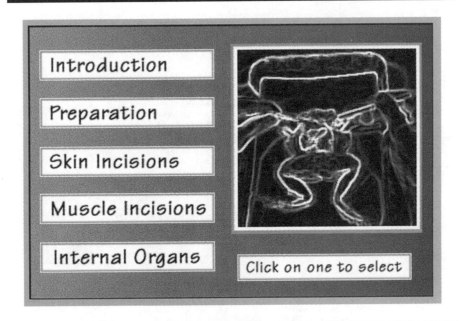

FIGURE 8.7:   This interactive frog dissection is a Web classic. Bravo!

Using HTML to Mark Up a Document

Now let's take a look at how all this is done. Marking up a document is a pretty simple matter of identifying what you want any given element to be and then literally *marking* it as that type of element (see Figure 8.8).

The markup, or *tag*, in HTML documents is surrounded by angle brackets, like this:

```
<title>
```

These tags usually come in pairs and affect everything between them. For example, surrounding a heading you'll see <h1> at the beginning, matching the </h1> at the end. … More on this as we go along.

```
<html>
<head>
<title>10 PM</title>
</head>
<body>
<h1>10 PM</h1>
<h2>by Brenda Kienan</h2>
<p>
        How many women lie in darkness in Quakertown, Lansdale, Perkasie;
considering their pasts, with the undusted rifle rack hanging over the bed and the
green afghan heaped and dragging from the arm of a chair onto the carpet where the
kids pulled it down and went on. Through the drawn shades the sounds of a thousand
crickets and wind sweeping between this trailer and the next. These are the elements
of redemption: the wind rising, rattling the corrugated plastic roof of the neighbor's
carport, the husband coughing over the droning tv news, the washer clicking and
getting louder as the clothes inside it spin out of balance. This is an ordering of events
that carries one day to the next.<p>
        How many women, each in her own separate darkness, surveying what might
have happened, while the rushing wind finds its way into heating ducts and whistles
through tin.<p>
        <i>Papa, it is vanishing.</i> The blue June evenings and the scent of dusty
pavement as a long-awaited rain falls. <i>I thought I'd still know, but I'm
drifting.</i> White tulips. Gold star confetti sprayed across starched tablecloths.
The priest's thick fingers holding a book.<p>
        How many women making a list, of the ways they might have gone, of the
friends they see in markets, marriages lost, pushing carts full of children, sugary
cereals, cheap meats. How many mornings of driving: her own child to another's care,
her husband (who's lost his license) to work, herds of teenagers in a yellow bus to
school. How many times the red-haired boy pushing his way to the seat behind her,
bringing her gifts of novelty pencils, a sandwich, cloisonn&eacute; earrings.<p>
        How many women wondering, each in her cool separate darkness, if the news
is yet over, if the wind will grow still.<p>
<h3>Copyright 1995 Brenda Kienan</h3>
</body>
</html>
```

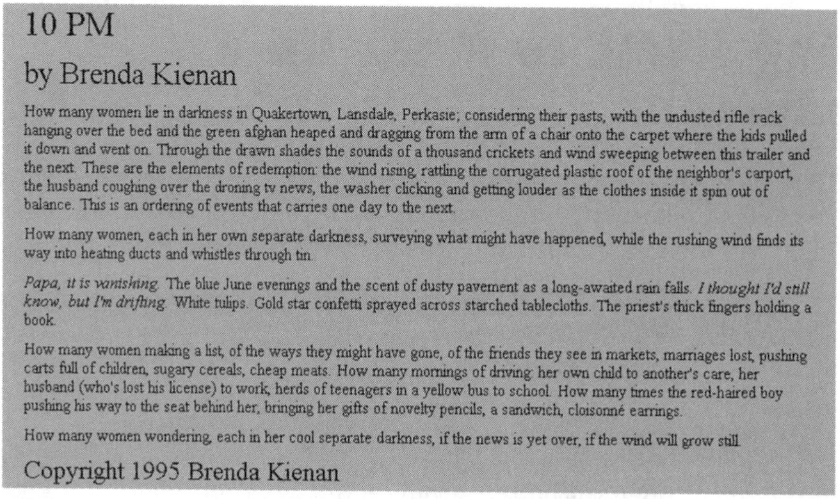

10 PM

by Brenda Kienan

How many women lie in darkness in Quakertown, Lansdale, Perkasie; considering their pasts, with the undusted rifle rack hanging over the bed and the green afghan heaped and dragging from the arm of a chair onto the carpet where the kids pulled it down and went on. Through the drawn shades the sounds of a thousand crickets and wind sweeping between this trailer and the next. These are the elements of redemption: the wind rising, rattling the corrugated plastic roof of the neighbor's carport, the husband coughing over the droning tv news, the washer clicking and getting louder as the clothes inside it spin out of balance. This is an ordering of events that carries one day to the next.

How many women, each in her own separate darkness, surveying what might have happened, while the rushing wind finds its way into heating ducts and whistles through tin.

Papa, it is vanishing. The blue June evenings and the scent of dusty pavement as a long-awaited rain falls. *I thought I'd still know, but I'm drifting.* White tulips. Gold star confetti sprayed across starched tablecloths. The priest's thick fingers holding a book.

How many women making a list, of the ways they might have gone, of the friends they see in markets, marriages lost, pushing carts full of children, sugary cereals, cheap meats. How many mornings of driving: her own child to another's care, her husband (who's lost his license) to work, herds of teenagers in a yellow bus to school. How many times the red-haired boy pushing his way to the seat behind her, bringing her gifts of novelty pencils, a sandwich, cloisonné earrings.

How many women wondering, each in her cool separate darkness, if the news is yet over, if the wind will grow still.

Copyright 1995 Brenda Kienan

FIGURE 8.8: In an HTML-coded document (above), you see tags (within angle brackets) surrounding the element to which they refer. In the resulting Web document (below), you do not see the tags—you see only the effect they have on the document displayed.

There are a few exceptions to the pairing of HTML tags, which we'll point out during the course of this chapter.

HTML tags can be written using upper- or lowercase letters—it doesn't matter.

In Figure 8.9 you can see all the elements of a basic HTML document. Take note of:

◆ The entire document enclosed between <html> and </html>

◆ The title of the document enclosed between <title> and </title>

◆ The header of the document enclosed between <h1> and </h1>

◆ The body of the document enclosed between <body> and </body>

In the sections that follow, we'll look at the basic HTML tags you can use in your documents. Remember as we go along that these tags are the same whether you are marking up a document in a word processor or in an HTML editor.

```
<html>                                                    Beginning of document
<title>The Page's Title Goes Here</title>                 Title
<h1>The Page's Title Is Usually Repeated Here</h1>        Header
<body>
Here is the body of the page.                             Body of document
</body>
</html>                                                    End of document
```

FIGURE 8.9: Here you can see the HTML coding for the basic elements of a Web document.

 If you're using a word processor to create an original document you intend for Web publication, you can, of course, simply write in the HTML coding as you go along; you don't have to write the document first and enter the tags afterward.

Every Document Must Have the "Required" Tags

Every HTML document must include certain tags, which essentially identify the document as an HTML document and, as such, show its beginning and end. Note that even these fundamental HTML tags come in
pairs—the <html> at the beginning of the document matches the </html>
at the end of the document.

Marking Up Heads

HTML supports six levels of heads. Each level of head will look different
when it's displayed in a Web browser such as Netscape. The highest level
(let's call this the "1" head) will be larger and more obvious; the lowest
level (the "6" head) will be smallest and most discreet.

 The actual way each head looks is different from one browser
to the next. In other words, HTML allows you to say what text
is a head, but not what the head will look like when User A
accesses it with Netscape, User B with Spyglass Mosaic, and
User C with Internet Explorer.

The text of the head should appear between two head tags <hn> and
</hn>, where n can be any number between 1 and 6. It is customary to
start your document with a head of level 1, to indicate the important
topic that comes first. You can follow a level 1 head with heads of lower
levels; you can also place new level 1 heads farther down in your document, as you please.

Beginning New Paragraphs

You must explicitly code each and every new paragraph of text by placing
the <p> tag at its beginning. You needn't close a paragraph with any coding,
however. This new paragraph business is one of the major exceptions to the
"opening and closing" paired tags that are the general rule in HTML.

 Web browsers will not start a new paragraph if you do not include the <p> tag, regardless of how your document looks in your word processor.

Changing the Justification of Paragraphs

When you use the <p> tag, what you'll get is the regular, left-justified paragraphs you're used to seeing most often in print. You can change the alignment of a paragraph—to make it either centered or right-justified—by embedding the `align` command in the <p> tag in that paragraph. Embedding the `align` command is a simple matter of inserting a space and a bit of text into the <p> tag between the p and the >.

For example, let's say you want the opening text of your home page centered on the screen. The coding would look like this:

```
<p align=center>Welcome to Lori's Home Page!
```

You'll have to mark the next paragraph with another <p> tag, of course, as you always have to do; unless you specify otherwise, that next paragraph will appear left-justified, as usual. Here are the commands you can embed to change any paragraph's justification:

The Command	Will Produce
align=center	Centered paragraphs
align=right	Right-justified paragraphs

 Be sure to include a space before the `align` command.

Inserting Ruled Lines

Rules, or ruled lines, are horizontal lines that you can use to separate parts of your document. To place a rule in your document, use the <hr> tag.

(See Figure 8.10.) Again, it's not necessary to indicate the end of the rule with a closing tag.

The <hr> tag inserts a shaded, engraved line that crosses your Web page (no matter what size the page appears to be on screen) from the left margin to the right.

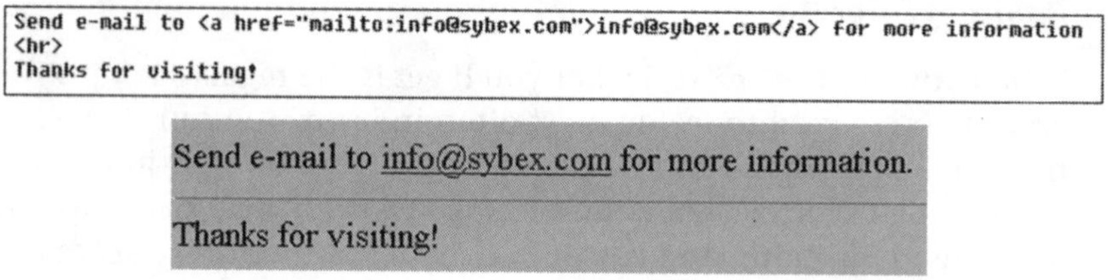

```
Send e-mail to <a href="mailto:info@sybex.com">info@sybex.com</a> for more information
<hr>
Thanks for visiting!
```

Send e-mail to info@sybex.com for more information.

Thanks for visiting!

FIGURE 8.10: The coding you see in the HTML document above results in the rule you see in the Web document below.

Netscape also allows you to vary the look of ruled lines by embedding commands in the <hr> tag (just like you can embed the align command in the <p> tag). You can embed as many commands as you like to achieve the effect you want. For example, if you would like the ruled line to be exactly 250 pixels wide and to be centered on the page, you can use the following code:

```
<hr width=250 align=center>
```

You can use these commands with the <hr> tag to change the look of ruled lines:

The Command	Will Produce a Ruled Line That Is...
size=n	n pixels thick
width=n	n pixels wide
width=n%	n percentage of the width of the page
align=left	Pushed up against the left margin (left-justified)
align=center	Centered on the page

The Command	Will Produce a Ruled Line That Is...
`align=right`	Pushed up against the right margin (right-justified)
`noshade`	A solid bar with no engraving or shading

Go ahead and play around with all these options to see what kind of ruled lines are most effective in your document.

Creating Lists

You can have two types of lists in a Web document: numbered and bulleted. In HTML lingo, numbered lists are called *ordered* lists, and bulleted lists are called *unordered* lists.

Ordered Lists

Ordered (numbered) lists result from text nested between the `<ol>` and `</ol>` tags. Each new item in the ordered list must start with the `<li>` tag. Unlike most other HTML tags, the `<li>` tag need not end with the `</li>` tag. For example, a numbered list of types of fruit would look like:

```
<ol>
<li>Apple
<li>Orange
<li>Cherry
</ol>
```

A Web browser would display the above list like this:

1. Apple
2. Orange
3. Cherry

When you're coding an ordered list, you need not enter the numbers. The HTML coding tells the Web browser to number the items sequentially in the order in which they appear.

Netscape also lets you control the type of numbering in an ordered list. To specify the type of numbering you want, you can embed the `type` command in the first `<ol>` tag. For example, if we modify our fruit list like this:

```
<ol TYPE=I>
<li>Apple
<li>Orange
<li>Cherry
</ol>
```

Netscape will display it with roman numerals, like this:

   I. Apple
  II. Orange
 III. Cherry

You can use the following commands to specify the type of numbering you want:

The Command	Will Produce
type=A	Uppercase letters, starting with A
type=a	Lowercase letters, starting with a
type=I	Uppercase roman numerals, starting with I
type=i	Lowercase roman numerals, starting with i
type=1	Arabic numerals, starting with 1

 Not all Web browsers "understand" the `type` options for numbers as Netscape does. If you create a page using these options and someone loads the page using a Web browser that doesn't allow for this, he or she will see the items listed using arabic numerals.

Unordered Lists

Unordered (bulleted) lists result from text nested between the `<ul>` and `</ul>` tags. This, of course, is similar to what you do to create an ordered list. Each new item in the bulleted list must begin with the `<li>` tag. This is exactly like what you do with each item in an ordered list; it is the o or u in the opening and closing tags that "tells" Netscape whether the list is to be numbered or bulleted—and, again, you need not bother with placing any type of bullets. They will appear when the document is viewed on screen wherever you have placed the <li> tag in your unordered list.

 Remember that the bullets will look different and will be of different sizes in the various Web browsers.

By default, Netscape uses solid discs as bullets, and it does not indent bulleted lists. You can change bullets to squares instead of discs. Doing so is a simple matter of embedding the type=square command in your opening <ul> tag, like this:

```
<ul type=square>
```

Other than that one little change, you create your bulleted list as described above. If you use the type=square command in this way, all bullets in your list will be neat, stolid squares.

Creating Links

Now we get to the heart of things. As you know well by now, the beauty of the Web is the way documents are interrelated through being linked—that's what makes the Web so wonderfully webby. Let's take a look behind the scenes at the HTML underpinnings of a link.

In HTML lingo, a link is really what's called an *anchor*, the opening code for which is <a. What the anchor looks like when it appears as a link in a Web document will differ depending on the Web browser being used, but usually it'll show up as underlined blue text. When you click on the link (the under-lined blue text), the anchor is activated, and the file with which it is associated (the other end of the link, if you will) is loaded and displayed on screen.

Here's an example of how this works in HTML: If you wanted the word *Internet* to appear in a document as a link, you'd code the word like this:

```
<a href="http://www.sybex.com/internet.html">Internet</a>
```

Then, when the document is viewed with any Web browser, such as Netscape, the word Internet will appear as a link. When a user clicks on it,

the file INTERNET.HTML will automatically be transferred from the HTTP server, and a list of Internet-related books will appear on screen.

 Remember, you must indicate the type of file to which you are linking; this will "tell" the Web browser employed by any given user how to deal with the file. When it comes to images, most Web browsers "out of the box" can deal only with GIF and JPG files. You'll need special viewers and players (as described in Chapter 11) to view images or play sounds in other file formats.

What's Behind That Sound, Graphic, or Video Link

In your Web roamings, you've probably found links that go not to HTML documents but perhaps instead to graphics, sounds, and videos. The URL in a link doesn't have to point to another HTML document; it can point to any type of file. For example, the anchor

```
<a href="http://www.iuma.com/IUMA/ftp/music/Madonna/
Secret.mpg">Madonna</a>
```

creates a link to the machine where a video clip from Madonna's Secret video is stored. When you click on the link, the video will be transferred to your computer, and a player for MPEG files will start up so that you can see the video—the trigger for that action is in the HTML coding shown above. You can create links to any type of file in this manner—just include the full path to the file in the URL.

Creating Glossaries

A *glossary* in a Web document is a special element designed to let you place definitions in your documents. Glossaries look a bit like lists when they are coded with HTML; the list of items this time must be surrounded by the tags <dl> and </dl>. Each defined term in the glossary starts with the tag <dt>. The definitions themselves follow the term to which they apply and begin with the tag <dd>. Neither <dt> nor <dd> tags need closing tags.

Here is a sample of coding for a glossary:

```
<dl>
<dt>Apple
<dd>A round fruit, often red in color when ripe but some-
times green or yellow
<dt>Orange
<dd>A round, orange fruit
<dt>Cherry
<dd>A small, round, red fruit
</dl>
```

The result of this sample coding will look like this:

Apple
> A round fruit, often red in color when ripe but sometimes green or yellow

Orange
> A round, orange fruit

Cherry
> A small, round, red fruit

Inserting Addresses

Address is a special HTML element that was originally designed to hold the address of the author of the page (the snail-mail address, the e-mail address, or both). Most Web browsers display this element in an italic font, smaller than body text. For example,

```
<address>
Daniel A. Tauber and Brenda Kienan
<br>Sybex
<br>2021 Challenger Drive
<br>Alameda, CA 94501
</address>
```

will appear as shown here:

Daniel A. Tauber and Brenda Kienan
Sybex
2021 Challenger Drive
Alameda, CA 94501

We've used the `<br>` tag in the above example instead of the `<p>` tag. The `<br>` tag inserts a line break without adding extra space between lines, as the `<p>` does.

Assigning Text Attributes

You are probably familiar with *text attributes* from word processors. Things such as bold, italic, and font color, which differentiate some text from the usual, are all known as *attributes* in a word processor. You can specify attributes such as these using HTML.

 Remember that none of the formatting or text attributes you might have in your word-processed document will carry over to your Web document—you must specify what you want using HTML coding.

The types of attributes you can specify using HTML are broken down into two classes:

◆ Physical
◆ Logical

The *physical* attributes specify how text characters will look: italic or bold, for example. They will be italic or bold no matter which Web browser is used for viewing (as long as the browser understands that particular type of formatting). The *logical* attributes specify the amount of emphasis you want to give to important text; you can choose to make text *big, small, emphasized,* or *strongly emphasized.* Different Web browsers will have different ways of displaying logical attributes (some may show strongly emphasized text as bold, others may show it as red or in a slightly larger size, for example). The choice of using logical or physical attributes is yours. Some people prefer to use physical attributes because they want to control the way the text finally looks. Other people prefer to use logical attributes because they convey "meaning" without specifying what the text should look like.

Physical Attributes

You can use physical attributes to make text appear bold, italic, super-script, or subscript.

The tags used to apply these attributes are summarized here:

To Get This Attribute	Use the Starting Tag	And the Ending Tag
Bold	`<b>`	`</b>`
Italic	`<i>`	`</i>`
Superscript	`<sup>`	`</sup>`
Subscript	`<sub>`	`</sub>`

You can use several attributes together simply by embedding them. Just be sure the opening tag that's first-in corresponds to the closing tag that's last-out. For example, to make the phrase <u>Bungee Jumping</u> both bold and italic, use the coding `<b><i>Bungee Jumping</i></b>`.

Logical Attributes

You can use logical attributes to give emphasis to text you feel is impor-tant. The way the text actually appears when viewed in a browser depends on the browser's individual way of handling these attributes. The logical attributes that you can use are:

To Get This Attribute	Use the Starting Tag	And the Ending Tag
Emphasis	`<em>`	`</em>`
Strong Emphasis	`<strong>`	`</strong>`
Big Typeface	`<big>`	`</big>`
Small Typeface	`<small>`	`</small>`

Here you can see the result of making text emphasized and strongly emphasized and viewing the text with Netscape:

Emphasis and **Strong Emphasis**

This is what big and small typefaces look like compared with the default, regular-sized font:

Big type and Small type

Changing Font Size

Netscape allows you to change the size of the font in your document. You can use this feature to vary text size, down to the letter. Changing the font size allows you to use effects such as large initial capital letters (an elegant way to display important text).

The font size in an HTML document has a base value of 3 (this doesn't mean 3 point sizes; it's an arbitrary number set by Netscape). To change the font size, you insert the `<font size=`*n*`>` tag wherever you would like it to apply, and you insert the closing tag `</font>` wherever you would like it to end. *N* is the new size of the font. You can express the new font size in one of two ways:

◆ you can set it as a value between 1 and 7, or

◆ you can set it relative to the size of the base font, by using a + or a - sign.

For example, to create large initial capital letters, you would use the following HTML coding:

```
<font size=+2>I</font>NITIAL <font size=+2>C</font>APS
```

You're telling Netscape to make the first letter of each word two sizes larger than the base font. Here is the result once you view the text with Netscape:

INITIAL CAPS

You can also change the value of the base font using the `<basefont=`*n*`>` tag. For example, if you would like all the text in your document to appear larger (say, size 4 instead of the default size 3), you would place the following HTML tag wherever you would like the base font size to change:

```
<basefont size=4>
```

Changing Font Color

Not only can you vary text size, you can specify colors for regular text, hyperlink text, *active* hyperlinks (ones that are in the process of being clicked), and *visited* hyperlinks (hyperlinks you have already activated). You set these colors by embedding commands in the <body> tag at the beginning of your HTML document.

As for the colors themselves, Netscape recognizes the *hexadecimal* color system. This system uses a six-digit code to specify the red, green, and blue balance of the color. This may seem like a bit of esoteric information, but you can use it to create beautiful effects on your page.

 Not all browsers "understand" the use of custom colors in an HTML document. Even those of your readers who are using Netscape may have monitors with limited or no color capability. Keep these caveats in mind when using color in your Web pages.

What's Out There

You don't have to memorize hex codes to be able to add color to your Web page. InfiNet's Color page lists about 100 colors you can choose from, along with their hexadecimal equivalents. Visit http://www.infi.net/wwwimages/colorindex.HTML to open this big box of color.

To specify colors, just embed the following commands in the <body> tag, where *n* is the hexadecimal code for the color you choose:

Use This Command	To Change the Color of
text="*n*"	Regular body text
link="*n*"	Hyperlink text
alink="*n*"	Active hyperlink
vlink="*n*"	Visited hyperlink

For example, if you would like to create a Web page with black text, green hyperlink text, hyperlinks that turn yellow while you click on them, and magenta after you've visited them (wow! what a color scheme), your <body> tag would look like this:

```
<body text="000000" link="00FF00" alink="FFFF00"
vlink="FF00FF">
```

Because the text color commands are embedded in the <body> tag, they can be set only once for each Web page. You cannot change text color halfway through your document, for example.

Using Special Characters

Some special characters are readily available in HTML. For example, you'll often want to use the special character for the copyright symbol (©), and that one's no problem—there's a code you can use for it. But HTML files are really plain text files, so you don't have access to some other special characters. The symbol that's used to indicate copyright for digital audio, a letter P enclosed in a circle, is one unfortunate example.

Some "special" characters you'd use fairly regularly in word-processed text, such as angle brackets and even the ampersand, have special meanings in HTML, which already you know if you've read earlier sections of this chapter.

To include characters such as these in your HTML document, you'll have to insert special escape codes in your file. Here are some examples:

For the Symbol	Which Means	Use the Code
&	Ampersand	&amp;
>	Greater-Than	&gt;
<	Less-Than	&lt;
®	Registered Trademark	&reg;
©	Copyright	&copy;

What's Out There

You can get a complete list of special characters and how to code for them at `http://hyperg.tu-graz.ac.at/T0x811b9908_0x00058490`.

Embedding Images

Images that appear as part of a Web page are called *inline images*. Although it is possible to place many, many inline images in your document, remember that including them will greatly increase the time required to load and view the document.

It's best in some circumstances to place thumbnails of images in your page—thumbnails load a lot faster than larger images—and link the thumbnail to the larger image, allowing users to download the bigger image if they want to and have time to wait for it. See <u>Mixing Elements</u>, the next section in this chapter.

Any image that you want to include as an inline image in a Web document must be in one of two graphics file formats: GIF or JPG. Let's look more closely at use of the ever-popular GIF format in this section.

Some Web browsers (including Netscape) can display inline images in JPG format. JPG files are much smaller in size than other image files, so they appear on screen much more quickly—a real advantage. The drawback for the publisher, however, is that not all Web browsers can display them. If you use JPG and a user tries viewing your document with a browser that can't handle JPG, all he or she will see is a little error message where the image should be.

You can use the `<img>` tag to place an inline image into your HTML document. For example,

```
<img src="http://www.sybex.com/sybexlogo2.gif">
```

will cause the image stored in the file SYBEXLOGO2.GIF on the machine to be displayed as part of the Web document.

A couple of other nifty things you can do with Netscape involve text wrapping around images on screen. To cause an image to appear to the left of text with the text wrapping around the image, use the `align=left` command, like this:

```
<img src="http://www.sybex.com/sybexlogo2.gif" align=left>
```

To cause an image to appear to the right of text with the text wrapping around the image, use the `align=right` command, like this:

```
<img src="http://www.sybex.com/sybexlogo2.gif" align=right>
```

What's Out There

You can scope out a helpful FAQ file for extensive tips on scanning images to use in your Web documents. To find the Scanning FAQ, use the URL `http://www.infomedia.net/scan`. Transparent GIFs are GIFs in which one of the colors is invisible. (You might want to do this if you'd like the background color the user's Netscape is using to be one of the colors in the image.) To find out how you can make your GIFs transparent, look into the URL `http://melmac.harris-atd.com/transparent_images.html`.

Changing the Background

We've talked about how you can use font colors and inline images to brighten up your pages. You can also change the way the background of your document looks by specifying a color or using an image as the backdrop for the document text (as opposed to the browser's default background color of gray or white).

The color and/or image you choose for your background should harmonize with the color of your text. We've seen quite a few examples of enthusiastic Web authors who pick flamboyant colors for their documents, only to render them unreadable.

Like changing text color, you change the way the document background looks by embedding commands into the <body> tag.

Not all Web browsers can display custom colors or images as backgrounds. For this reason, be sure your document depends on the overall design of text and graphics—not on the background—to look good.

Setting the Background Color

Changing the background color of your document from the default background to something more interesting is an easy way to lend drama and allure to your page. To specify a background color, use the bgcolor=n command, like this:

```
<body bgcolor="000000">
```

More and more Web browsers recognize Netscape-specific design features such as nifty background colors, but some older or less capable browsers can't interpret the bgcolor command. When a page that uses this command is accessed by a browser that doesn't recognize background color, the browser will just ignore the command and use whatever its default background color is—probably gray or white. No harm done.

Using an Image for Your Background

Another way to spice up your document is to use an image for its background. You can use any GIF or JPG graphic file as your background image (any browser that recognizes custom backgrounds can also display JPG images). For example, many companies like to use dimmed versions of their logos as background graphics—kind of like a watermark in expensive stationery (see Figure 8.11).

 Netscape <u>tiles</u> the graphic you specify as a background to make it fill up the entire window. That is, it will repeat the graphic in its original size until it covers the page's viewing area.

To specify a GIF or JPG file as your background image, use the command, like this:

```
<body background="clouds.gif">
```

Mixing Elements

Just as you can create ***bold-italic*** text by embedding the italic tag within the bold tag, you can embed one type of HTML element within another element. For example, you might want to create an unordered (bulleted)

FIGURE 8.11: Microsoft uses its logo as a background graphic.

list in which each element is a link to another Web page. In fact, if you think about it, your entire HTML file is embedded between the `<html>` and `</html>` tags; so everything in your document is already embedded between two standard HTML tags.

Another practical use for embedded HTML tags is a link that leads to an image. In that case, the inline image tag is embedded inside the link tag. (And this, dear reader, takes us to the next section.)

Using Pictures As Links

To make an image act as a link to another document, you can use the link tag, `<a`, followed by indicators of what you're linking to, followed by `</a>`. In a nutshell, here's what you do: Where you'd normally place the text the user will click on to activate the link, you can instead place the tag to display an inline image. For example, if you have an image called tocatalog.gif, you could place

```
<a href="http://www.sybex.com/catalog.html"><img
src="http://www.sybex.com/tocatalog.gif"></img></a>
```

in your Web document to create a link to the page stored in the file CATALOG.HTML. This causes a Web browser to display the image TOCATALOG.GIF with a border around it. When a user clicks anywhere in the picture, the link will become activated, and, in this case, the Catalog page indicated will appear.

 Some Web pages have graphic links <u>without</u> borders around them. Usually, however, the context of a graphic makes clear if it is a link or not.

Creating Lists of Links

Let's say you want a list of links. To do this, create an ordered or unordered list, placing a link as each item in the list. For example,

```
<ul>
<li><a href="http://www.sybex.com/index.html">Sybex's Home
Page</a>
<li><a href="http://www.sybex.com/catalog/catalog.pl">Sy-
bex's Catalog</a>
```

```
<li><a href="http://www.sybex.com/internet.html">Sybex's
List of Internet Books</a>
</ul>
```

produces a bulleted list with three items, each of which is a link to another page:

- Sybex's Home Page
- Sybex's Catalog
- Sybex's List of Internet Books

Creating a Simple Home Page

Great. Now, having read this chapter, you know all the HTML tags that go into creating a simple page. Let's go step by step through creating a home page. We'll use Word for Windows 95 to do this, and when we're done, we'll save the file as a plain text file.

Java: The Hot Ticket to Live Action

If you've been out Websurfing of late, you've probably come across sites that include "live action." These are examples of Netscape's support for *Java*, a programming language developed by Sun Microsystems that enables a vast new frontier of interactivity. Using Java, developers can create little applications called *applets*, which, when they're embedded in HTML documents, create dazzling effects such as animation that might be used in games or for illustrations; ticker tape feeds for news, sports, and stock data; real-time interactivity that can be used for anything from crossword puzzles to the sharing of medical data; and handy gadgets such as mouse pointers that change shape when you drag them over something. Creating Java applets requires a fairly high level of programming knowledge and, as such, is beyond the scope of this book. Still, you should know that it is an option should you decide to become a Web-publishing guru. Java is also discussed briefly in Chapters 3 and 6 of this book.

To follow along, start up Word and open a new, empty document window.

Just about everything we do here you can do in any word processor. If you use a different word processor—WordPerfect, for example—you can follow along, substituting as necessary the functions and commands your word processor uses.

1. In your blank, new document window, type **\<html\>** and press ↵ to start your page. (Remember that all HTML documents should be surrounded by the \<html\> and \</html\> tags. We'll put in the \</html\> later, at the end of these steps.)

2. Now type **\<title\>Herkimer Uglyface's Home Page\</title\>** and press ↵. (You can replace Herkimer Uglyface with your own name, which is probably more attractive anyway.) This will make the title of your home page appear in the title bar when your page is viewed by a user.

3. Now type **\<h1\>Herkimer Uglyface's Home Page\</h1\>** and press ↵. This will make the title of your home page appear at the top of your home page. (Although it's customary to use the same text for the title and the first head, you can actually enter whatever you want in place of "Herkimer Uglyface's Home Page" here.)

4. Now we are ready to enter some body text, so type **\<body\>** and press ↵. This will tell the Web browser that what follows is the body text of the document.

5. Type in a few paragraphs of body text. Remember as you do this to use the \<p\> tag at the beginning of every new paragraph.

6. If you want people viewing your page to reach you by e-mail, you can add a link to your e-mail address. Type **\<a href="mailto:** followed immediately by your e-mail address (with no space after). After your e-mail address (again no space should follow the address), type **">.** (Don't type that last period. It's only there to make our editor happy.) Press ↵.

7. Once you have typed the body text for your page, and added your e-mail link if you chose to, type **\</body\>** to end the body text and **\</html\>** to end the document. These two HTML tags match their counterparts at the beginning of the document. You can press ↵ after each of these tags if you're a stickler for aesthetic consistency, but it's not necessary.

Now it's time to save the document. (Remember, we're using Word for Windows 95 for this demo.)

1. From the Word menu bar, select File ➤ Save As. The Save As dialog box will appear.

2. In the Save As dialog box, click on the down arrow next to the text box labeled Save as type. A list of file types recognized by Word will appear. From this list, select Text Only (see Figure 8.12).

3. Type a path and a filename for the file in the File name text box. If you're saving the file to your hard disk and placing it in your Netscape directory, the path will probably be C:\PROGRAM FILES\NETSCAPE. Our hero, Herkimer Uglyface, named his file HERKPAGE.HTM—you can name yours what you like, but you'll have to end the file with the extension .HTM, because this is an HTML file you are saving.

4. Click on the OK button to save the file.

When Word is finished saving the file, the Save As dialog box will close automatically. You can now exit Word. Don't be alarmed if it asks if you want to save changes to your file when you exit even though you just saved the file as a text file. Just answer No and continue to exit Word for Windows.

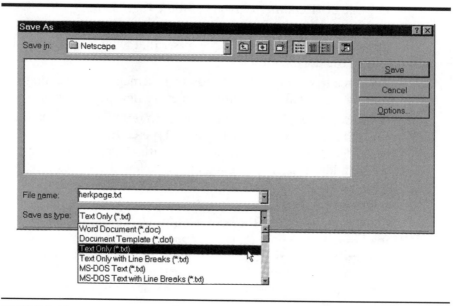

FIGURE 8.12: In the list of file types, select Text Only.

Don't answer Yes when Word asks if you want to save changes to your file when you exit after having saved the file as a text file; if you do, Word will overwrite your text file with a Word file.

Good work. We're ready to look at the file with Netscape to see how it turned out.

Using Netscape to Check Your HTML Document

You've created an HTML document and saved it as a text file on your hard disk. Before you make your page public, you'll want to test it. You can use Netscape to see what your finely crafted page will look like when it's viewed with a Web browser. To load a file from your hard disk into Netscape, follow these steps:

1. Start Netscape and select File ➤ Open File from the menu bar. The Open dialog box will appear.

2. In the Open dialog box, highlight the filename you gave your page. (The Open dialog box works here just as it does in any Windows application.)

3. Click on the OK button. The dialog box will close, and in a few seconds your home page will appear on screen, in the form of a beautiful Web document!

You won't be able to fix typos or other errors or add things to your HTML document while you are viewing it with Netscape. If you want to make changes, close Netscape, open up your word processor, and make the changes there. Then, you can save the modified file, and reopen it in Netscape to see the changes you just made.

Making Your HTML Document Available to the World

Having created a wonderful HTML document on your own computer, you'll want to make it available to the world. As a Web publisher, you can, if you have a big pile of money, buy a machine and set it up as a Web server. This is simply not practical for most people; so we're going to skip it. You can also, if you have access to a Web server at a university or elsewhere, sneak your page onto that server (but don't say we said so). A third option, more practical for a lot of people, might be to publish your page with the help of your Internet service provider.

Many Internet service providers (and even some commercial online services) offer you the option of publishing your Web page on their server as a perk for your use of their service. Unfortunately, however, this is sometimes not free—check with your service provider about costs, and if there is an unreasonable charge, switch providers.

The technical specifics of making your Web pages available to the world vary from one Internet service provider to another; so we cannot go into great detail in this book. Contact your service provider to see how it recommends that you make your documents available to the Internet public.

For your HTML documents to become available to the world, they must be stored on an FTP or HTTP *server* computer that is connected to the Internet. This, for all practical purposes, is not going to be your stand-alone PC with a dial-up connection to the Internet. It'll be a specially outfitted computer that belongs to your Internet service provider. Your service provider will tell you how to transfer your files to its machine and which URLs people should use to access your page.

When Your Page Is Ready, Publicize It

One of the worst tragedies in publishing of any sort is a wonderful piece of work that goes unnoticed because *nobody knows it's there*. Don't let this happen to your Web page. Sure, some people are bound to stumble across it; but you probably want lots and *lots* of people to see it—otherwise, why publish it on the Net?

Some fairly obvious ways to publicize your page include printing the URL on your business card (if that's appropriate) or in ads if yours is a commercial venture. Some magazines list the addresses of Web sites, sometimes for a small fee. But let's look at using the Net itself as a vehicle for publicity.

In Chapter 5, we showed you some great starting places for Internet exploration, including the Netscape What's New page and a bunch of meta-indexes such as Magellan, Yahoo, and GNN. There are also loads of smaller, more focused indexes on the Net that specialize in all sorts of areas of interest, from Hellenic studies to humor, technology law, the state of Georgia, and zoos. You can get your page listed in many of these big or small indexes quite easily. In a typical example, you can just fill in a brief on-screen form describing your site and providing the pertinent details—such as your URL. Then you can select as many or as few indexes as you'd like your site to appear in, click on an oh-so-easy Submit button, and—wham-o!—an announcement of your site's birth is blasted off into all the appropriate places in cyberspace in no time flat. (For those of us who had to track these things down and fill out individual forms in the dark ages of late 1994, this is just incredible.)

Another venue for announcing your page might be various carefully selected Usenet newsgroups. Again, you can do this via announcement services; just be sure to choose appropriate newsgroups based on whether their topics are related to the topic of your page. Be discreet—no one wants to get junk mail in newsgroups any more than in "real" life. Make sure your announcement to specific newsgroups is timely, relevant, to the point, and respectful of that particular newsgroup's culture.

What's Out There

Pointers to Pointers, an excellent service that blasts out an announcement introducing your Web page to dozens if not hundreds of meta-indexes, specialty indexes, newsgroups, and more, is free for you to use at `http://www.homecom.com/global/pointers.html`. There are plenty of these services you can use, though some charge a fee and not all are as comprehensive as Pointers to Pointers. (Please heed the request posted on the Pointers to Pointers page not to abuse this wonderful service by posting your page more than once here or at more than one service.) To find more of these announcement services, you can go to the Yahoo List of Announcement Services at `http://www.yahoo.com/Computers_and_ Internet/Internet/World_Wide_Web/Announcment/Services`.

If your page is of a commercial nature, you can list it in indexes devoted to commercial sites; for example, you can list your commercial site for free along with thousands of other companies in Open Market's Commercial Sites Index.

What's Out There

Open Market's Commercial Sites Index can be found at `http://www.directory.net`.

You can also announce your page via Internet mailing lists such as Net-Happenings. NetHappenings, by the way, is a wonderful way to stay current on (guess what) what's happening on the Internet. To subscribe to NetHappenings, send e-mail to `majordomo@lists.internic.net`; in the body of your message, type **subscribe <net-happenings>**.

You can trade links with others who've published pages on related topics (or even unrelated topics). You can also add the URL of your page to a signature that will appear at the bottom of your e-mail messages. That way, every time you send out e-mail, a subtle advertisement of your page will appear with the mail. And finally, you can embed the URL for your page into an e-mail message and send that out. To find out how, read on.

It's important to avoid *spamming*—the unnecessary junking up of people's e-mail in boxes with messages of no interest to them. In general, consider the nature of your page and tailor your choice of where to announce it accordingly. But do announce it—no one will know it is there if you don't.

HTML in Netscape's Electrifying E-Mail

In a hot development new to Netscape Navigator version 2, you can embed hyperlinks, inline images, and other HTML tags right into the body of your e-mail messages, effectively transforming them into working HTML documents. Figure 8.13 shows an e-mail message with an image embedded in it.

With this new integrated e-mail capability, readers of your e-mail messages can, for example, jump directly to a Web page without a second thought. No more cutting and pasting URLs from your e-mail into the Open Location dialog box; it's as if your e-mail messages were mini Web pages in and of themselves! Of course, the hyperlinks and other HTML tags you embed in your e-mail messages will work as links only for those of your readers who are also using Netscape Mail. (If you send a Netscape-enhanced e-mail message to someone with a run-of-the-mill e-mail program, the message will look like an average, run-of-the-mill message—it won't have any nifty hyperlink text or inline images in it.)

Using HTML in e-mail messages is basically a two-step process. First you must create an HTML file you want to add to your e-mail. Then you must attach the file to an e-mail message. Chapter 4 showed you the ins and

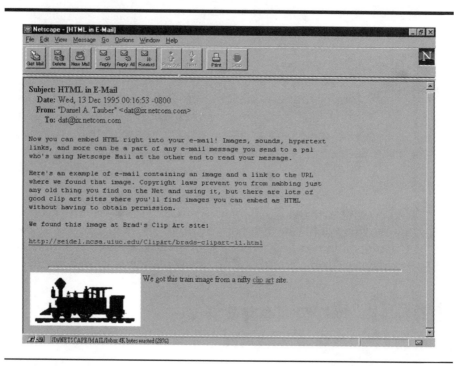

FIGURE 8.13: You can embed links, images, and other HTML right into your e-mail messages.

outs of Netscape Mail, and now that you've read this chapter, you know the basics of HTML. Roll this all together with another step or two, and you're set. Here are the details:

1. Follow the steps and guidelines throughout earlier sections in this chapter to create a file with any of the HTML trappings you want. You can use any of the tags we discuss in this chapter in HTML e-mail. As an example, to embed a URL in your e-mail, open your word processor and type **<html>Take a look at this <a href="http://www .dnai.com/~vox/netscape">Netscape</a> page</html>**. (Not the period at the end; it's just there to stop the sentence.) This will become a brief HTML file that will be the body of your e-mail message. Note that the word *Netscape* is linked to a URL. Give this document a descriptive name with the extension HTM (NETMSG.HTM, for example) and save it as a text file. Close your word processor.

2. Start Netscape and create a new e-mail message as described in Chapter 4's quick and easy instructions.

3. After you enter the recipient and subject of the message in the Message Composition window as usual, click on the Attachment button. The Attachments dialog box will appear.

4. In the Attachments dialog box, click on the Attach File button. The Enter File to Attach dialog box will appear.

5. In the dialog box's list of files, highlight the name of the file you just created and click on the Open button. The Enter File to Attach dialog box will close, and the Attachments dialog box will reappear, this time with the file you just selected listed in its large list box.

6. Click on the Attachments dialog box's OK button. The dialog box will close, and the Message Composition window will be visible. The name of the HTML file you created will appear in the Message Composition window's Attachments text box.

7. Now send off your HTML file, just as you would any other e-mail message, by clicking on the Message Composition window's Send Message button.

When your message arrives, the HTML file you created will look just like any other e-mail message, but it will contain whatever HTML functionality you built into it—in our example, the word *Netscape* will actually be a link to a Web page. The pal we sent it to will be able to click on the Netscape link and will be zapped right over to a page about this book.

 If you write a regular e-mail message and you attach an HTML file to it, the recipient will see the e-mail message you entered appearing as he or she always does, but followed by a ruled line and then the HTML file you are sending. For example, if you send an e-mail message that says "Check this out" with an attached HTML file containing an image, the message will appear first, followed by a rule, followed by the image. (Again, see Figure 8.13.)

That's all there is to using HTML tags in your e-mail. You can experiment with using the different HTML options discussed in this chapter in your e-mail messages.

What's Next?

Well. Now you know all you need to know to browse the Web, search for what you find intriguing or useful, create your own home page, and include HTML in your Netscape e-mail messages. In Chapters 9 and 10, we're going to cover the nitty-gritty technical details: How to get connected and install Netscape. Then, in Chapter 11, we'll show you how to get some nifty viewers and players from the Internet itself.

Part Three:

Getting Started with Netscape

Laying the Groundwork for Installing Netscape

Roll up your sleeves—this is the part where we get down and dirty and put things together. In this chapter, we're going to get you on the Net, set up your Internet connection, and *go get Netscape* from the Internet itself.

Before you can start cruising the Internet with Netscape Navigator—or even download the program to your computer—you have to have your Internet connection ready to go. Until recently, connecting your stand-alone home computer to the Internet meant installing complicated software on your computer—called SLIP/PPP software—and configuring it with information about your Internet service provider. Two recent events have made connecting to the Internet much easier:

◆ Windows 95 includes the software you need to access the Internet via any Internet service provider (you don't need separate, special SLIP/PPP software any more, though you do need a SLIP/PPP account).

◆ Many commercial online services (such as CompuServe) now offer Internet access to their subscribers as part of their services.

Internet Service Providers and Commercial Online Services: The Big Difference

Believe it or not, commercial online services such as CompuServe and America Online are not part of the Internet. They do provide Internet access these days, but in actuality, commercial online services are separate, distinct entities—what's the difference? Well, a commercial online service provides content, such as online magazines, consumer reports, and reference materials; forums in which people discuss their interests; contests; and online access to celebrities—whatever's deemed commercially viable and of interest—to subscribers who pay a (usually monthly) fee for that service. As part of all this, the commercial online services have begun to provide access to the Internet as well. An Internet service provider gives you access to the Internet for a (usually monthly) fee, but does not usually provide any content whatsoever—all the content, in this case, comes from the Internet itself. Commercial online services often charge extra for some "premium" aspect of their services; they may also charge for receipt of e-mail. Internet service providers generally charge only for access time, not for any kind of premium stuff....Now you know.

In this chapter we'll cover the major ways to get connected and get Netscape:

◆ Using Windows 95 Dial-Up Networking to access the Internet via any of a lot of Internet service providers

◆ Using Netcom NetCruiser software to access the Internet

◆ Using software provided by some of the major commercial online services—CompuServe or Microsoft Network—to access the Internet

If you're just getting started using the Internet, you may want to read this entire chapter before you decide which method of connecting is best for you. If you already have an account with an Internet service provider, turn to the section titled *Getting Connected via Windows 95 Dial-Up Networking*; if you have an account with Netcom's NetCruiser, turn to the section titled *Getting Connected via Netcom NetCruiser*; if you have an account with CompuServe, turn to the section titled *Getting Connected via CompuServe NetLauncher*; and if you have an account with the Microsoft Network, turn to the section titled *Getting Connected via the Microsoft Network*.

Depending on the type of Internet connection you use (Windows 95 Dial-Up Networking, NetCruiser, NetLauncher, and so on) you'll get and use either the 32-bit or 16-bit version of Netscape. Turn to *A Tale of Two Versions* in Chapter 10 for details.

Why didn't we cover America Online and Prodigy here? Well, as of this writing, you cannot run Netscape with America Online or with Prodigy. Maybe that'll change soon....

Getting Connected via Windows 95 Dial-Up Networking

When it comes to using an Internet service provider and your Windows PC to access the Internet, there are two eras: Before Windows 95, and after Windows 95. Before Windows 95, setting up your Netscape connection with an Internet service provider was a big drag. Not only did you have to have a SLIP/PPP account with an Internet service provider, you also had to install several separate pieces of software (including special SLIP/PPP software that "introduced" your Internet service provider to Netscape at the beginning of every session). Then you had to configure your machine and all this software to work neatly together—it might have taken a whole day!

What's Out There

You can get the latest news about Dial-Up Networking on Windows 95.com's TCP/IP set-up page at `http://www.windows95.com/connect/tcp.html`.

You still need an account with an Internet service provider, but you're saved all that other hassle, because Windows 95 includes all the software you need to get connected to the Internet. You do still need a SLIP/PPP account, but you don't need special SLIP/PPP software. You can use Windows 95 Dial-Up Networking with just about any Internet service provider that offers SLIP or PPP, and these days, lots of them do.

 Getting connected to the Internet via Windows 95 Dial-Up Networking is just one of several options for connecting your computer. Later in this chapter, we'll show you how to get connected via some other popular options, such as Netcom NetCruiser, CompuServe NetLauncher, and the Microsoft Network.

What You Need

Let's face facts. Netscape (as you find it on the Internet) just isn't one of those programs you can take out of the box and expect to install itself. Netscape has many wonderful attributes, but unfortunately that's not one of them. To run Netscape on your Windows PC using an Internet service provider, you need:

◆ An account with an Internet service provider

◆ Netscape itself

◆ Windows 95 Dial-Up Networking Software (which comes with Windows 95)

Setting up an account with an Internet service provider is up to you. Suffice it to say, the most important considerations in selecting an Internet service provider are:

◆ Whether it provides a local access phone number so that you can avoid long distance charges

◆ Whether it offers SLIP/PPP accounts

You also need a Windows PC with at least 8MB of RAM (12MB or more is a lot better), 10MB of available hard disk space, and a fast modem (at the very least 9600 bps, although 14,400 bps or 28,800 bps is much better). Except for the modem, this is the same stuff you need to run most Windows programs, so you're probably set.

In the section that follows this one, we'll talk a bit more about choosing an appropriate Internet service provider. Appendix B lists some reputable Internet service providers you can contact if you like; but read on first so that you'll know what you need.

If you'd like more information about Internet basics, look into The ABCs of the Internet by Christian Crumlish (Sybex, 1996). This book walks you through many aspects of the Internet and includes a comprehensive list of Internet service providers.

By the way, getting Netscape will probably be a matter of going out on the Internet and downloading an evaluation copy of the software; we'll go over that in an upcoming section of this chapter. You can also get Netscape in a box from any of many retail outlets, but we're going to leave it to the documentation in that box to tell you how to install Netscape if you go that route.

Okey dokey, let's get cracking. Before we do, however, a few words of caution: This section is going to deal with material that's a little more technically demanding than what we've done so far in this book. Setting up Windows 95 Dial-Up Networking involves a lot of making little "pieces" work together. Don't let this discourage you—take your time, have patience, read carefully, and ask your Internet service provider for help if you get stuck.

Take into consideration the willingness of an Internet service provider to help you get your Windows 95 Dial-Up Networking when you choose whether to set up an account with that service provider—it's an indication of that company's overall attitude toward customer service.

In the end you'll have Netscape running, and it'll be well worth your effort.

Selecting an Internet Service Provider

You need to think about some things as you select an Internet service provider to work with Netscape. Let's go over the important points.

Ask about SLIP/PPP

If you're going to run Netscape on a home computer equipped with a modem (that's what we're here for, isn't it?), you're going to need a SLIP account *or* a PPP account. The Internet service providers that offer SLIP/PPP are different from commercial online service accounts such as CompuServe or America Online.

SLIP stands for *Serial Line Internet Protocol,* and PPP stands for *Point-to-Point Protocol*. Some Internet service providers offer one, some offer the other, some offer both. For your purposes at home, they are equivalent; either kind of account will allow you to run Netscape just fine (that's why we talk about them as a unit, using "SLIP/PPP" for shorthand).

In telecommunications jargon, SLIP/PPP allows you to send TCP/IP packets (see Chapters 1 and 2) over a serial communications device—a *modem*. Remember, while you are logged on to your SLIP/PPP account, your machine at home *is actually part of the Internet*. Maybe that's worth repeating. You're not logged on to the Internet the way you are logged on to a BBS when you call one—in that case your single machine is accessing the single machine on which the BBS resides. When you log on to the Internet, your machine becomes part of the network of millions of computers that make up the Internet, and you can communicate with any one of them by sending and receiving e-mail, files, or whatever.

Consider the Costs

A major consideration in selecting a service provider is cost. Essentially two costs are involved: a monthly or hourly fee you pay the service provider for access, and the fee you pay (or do not pay if you are clever and find a service provider with local access) to the phone company for long distance charges. *Shop around for a good deal*, and when you ask about the deal, remember to ask about a local access number.

You can find information about Internet service providers in your area in local computer publications. And you can find information about the national providers in national computer magazines—you'll find no shortage of them, and one is bound to be perfect for you. (See Appendix B.)

You can generally expect to pay somewhere in the neighborhood of $25–$50 a month for a SLIP/PPP account with an Internet service provider, plus (sometimes) a one-time setup or registration charge.

Ask about technical support too. Is it available by telephone seven days a week or only through e-mail? Is the provider's technical support group fully staffed? Are people available at the time you'll call? If you have pals you can consult, ask them about the quality of support and the provider's reputation for reliability.

Make Note of Some Technical Details

Once you choose a provider, you can usually set up your account over the telephone. It should take only a few days (if that) for your service provider to get you going.

But let's back up a minute. While you've got them on the line, find out some technical information you'll need to set up Windows 95 Dial-Up Networking for use with Netscape. Make note of the answers as you go—we'll use this information later in this chapter. Specifically, ask for the following information:

- ◆ The IP Address assigned to your machine at home (unless your provider "dynamically assigns" an IP address)
- ◆ The IP Address of the provider's primary domain name server
- ◆ The IP Address of the provider's secondary domain name server, if any

If you're already familiar with addresses in the `domain.names.separated` `.by.periods` format, you'll know that `violet.berkeley.edu` is a machine at the University of California, Berkeley. This is *not* what you want here, however. In our discussion in Chapters 1 and 2, we described how an address such as `violet.berkeley.edu` is the easier-to-remember version of what's really a numeric address. You want the IP address in a *numeric* format—numbers separated by periods—such as `126.54.32.1`.

Ask for the four-number address the provider is assigning to your computer. *Every* computer on the Internet has such an address, called an *IP (Internet Protocol) address*. Note that some providers assign your machine a permanent IP address; others assign an IP address "dynamically," meaning that each time you log on to your SLIP/PPP account, the provider's server automatically assigns your computer an address for use in that session only.

If your provider assigns your machine a permanent IP address, write it here:

_____._____._____._____

If your provider assigns an IP address dynamically, just leave these blanks blank.

Last, you will need to know the IP address of your service provider's primary and, if it has one, secondary domain name servers. Write these addresses here:

_____._____._____._____

_____._____._____._____

In addition to the IP addresses above, you also need the names of a few servers that your Internet service provider maintains:

◆ News (also know as NNTP) server
◆ Mail (also know as the POP3 and SMTP) servers. This may be a single server, or it may be two different servers.

Write the name of the news server here:

_____

You'll use these server names in the next chapter when you get Netscape running. You don't need the numeric IP addresses here. Simply entering the servers' names, such as news.abc.com, is fine.

Now write down the name of the POP3 and SMTP servers here (if the same server is used for both, simply write down the name twice).

_____

_____

There is one teensy caveat here: If you want to connect via a SLIP account (rather than PPP), you'll need the CD-ROM version of Windows 95. The CD-ROM version includes both SLIP and PPP capability; the diskette version does not include the Windows 95 SLIP driver. PPP is more commonly offered than SLIP, however, and PPP has some performance advantages over SLIP. So unless you have some special reason to want SLIP, the PPP driver that comes with Windows 95 will probably fit your needs.

Installing Windows 95 Dial-Up Networking

Now that you have an account with an Internet service provider, you are ready to install and set-up Dial-Up Networking. (Actually, you can go ahead and install Dial-Up Networking before you have your Internet service provider account; you just can't finish installing and using it until you get the account information from your provider.) You must (obviously) *install* Dial-Up Networking before you can use it to connect to your Internet service provider. If, during your installation of Windows 95, you indicated that you wanted Dial-Up Networking installed, it'll be there, but the Windows 95 installation process does not automatically assume that you want Dial-Up Networking. You can install Dial-Up Networking now if you need to, using the Add/Remove Software Component Control Panel. To do so, follow these steps:

1. From the Start menu, select Settings ➤ Control Panel. The Control Panel window will appear.

2. In the Control Panel window, double-click on the Add/Remove Programs icon.

   Add/Remove
   Programs

   The Add/Remove Programs Properties dialog box will appear (see Figure 9.1).

3. Along the top of the dialog box, you'll see a number of tabs. Click on the Windows Setup tab, and the window's contents change to show which portions of Windows 95 have been installed on your computer.

Laying the Groundwork for Installing Netscape

Click here to display installed Windows 95 components.

Click here to display Communications components.

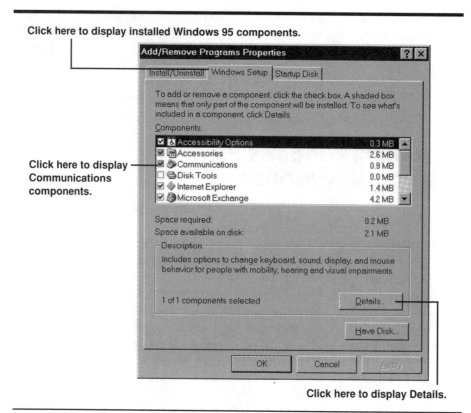

Click here to display Details.

FIGURE 9.1: You can use the Add/Remove Programs Properties dialog box to add Windows 95 Dial-Up Networking component to your computer if you don't have this gem installed already.

4. Because Dial-Up Networking is all about communicating, it is grouped with other communications options in Windows 95. Click on the Communications entry in the Components list along the left side of the dialog box, and then click on the Details button. The Communications dialog box, which is shown in Figure 9.2, will appear showing the Windows 95 communications options you can install.

5. In the Communications dialog box, click on the checkbox next to the Dial-Up Networking entry. (This indicates that you want to install Dial-Up Networking on your computer.) Now, click on the OK button to continue. The Add/Remove Programs Properties dialog box will reappear.

FIGURE 9.2: In the Communications dialog box, you can select Windows 95 communication components for installation. Here we have selected the Dial-Up Networking component.

6. In the Add/Remove Programs Properties dialog box, click on the OK button to start installing Dial-Up Networking. Windows will ask you to insert either the Windows 95 diskettes or the CD-ROM as files are copied from them to your computer. Insert the diskettes or CD-ROM as requested.

7. When Dial-Up Networking is installed, a dialog box will appear telling you that you must restart your machine before Dial-Up Networking will actually work.

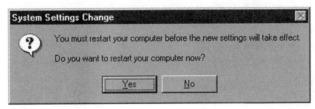

Click on the Yes button to finish installing. Your computer will restart and Windows 95 will start running again.

When your machine restarts, Dial-Up Networking is installed. You will not see any obvious changes as a result of the installation (except that you will have a new icon in your My Computer window called Dial-Up Networking). Even though you now have the software required to access your Internet service provider, you still need to:

◆ Create a new connection for your Internet service provider

◆ Enter information about your Internet service provider

Once you complete these two steps, you'll be ready to start using the Internet.

Introducing Dial-Up Networking to Your Internet Service Provider

Now you're going to set up Dial-Up Networking to work with your Internet service provider. In particular, you'll

◆ Create the connection that tells Dial-Up Networking the telephone number to dial for your Internet service provider

◆ Configure the connection so that Dial-Up Networking knows how to access the Internet via your Internet service provider

We are now ready to start creating the connection you'll use to hook up with your Internet service provider.

If your PC is on a LAN (a Local Area Network), you must contact your Network Administrator before you configure Dial-Up Networking—otherwise you can make a real mess of things and cause that person a lot of grief.

1. From the Start menu, select Settings ➤ Control Panel. The Control Panel window will appear.

2. In the window, double-click on the Network icon.

Network

The Network dialog box (shown in Figure 9.3) will appear.

3. In the Network dialog box , click on the Add button. The Select Network Component Type dialog box will appear (see Figure 9.4).

4. Now, in the Select Network Component Type dialog box's list box, double-click on the word Protocol. The Select Network Protocol dialog box will appear (see Figure 9.5).

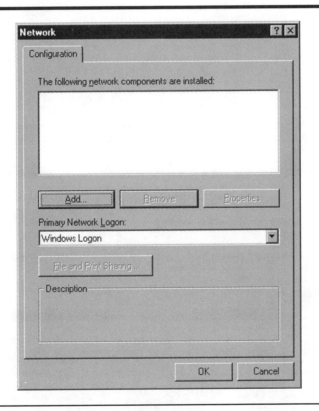

FIGURE 9.3: The Network dialog box is where you set up all aspects of networking in Windows 95, including access to the Internet.

5. Along the left side of the Select Network Protocol dialog box, you will see a list box labeled Manufacturers. In the list, highlight Microsoft, and you will see a list of network drivers—the software that Windows uses to communicate over a network such as the Internet.

6. In the list of network drivers (which you can see in Figure 9.5), click on the entry titled TCP/IP (remember, TCP/IP is the Internet protocol we discussed in Chapter 2).

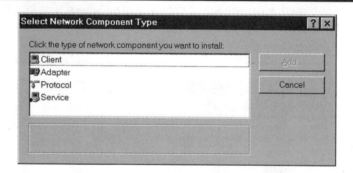

FIGURE 9.4: The Select Network Component Type dialog box

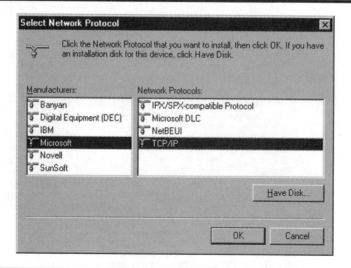

FIGURE 9.5: The Select Network Protocol dialog box with Microsoft and TCP/IP highlighted

7. With the TCP/IP entry highlighted, click on the OK button. The Network dialog box will reappear, with TCP/IP now listed in the Network Components list as shown in Figure 9.6.

8. When you installed Dial-Up Networking, Windows set it up to access a bunch of networks, such as Microsoft NT and Novell Netware, in addition to the Internet. In this step, we'll remove the pieces that are used to access these other networks, just leaving what is required to access the Internet. In the Network dialog box's Network Components list, highlight IPX/SPX Compatible Protocol, and click on the Remove button, and then highlight NetBEUI, and click again on the Remove button. Finally, highlight File and Printer sharing for Microsoft Networks and click once more on the Remove button. Figure 9.7 shows the Network dialog box after removing the IPX/SPX, NetBEUI, and File and Printer Sharing components.

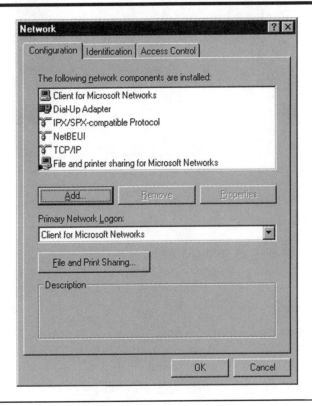

FIGURE 9.6:   TCP/IP is now listed under Network Components.

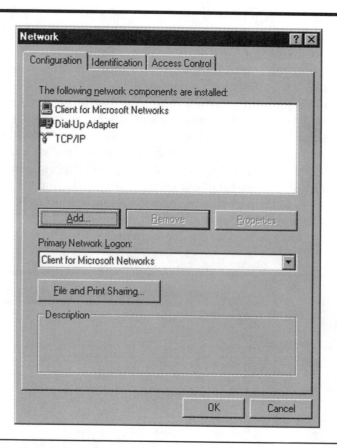

FIGURE 9.7: Here is the Network dialog box after the unnecessary network components have been removed.

If your machine is on a LAN, messing around too much with this list can really wreak havoc. Please, please talk to your network administrator first.

9. At this point, only Client for Microsoft Networks, Dial-Up Adapter, and TCP/IP should appear in the Network Components list. If this is so, click on the OK button to continue. The Network dialog box will close, leaving you with your familiar desktop.

You've established all the network settings required to access the Internet using Dial-Up Networking. Now you have to create the actual Dial-Up Networking connection, which means in essence that you must provide Windows with detailed information about your Internet service provider.

Creating a New Dial-Up Networking Connection

To actually use Dial-Up Networking, you create something called a *connection*. According to Microsoft, a connection holds information about your Internet service provider—for example, its telephone number. Once you have created the connection, you can use Dial-Up Networking by double-clicking on the Connections icon on the desktop.

 You need to have a modem installed in your computer and configured for Windows 95 in order to use Dial-Up Networking. If you don't have this stuff all together, you'll be prompted to rectify matters during this setup procedure.

To create a connection, follow these steps:

1. When you installed Dial-Up Networking, Windows created a new icon in the My Computer window called Dial-Up Networking. Open the My Computer window by double-clicking on the My Computer icon on the desktop. Now double-click on the Dial-Up Networking icon.

Dial-Up
Networking

The Dial-Up Networking window will appear. As you create Dial-Up Networking connections, they will appear in the Dial-Up Networking window as icons.

2. In the Dial-Up Networking window, double-click on the Make New Connection icon. You double-click on this icon whenever you want to create a new connection for Dial-Up Networking. The Make New Connection dialog box will appear, as shown in Figure 9.8.

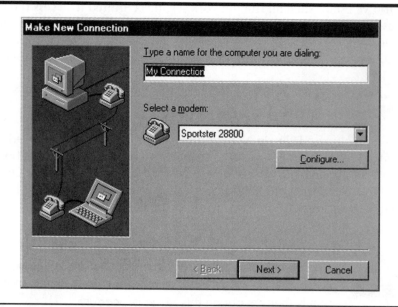

FIGURE 9.8: In the Make New Connection dialog box, you'll provide detailed information about your Internet service provider.

3. In the Make New Connection dialog box, type a name for the connection—the name of your Internet service provider is a logical choice—in the Type a Name for the Computer You Are Dialing text box. Don't press the ↵ key after you enter the name; we still need to enter some additional information in this dialog box before moving along.

4. In the Select a Modem pull-down list, select the modem you plan to use. Odds are that you have only a single modem installed on your computer, so this should be simple—you probably won't have to make any changes to this item.

5. Now click on the Next button to move to the next Make New Connection dialog box (don't get confused—all the dialog boxes used to create the connection have the same title). In this dialog box, enter the phone number you will use to dial up your Internet service provider, as shown in Figure 9.9.

6. First, type the area code in the Area Code text box, and then type the telephone number in the Telephone Number text box.

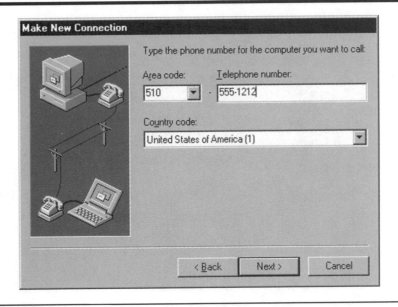

FIGURE 9.9: In the second Make New Connection dialog box, enter your Internet service provider's phone number.

Do not enter a 1 or any other special access numbers before the area code. Windows treats all those special access digits specially—you specify them when you set up your modem.

7. Now in the Country Code pull-down list, select the country where your Internet access provider is located. (Odds are this already indicates the correct country, unless you are calling internationally for your Internet access.) Click on the Next button to continue. The last Make New Connection dialog box will appear, as shown in Figure 9.10.

8. The last Make New Connection dialog box informs you that you have successfully created the connection.

Click on the Finish button to finish creating the connection, or if you see a boo-bette, click on the Back button to return to the previous Make New Connection dialog box so that you can fix it. (You can travel back and forth through the Make New Connection dialog boxes by clicking on the Next and Back buttons. When you're done

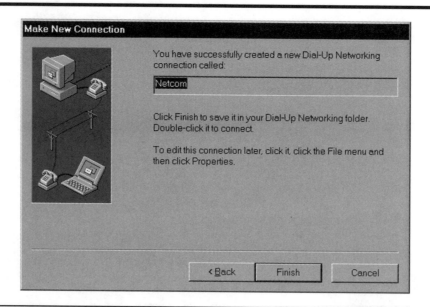

FIGURE 9.10: A dialog box like this one will tell you that you've successfully created your connection.

making corrections, simply click on the Next button until you get to the last Make New Connection dialog box and then click on the Finish button.)

The Dial-Up Networking window will appear on the desktop (as shown in Figure 9.11) listing the new connection that you just created. Now it's time to actually introduce your Internet service provider to your machine and to Windows.

Configuring Your Dial-Up Networking Connection

You've created the connection for your Internet service provider, and in the process of that you specified your Internet service provider's name and telephone number. Now you must specify all that other information you got from your Internet service provider when you set up your account (remember that from the earlier section?). That's all part of *configuring* (setting up) your connection.

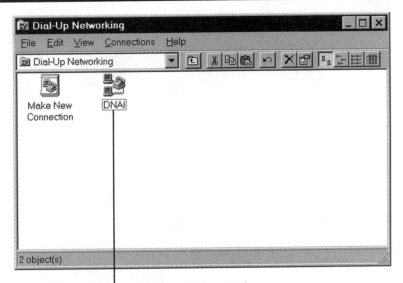

Here is the connection you just created.

FIGURE 9.11: The new connection you just made appears in the Dial-Up Networking window.

Follow these steps:

1. In the Dial-Up Networking window, which should still appear on your desktop, right-click on the icon for the connection you just created. A menu will appear.

Note that the name of the icon will depend on the name you entered in the first Make New Connection dialog box in the last section. It is probably the same name as your Internet service provider. In the menu, select Properties. The Properties dialog box will appear, as shown in Figure 9.12

2. In the Properties dialog box (again, see Figure 9.12), click on the Server Type button. The Server Types dialog box will appear (see Figure 9.13).

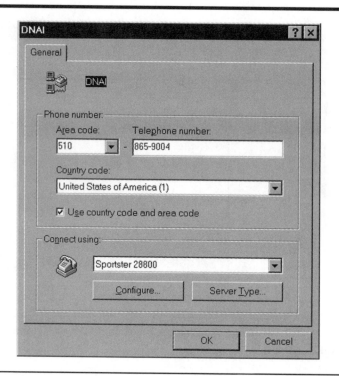

FIGURE 9.12: Here is the Properties dialog box. The name of your Internet service provider will appear in the title bar.

3. In the Server Types dialog box, you'll specify a number of things about your Internet service provider. In the Type of Dial-Up Server drop-down list, the phrase *PPP: Windows 95, Windows NT 3.5, Internet* should appear. If you don't see this phrase, pull down the Type of Dial-Up Server list and select the entry

PPP: Windows 95, Windows NT 3.5, Internet

You can also use Dial-Up Networking to make a SLIP connection, though we're just describing the more common PPP connection here. To use SLIP to connect to the Internet, you need to install the SLIP driver that comes only on the Windows 95 CD-ROM (not on the diskettes). Refer to the Windows 95 Resource Kit, also on the Windows 95 CD-ROM, for details.

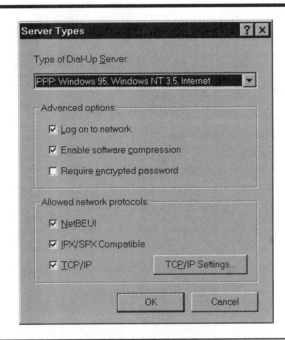

FIGURE 9.13: In the Server Types dialog box, you'll verify that PPP is selected as the service type.

4. Now, in the Server Types dialog box, click on the TCP/IP Settings button, and the TCP/IP Settings dialog box will appear (see Figure 9.14).

5. In the Specify an IP Address text box in the TCP/IP Settings dialog box (see Figure 9.14), enter the IP address assigned to you by your Internet service provider. If your provider uses dynamic IP—in other words, if it gives you a new IP address each time you connect—simply select the Server Assigned IP Address button.

6. In the Primary DNS (Domain Name Server) box, enter the IP address of your Internet service provider's Primary Domain Name Server. Again, if your Internet Service Provider assigns you a DNS server every time you connect, select the Server Assigned Name Server Addresses button.

7. If your Internet service provider gave you the IP address of a Secondary Domain Name Server, enter its address in the Secondary DNS text box. A Secondary Domain Name Server is not required, however; so if you don't happen to know it, leave this field blank.

Click here if a new IP address is assigned
each time you call.

Enter your IP address here.

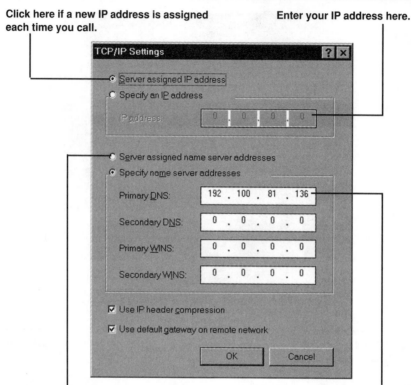

Click here if a different Domain Name Server
address is assigned each time you call.

Enter the Domain Name Server
address here.

FIGURE 9.14: In the TCP/IP Settings dialog box, you'll enter all that pertinent
information you got from your Internet service provider.

8. You're finished with this bit; so click on the OK button. The Server
Types dialog box will reappear.

9. In the Server Types dialog box, click on the OK button, and the Properties dialog box will reappear.

10. Finally, in the Properties dialog box, click on the OK button to save
the information you just entered. The Dial-Up Networking window
will appear on the desktop again.

You have entered all the information necessary to access the Internet via
your Internet service provider and Dial-Up Networking. You are now
ready to connect to the Internet.

Actually Connecting!

Now that you've created and configured your connection you are ready to actually connect to the Internet. Remember, you must start up the connection before you use Netscape. This connection is what allows Netscape or any other Internet application on your computer to talk to the world. To connect, follow these steps:

1. The Dial-Up Networking window should still be displayed on your screen. In the Dial-Up Networking window, double-click on the icon for the connection you created. The Connect To dialog box will appear, as shown in Figure 9.15.

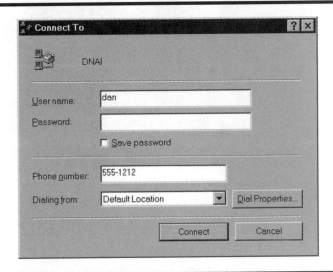

FIGURE 9.15: The Connect To dialog box will appear when you double-click on a connection in the Dial-Up Networking window.

2. In the Connect To dialog box, click on the Connect button. Windows dials the phone number you specified and then waits for your Internet service provider to answer. Leave the User name and Password fields blank—they are used only when connecting to other types of networks, not when connecting via Dial-Up Networking.

3. You'll hear your modem dialing your Internet service provider. When you're actually connected, a dialog box will appear to let you log in to your account. What this dialog box looks like depends on your Internet service provider's preferred look and feel; Figure 9.16 shows one that is more or less typical.

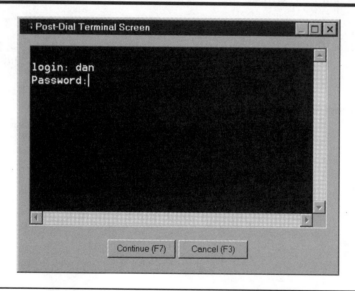

FIGURE 9.16: A dialog box that looks something like this one will let you log in to your account.

4. Log in to your account according to the instructions your provider has given you—the actual procedure varies from one provider to another.

5. Once you are logged in, click on the Continue button.

A small dialog box will appear showing how long you've been connected.

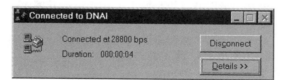

This dialog box remains in view until you disconnect from the Internet. You can minimize this dialog box by clicking on its Minimize button in the upper-right corner of your screen. That will get it of your way.

Now—once you get Netscape—you can start it up. Netscape will use Dial-Up Networking as its go-between to make the vital connection to your Internet service provider.

Getting Netscape from the Internet via Dial-Up Networking

Now we can go on to our bigger purpose—getting a copy of Netscape so that we can install and use it. As we mentioned earlier, you can get Netscape from the Internet itself or, more specifically, from the FTP site of Netscape's manufacturer. An FTP site is basically a public archive of files accessible to anyone on the Internet who has an FTP program (like you, now that you've got Dial-Up Networking all set up).

The FTP program that comes with Windows 95 is character-based, meaning that it does not appear in the nifty way that Windows programs do; you'll have to type text-based commands to get it to work.

Here's what you do to get Netscape:

1. If you are not still connected to the Internet, connect now, using the instructions in the preceding section.

2. From the Start menu, select Run. The Run dialog box will appear.

3. In the Run dialog box, type **ftp ftp.netscape.com** in the Open text box and press the ↵ key. A window will appear, as shown in Figure 9.17.

Only so many people can use Netscape's FTP server at once. You may have to try several times or at odd hours (like at 2:00 AM) before you can connect successfully. The absolute worst time to do this, in fact, is noon. It seems like every soul on the face of the earth is on the Net at lunchtime; so it's better not to do your FTPing over a ham sandwich.

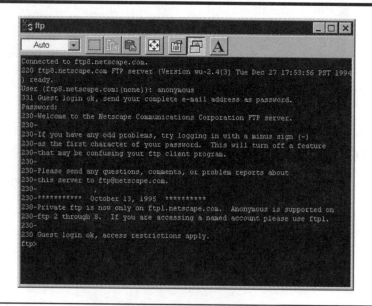

```
ftp                                                        _ □ X
Auto    ▼  □ ⬚ ⬚ ⬚ ⬚ ⬚ A
Connected to ftp8.netscape.com.
220 ftp8.netscape.com FTP server (Version wu-2.4(3) Tue Dec 27 17:53:56 PST 1994
) ready.
User (ftp8.netscape.com:(none)): anonymous
331 Guest login ok, send your complete e-mail address as password.
Password:
230-Welcome to the Netscape Communications Corporation FTP server.
230-
230-If you have any odd problems, try logging in with a minus sign (-)
230-as the first character of your password.  This will turn off a feature
230-that may be confusing your ftp client program.
230-
230-Please send any questions, comments, or problem reports about
230-this server to ftp@netscape.com.
230-
230-**********  October 13, 1995  **********
230-Private ftp is now only on ftp1.netscape.com.  Anonymous is supported on
230-ftp 2 through 8.  If you are accessing a named account please use ftp1.
230-
230 Guest login ok, access restrictions apply.
ftp>
```

FIGURE 9.17: We are using FTP to log in to Netscape's FTP site on the Internet.

4. Near the top of the FTP window, you should see a line that says *User*, followed by the name of a computer on the Internet. Netscape has things set up so that when you access `ftp.netscape.com`, you are actually accessing any of a number of identical FTP servers. Don't worry—each server contains the same set of files. The Netscape folks do it this way so that the thousands of simultaneous FTP connections they get when they release a new version of Netscape won't bring the house down. We are using anonymous FTP to get Netscape; so at the User prompt mentioned earlier in this step, type **anonymous** and press ⏎. A request for a password will appear.

5. It is customary to enter your e-mail address as a password when using anonymous FTP. This gives the people who run the FTP site some information about who is using their site. Go ahead and type your e-mail address and press the ⏎ key. A welcome message will appear.

Steps 4 and 5 describe the standard conventions for using anonymous FTP.

6. Netscape is in the directory /NETSCAPE/WINDOWS on Netscape's FTP server. Type **cd /netscape/windows** and press ↵ to change to the directory that holds Netscape for Windows. (Note that those are forward slashes instead of the familiar backslashes used by DOS.) A message describing Netscape and its licensing terms will appear.

7. Now type **bin** and press the ↵ key. The bin command tells FTP that you are transferring binary files instead of ASCII text files.

8. You must now specify where on your local computer the file you transfer should be stored. Type **lcd c:** and press the ↵ key. This tells FTP to store files that you transfer in the root directory of your C: drive.

9. Now type **ls** and press the ↵ key. You should see a list of files like those shown in Figure 9.18. In the list of files, you'll see one called N32E20.EXE. This is the one that contains Netscape Navigator for Windows 95.

10. We are now ready to copy Netscape from Netscape's FTP server to your machine. Type **get n32e20.exe** and press the ↵ key. This file is more than 2MB in size; it may take 30 minutes or so to arrive. The FTP prompt will return on screen when the transfer is finished.

11. When the transfer is finished and the files are on your machine, type **quit** and press the ↵ key to quit FTP. The Windows 95 desktop will appear again.

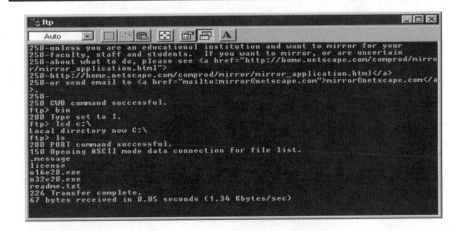

FIGURE 9.18: In this list of files you'll see one called N32E20.EXE. That's the one you want.

Now Netscape is on your machine; let's disconnect from the Internet, just for practice. This is something you'll have to do pretty much every time you shut down Netscape; it's the technique for closing down your Dial-Up Networking Internet connection.

12. Earlier, you minimized the Connected To dialog box to get it out of your way. Now you need to see it again. Click on the Connect To button on the Task Bar, and the dialog box will reappear.

13. In the Connected To dialog box, click on the Disconnect button. The Connected To dialog box will close, and your connection to the Internet will be snapped.

You made it! You've got a copy of Netscape, just waiting to be installed and configured on your machine. So, when you're ready, turn to Chapter 9 and let's install it already.

Getting Connected via Netcom's NetCruiser

NetCruiser is a popular all-in-one Internet access package from Netcom that provides not only Internet access, but a really nifty point-and-click interface (see Figure 9.19) that's great for beginners and powerful enough to grow into once you've got some experience under your belt. NetCruiser software works only with Netcom's Internet service, not with other Internet service providers. NetCruiser includes access to all the popular features of the Internet—including the World Wide Web—but its Web browser is notoriously weak, lacking many of the more advanced features found in Netscape and loved by millions. Because of this combination of factors, many people enjoy running Netscape on top of NetCruiser, which is in many ways the best of both worlds.

You can use Netscape with NetCruiser version 1.60 or newer; older versions of NetCruiser don't support Netscape. The good news is that if you have an older version of NetCruiser, you can upgrade to a newer version quickly via a handy menu item on the NetCruiser File menu.

FIGURE 9.19: NetCruiser lets you cruise the Internet using a simple point-and-click interface. You can also run Netscape on top of NetCruiser.

What's Out There

You can find out more about Netcom and NetCruiser from Netcom's home page at http://www.netcom.com.

What You Need

To run NetCruiser, you need a Windows PC with 8MB of memory and about 8MB of free disk space. A 9,600 bps modem is the minimum; a 14,400 or even 28,800 bps is better. You also need NetCruiser itself. You can often pick up the disk for free at trade shows or computer stores, but it will come without documentation. Perhaps the best way to get NetCruiser

is along with a terrific book, *Access the Internet*, written by David Peal and published by Sybex, that will tell you all about using NetCruiser.

Installing NetCruiser is an incredibly simple matter that is described in a phrase on the disk and in detail in the book. Here, we're going to focus on getting Netscape by using NetCruiser, and then on making a Netscape connection via your NetCruiser account.

Getting Ready to Run Netscape with NetCruiser

As mentioned, this section assumes you have NetCruiser and that you've installed it and made your first NetCruiser Internet connection. Now you need to set up NetCruiser to allow Netscape to run—it's no big deal. All you have to do is tell NetCruiser that it should accept third-party Internet programs such as Netscape to run in conjunction with it. To do so, follow these easy steps:

1. With NetCruiser running and connected to the Internet, select Settings ➤ Startup Options from the NetCruiser menu bar. The Startup Options dialog box will appear.

2. In the dialog box, click on the Autoload Netcom's Winsock.dll checkbox. A checkmark will appear in the checkbox. This tells NetCruiser to allow third-party Internet applications such as Netscape to access the Internet while NetCruiser is running.

3. Click on the OK button. The NetCruiser main window will reappear.

Wasn't that easy?

Getting Netscape from the Internet via NetCruiser

Now that you have NetCruiser set up to allow you to run Netscape, you are almost set. But you're missing one crucial piece of stuff: Netscape. In this section you'll learn to download Netscape to your computer using NetCruiser. In the next chapter you will learn how to install Netscape. To get Netscape, follow these steps:

1. Start up NetCruiser and get connected as you usually do.

2. From the NetCruiser menu bar, select Internet ➤ FTP Download. The Site Chooser: FTP dialog box will appear, as shown in Figure 9.20.

3. In the Site Chooser: FTP dialog box's Site text box, type `ftp.netscape.com` and press the ↵ key. A window titled *FTP To: ftp.netscape.com* will appear, with space in it for you to enter a username and a password. Don't do that; just leave what's there in place.

4. Now click on the OK button to accept the default entries. A dialog box displaying information about Netscape's FTP server will appear.

5. After reading the information in the dialog box, you can close the dialog box by clicking on its close box in the upper-right corner. You should now see a window titled *FTP To: ftp.netscape.com*, as shown in Figure 9.21.

6. The FTP To window is split into two sections—the upper part of the window contains directory names, and the lower part of the window contains filenames. Scroll the list until you see the NETSCAPE directory, and then double-click on it. The contents of the top part of the

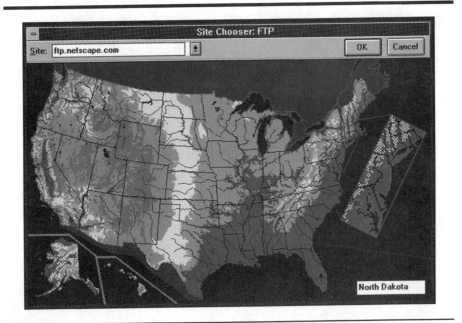

FIGURE 9.20: The Site Chooser: FTP dialog box after we entered the address of Netscape's FTP server

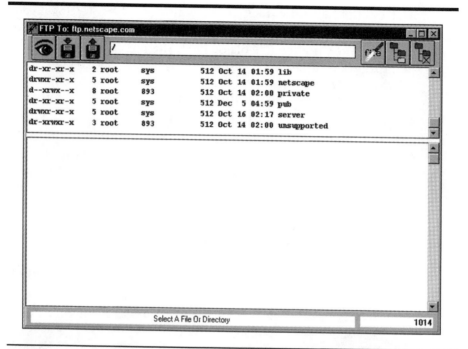

```
FTP To: ftp.netscape.com                                              _ □ ×
  👁  📥  📤  /                                          free  🗂  🗂

dr-xr-xr-x    2 root    sys       512 Oct 14 01:59 lib          ▲
drwxr-xr-x    5 root    sys       512 Oct 14 01:59 netscape
d--xrwx--x    8 root    893       512 Oct 14 02:00 private
dr-xr-xr-x    5 root    sys       512 Dec  5 04:59 pub
drwxr-xr-x    5 root    sys       512 Oct 16 02:17 server
dr-xrwxr-x    3 root    893       512 Oct 14 02:00 unsupported
                                                                ▼

                                                                ▲




                                                                ▼
                    Select A File Or Directory          1014
```

FIGURE 9.21: You'll use the <u>FTP To: ftp.netscape.com</u> window to transfer Netscape from Netscape's FTP server to your computer using NetCruiser.

window will change to show the directories in the NETSCAPE directory.

7. Now double-click on the WINDOWS directory in the top part of the window. The bottom part of the FTP To window will change to list the files located in the WINDOWS directory.

8. Locate the file named N16E20.EXE in the lower part of the window, and double-click on it. NetCruiser will display a dialog box asking if the file is a binary or a text file.

9. Click on the Binary File button, because we are transferring a binary file. The Save As dialog box will appear, as shown in Figure 9.22.

10. In the File Name field of the Save As dialog box, type **c:\n16e20.exe** and press ↵. Netscape will transfer the file you need to your local computer. You can see the progress of the file transfer in the status bar along the bottom of the FTP To dialog box.

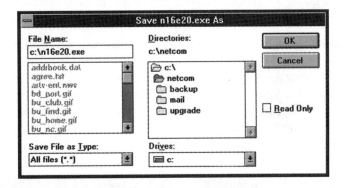

FIGURE 9.22:   In the Save As dialog box, type Netscape, which is of course the name you want the program to have on your local machine once it's been downloaded.

11. When the transfer is finished, close the FTP To window by clicking on its close box in the upper-right corner.

You now have a copy of Netscape Navigator on your computer, and you are totally ready to install it. Chapter 10 covers installing Netscape on your computer.

Getting Connected via CompuServe's NetLauncher

CompuServe's services have grown in the recent past to include quite credible Internet access via NetLauncher. NetLauncher comes with a Web browser, but many people enjoy running Netscape on top of NetLauncher because of Netscape's many state-of-the-art features.

What You Need

To run CompuServe's NetLauncher you need a Windows PC with 8MB of memory and about 8MB of free disk space. A 9600 bps modem is the minimum; a 14,400 or even 28,800 bps is better. You also need a CompuServe account and the software (WinCIM) that goes with that. Disks that will

get you going are frequently bundled with magazines and modems for free and are also often available at trade shows or in computer stores.

Installing WinCIM and setting up a CompuServe account is very easy; you'll be walked through that process on screen when you pop the disk into your machine. For a good, detailed description in print, refer to the book *Your First Modem*, written by Sharon Crawford and published by Sybex. Here, we'll focus on getting Netscape by using CompuServe's WinCIM and then on making a Netscape connection via your CompuServe/NetLauncher combo.

What's Out There

You can get information about CompuServe from its home page at `http://www.compuserve.com`.

Getting NetLauncher

CompuServe makes NetLauncher available to all its members free of charge— well, the software is free of charge. You will have to pay CompuServe for your connect time, of course. You can often find NetLauncher on diskette in magazines and at trade shows; you also have the option of downloading it from CompuServe's Internet forum.

What's What Here, Anyway?

Several pieces of software are involved in this set of procedures. WinCIM is the software CompuServe gives you so that you can access CompuServe's online service. NetLauncher is CompuServe's Internet access software, which lets you use your CompuServe connection to get onto and use the Net. (Remember, CompuServe is not part of the Internet; it's a separate kind of service.) Spry Mosaic is the Web browser portion of NetLauncher, and Netscape is of course the Web browser of choice, which you'll probably want to run instead of Spry Mosaic once you get all this stuff in place.

In this section, we'll show you how to use CompuServe's WinCim software (that's the software you usually use to access CompuServe) to download NetLauncher from CompuServe. To do so, follow these instructions:

1. Start WinCim as usual, and the Services window will appear, as shown in Figure 9.23.

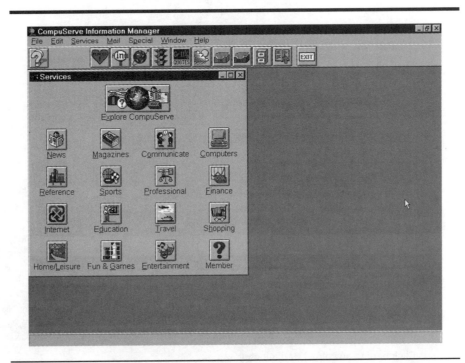

FIGURE 9.23: In WinCim's Services window, you can double-click on the Internet icon to go to CompuServe's Internet forums.

What's Out There

While using WinCim, you can access CompuServe forums specially focused on using the Internet. Simply Go Internet to access these forums.

2. Double-click on the Internet icon, and the Internet window will appear, as shown in Figure 9.24. From this window, you can navigate CompuServe's Internet forums, where you'll find discussions and loads of information—and even software—related to the Internet.

3. In the Internet window, double-click on the Direct Internet Access (Dial PPP) entry (again, see Figure 9.24). The Dialup PPP window will appear.

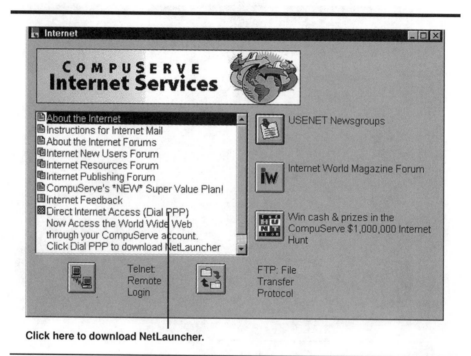

Click here to download NetLauncher.

FIGURE 9.24: CompuServe's Internet forums offer Internet discussions, information, and even software.

4. Now, in the Dialup PPP window, double-click on Download Net-Launcher. A dialog box will appear detailing the NetLauncher license agreement. Read the agreement and decide whether you want to abide by it.

5. Once you have read the license agreement, and if you agree to it, click on the Retrieve button to continue downloading NetLauncher. The Save As dialog box will appear.

6. You don't have to enter anything in particular in the Save As dialog box; simply click on the OK button to accept the default entries of saving NetLauncher as CNL.EXE in the C:\CSERVE\DOWNLOAD directory. A new dialog box will appear (see Figure 9.25), with a status bar that reflects the remaining time it will take to complete the downloading process.

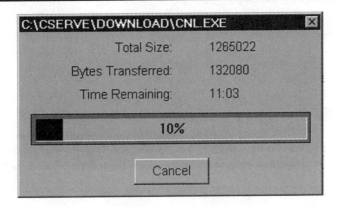

FIGURE 9.25: You can watch the progress of downloading NetLauncher by keeping your eye on the progress meter in this dialog box.

As NetLauncher is transferred to your computer, the status bar in the dialog box will move. Downloading NetLauncher will take about 20 minutes; so you may want to go away, have a cuppa joe, and then come back.

7. Now that you've downloaded NetLauncher, you no longer need to run WinCim; you can proceed without your CompuServe connection going. What's more, you don't *want* to keep running WinCIM, because you don't want to pay CompuServe for any more connect time than necessary. Quit WinCim now by selecting File ➤ Exit from the menu bar. The familiar desktop will be visible once more.

That's all there is to downloading NetLauncher. In the following section we'll show you the next bit of business—how to install NetLauncher so that you can access the Internet using your CompuServe account.

Installing NetLauncher

Now that you have NetLauncher downloaded to your computer, the time has come to install it. Installing NetLauncher is easy. You simply run the installation program that comes with NetLauncher, and it takes care of just about everything involved in configuring your computer for Internet access. In this section, you'll install NetLauncher, and then you'll be able to access the Internet using Spry Mosaic—the Web browser that comes as part of NetLauncher. In the next section we will use Spry Mosaic to download Netscape from the Internet.

Spry Mosaic is quite a workable Web browser; it lacks some of Netscape's features but is generally just fine. If you want to learn more about using Spry Mosaic, you might want to check out our book <u>Mosaic Access to the Internet</u> (Sybex, 1995), which includes the Spry Mosaic software and covers the basic features of Spry Mosaic. Or you might want to check out the CompuServe Internet forums for discussions on Spry Mosaic.

To install NetLauncher on your computer, follow these instructions:

1. From the Windows 95 Start menu, select Run. The Run dialog box will appear.

2. In the Run dialog box, type **c:\cserve\download\cnl.exe** and press ⏎. In a few seconds, the CompuServe NetLauncher Installation window will appear (see Figure 9.26).

3. Click on the Proceed button. A dialog box will appear, asking for the location of your CompuServe directory (usually C:\CSERVE).

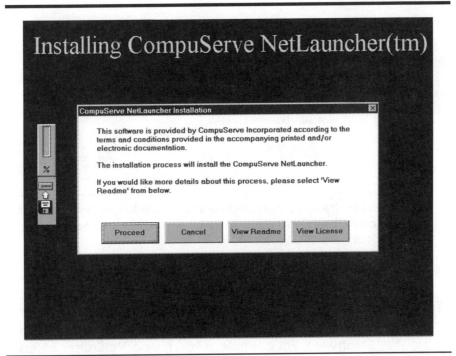

FIGURE 9.26: You'll use the CompuServe NetLauncher Installation program to install NetLauncher on your computer.

4. In this dialog box, enter the location and name of your CompuServe directory—the directory that holds your WinCim software. Unless you adventurously installed WinCim in an atypical location, you can simply accept the default entry, which will be C:\CSERVE. Click on the OK button to continue.

5. The installation program will search for any errant files on your machine that may conflict with NetLauncher. (Isn't that clever?) If it finds any, the dialog box shown in Figure 9.27 will appear, asking if the offending files should be renamed (from WINSOCK.DLL to WINSOCK.000). If this dialog box appears, you should click the Rename button to rename the dangerous files—that will get them out of the way without destroying them. Keeping them around under a different name is a good idea in case you find yourself needing them later.

Laying the Groundwork for Installing Netscape

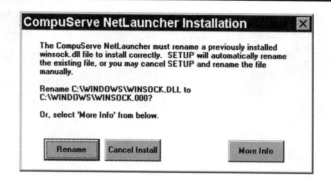

FIGURE 9.27: The CompuServe NetLauncher Installation program searches for and disables conflicting Internet access software by renaming the relevant file (WINSOCK.DLL) WINSOCK.000.

NetLauncher shrewdly tries to disable any other Internet access software you have on your computer. After installing Net-Launcher, you may have trouble using other Internet access software. For example, if you have a NetCruiser account in addition to your CompuServe account, some aspect of Net-Cruiser might be disabled by the installation of NetLauncher. (This business is fierce!) If this happens, consult the various companies' tech support people and the CompuServe Internet forums for help.

6. A progress meter in the middle of the screen will show that files are being installed on your computer. Once the installation is complete, a dialog box will appear, telling you that everything (presumably) went okay.

7. Click on the OK button to finish installing NetLauncher.

Once the Installation is finished, Spry Mosaic will start up and connect you automatically to the Internet via CompuServe. Leave Spry Mosaic running; we'll use it in the next section to download Netscape to your computer.

Getting Netscape from the Internet via NetLauncher

You're all set to download Netscape to your computer using your Net-Launcher connection to the Internet. Spry Mosaic will still be running; you'll use it to download Netscape.

To download Netscape, follow these steps:

1. From the Spry Mosaic menu bar, select File ➤ Open URL. The Open URL dialog box will appear.

2. In the text box of the Open URL dialog box, type `ftp://ftp.netscape.com/netscape/windows` and press ⏎. The contents of the /NETSCAPE/WINDOWS directory on Netscape's FTP server will appear in the Spry Mosaic window as shown in Figure 9.28.

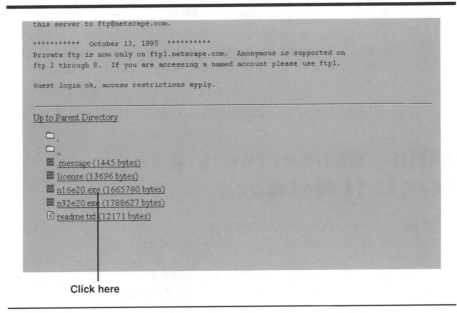

```
this server to ftp@netscape.com.

*********** October 13, 1995 **********
Private ftp is now only on ftp1.netscape.com.  Anonymous is supported on
ftp 2 through 8.  If you are accessing a named account please use ftp1.

Guest login ok, access restrictions apply.
```

Up to Parent Directory

📁 .
📁 ..
🗎 message (1445 bytes)
🗎 license (13696 bytes)
🗎 n16e20.exe (1665780 bytes)
🗎 n32e20.exe (1788627 bytes)
🗎 readme.txt (12171 bytes)

Click here

FIGURE 9.28: The contents of Netscape's FTP server as displayed by Spry Mosaic

Netscape's FTP servers are so popular that they're often over-worked, and sometimes they just plain don't respond to anonymous FTP requests. The worst time to do something like this is lunchtime, when everybody seems to be on the Net and many procedures slow to a crawl—and it gets really bad the week after Netscape announces the availability of new software. You may have to try several times or at odd hours (like at 2:00 AM) before you can connect successfully.

3. You'll have to indicate which of the listed files you want to download; click on the link <u>n16e20.exe</u>. That's the one. The Save As dialog box will appear.

4. In the Save As dialog box, type **c:\n16e20.exe** in the File Name text box and press ↵. The Save As dialog box will disappear as the file transfer begins.

5. As the file is transferred from Netscape's FTP server to your computer, the status bar along the bottom of the Spry Mosaic window will show the procedure's progress. When the status bar has moved all the way to the right side, the file transfer is complete.

It's time now to install Netscape. Turn to Chapter 10 for detailed directions.

Getting Connected via the Microsoft Network

The Microsoft Network is Microsoft's very own online service, designed to work in tandem with Windows 95. Starting with version 1.05 of the Microsoft Network software, you have full access to the Internet from your computer—you won't even need Windows 95 Dial-Up Networking. If you have an earlier version of Microsoft Network, however, (which you very well may, because early copies of Windows 95, of course, included earlier versions of Microsoft Network), you'll have to download an update from the Microsoft Network's Internet Center. (You'll also find directions and support for doing this at the Internet Center.)

What You Need

You can run Microsoft Network on any computer that runs Windows 95 and is equipped with a modem. For best performance, you should have at least 8MB of RAM. The Microsoft Network software takes up an additional 10MB of disk space. You also need a 9600 bps or faster modem—14,400 or even 28,800 bps is much better.

Getting Ready to Run Netscape with Microsoft Network

There isn't much to this; the Windows 95 installation process installs the Microsoft Network. If you have Windows 95 installed on your machine, you're set. So why doesn't everyone go this route? Well, it's easy—Microsoft made it no trouble at all—but it ain't cheap, and it's certainly not as fast as it could be. Nonetheless, it's the most no-brain method of getting connected. So let's move along to the part where you *do* something....

Getting Netscape from the Internet via Microsoft Network

Microsoft Network comes with the Microsoft Web Explorer—yet another Web browser similar to Netscape but lacking its power. We're going to use the Web Explorer to download Netscape Navigator to your computer. To download Netscape using Microsoft Network's Web Explorer, follow these steps:

1. In the Windows 95 desktop, double-click on The Internet icon.

The Internet

The Microsoft Web Explorer will start, as shown in Figure 9.29.

2. From the Microsoft Web Explorer menu bar, select File ➤ Open. The Open Internet Address dialog box will appear.

3. In the Open Internet Address dialog box's Address text box, type `ftp://ftp.netscape.com/netscape/windows`. Press ↵. In a few seconds, the contents of Netscape's FTP server will appear, as shown in Figure 9.30.

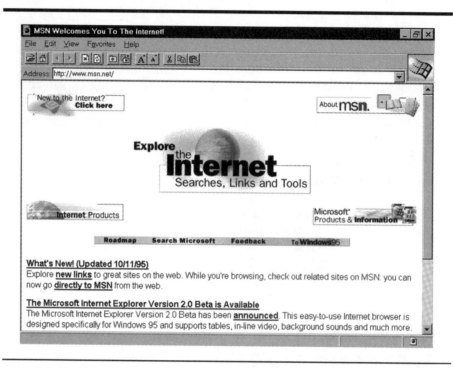

FIGURE 9.29: The Microsoft Network online service comes with Microsoft Internet Explorer, a Web browser.

4. Click on the link n32e20.exe. The Confirm File Open dialog box will appear, as shown here.

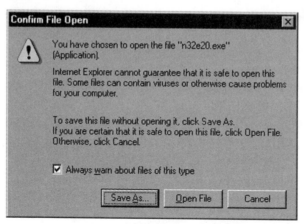

```
any underlying information or technology except in full compliance with
all United States and other applicable laws and regulations.  In particular,
but without limitation, none of the Software or underlying information or
technology may be downloaded or otherwise exported or re-exported (i) into
(or to a national or resident of) Cuba, Haiti, Iraq, Libya, Yugoslavia,
North Korea, Iran, or Syria or (ii) to anyone on the US Treasury
Department's list of Specially Designated Nationals or the US Commerce
Department's Table of Deny Orders.  By downloading the Software, you are
agreeing to the foregoing and you are representing and warranting that you
are not located in, under control of, or a national or resident of any
such country or on any such list.

REDISTRIBUTION and MIRRORING
<font size=+2><b>Redistribution Not Permitted</b></font> --
unless you are an educational institution and want to mirror for your
faculty, staff and students.  If you want to mirror, or are uncertain
about what to do, please see <a href="http://home.netscape.com/comprod/mirror/mirror_application.html">
http://home.netscape.com/comprod/mirror/mirror_application.html</a>
or send email to <a href="mailto:mirror@netscape.com">mirror@netscape.com</a>.
```

Up one level

Name	Size	Modified	Type
.message	2KB	Sep 28 01:21	File
license	14KB	Sep 27 22:47	File
n16e20.exe	1627KB	Sep 27 22:50	File
n32e20.exe	1747KB	Sep 27 22:49	File
readme.txt	12KB	Sep 27 22:47	File

Click here

FIGURE 9.30: The Netscape FTP server as seen from the Microsoft Internet Explorer

5. In the Confirm Open dialog box, click on the Save As button.

6. In the Save As dialog box's File Name text box, type **c:\n32e20.exe**. Press ↵. The file will transfer from Netscape's FTP server to your machine. You can monitor the transfer progress by looking at the bar that appears along the right side of the status bar at the bottom of the Web Explorer window.

When the transfer is done, quit the Web Explorer by selecting File ➤ Exit. The now familiar Windows 95 desktop will reappear. You'll have a copy of Netscape on your machine, and you're ready to start installing it. Turn to the next chapter for the scoop on installing Netscape.

Forging Ahead

Whether your preferred connectivity option is Windows 95 Dial-Up Networking, Netcom NetCruiser, CompuServe NetLauncher, or the Microsoft Network, you now have a connection to the Internet going and a copy of Netscape sitting on your hard drive. In the next chapter you'll actually install Netscape, which is a simple enough process. Then, with Netscape installed, you'll be fully equipped to start cruising and using the very wonderful World Wide Web.

Getting Netscape Navigator Going

In Chapter 9 we walked you through actually getting Netscape by downloading the appropriate version from the Internet. In this chapter, we're going to make the software work. First, we'll install it (a simple, largely automatic process), then we'll make it run, and finally we'll show you how to make some minor changes to enhance operations.

Installing Netscape Navigator

Installation varies slightly between the 32- and 16-bit versions of the program. If you are using Windows 95 Dial-Up Networking or the Microsoft Network to connect to the Internet, you downloaded the 32-bit version of Netscape and should follow the directions in the *Installing the 32-bit Netscape Navigator* section. If you are using Netcom NetCruiser or CompuServe NetLauncher, follow the directions in the *Installing the 16-bit Netscape Navigator* section.

A Tale of Two Versions

There are two versions of Netscape Navigator 2. One, the 32-bit version, works with Windows 95 Dial-Up Networking and the Microsoft Network. It offers full Java capability and faster, more reliable response than the other version, the 16-bit version. The 16-bit version works with Compu-Serve NetLauncher, with Netcom NetCruiser, and with many other types of Internet access software. The real difference between these versions is that the 32-bit version works only with a 32-bit operating system—Windows 95, in other words. If you're still using Windows 3.1 or Internet access software that's based on Windows 3.1, you need the 16-bit version of Netscape Navigator 2.

Thus, the file you downloaded in Chapter 9 would have been one file or another, depending on whether you needed the 32-bit version or the 16-bit version. If you are using Windows 95 Dial-Up Networking or the Microsoft Network to connect to the Internet, you downloaded N32E20.EXE—the 32-bit version. If you are connecting with Compu-Serve NetLauncher or Netcom NetCruiser, you downloaded N16E20.EXE—the 16-bit version.

Installing the 32-Bit Version

The 32-bit version of Netscape Navigator works with 32-bit Internet connection software, such as Windows 95 Dial-Up Networking or the Microsoft Network.

Here's how to install it:

1. Click on the Windows 95 Start button to display the Start menu, and select Run. The Run dialog box will appear.

2. In the Open field of the Run dialog box, type **c:\n32e20** and press ↵. A dialog box will appear with a message confirming that you are about to install Netscape Navigator.

3. Click on the Yes button. A dialog box titled Extracting will appear briefly, followed by another welcoming you to Netscape's own Setup program.

4. Click on the Next button to proceed. The Choose Destination Location dialog box will appear, as shown in Figure 10.1. Netscape's Setup program will put Netscape in a folder called C:\Program Files\Netscape\Navigator unless you tell it to do otherwise.

It's best to let this happen, but if you really, really want to, you can specify another folder by clicking on the Browse button to display the Choose Directory dialog box. In the Path field of the Choose Directory dialog box, enter the name of the folder into which you want to install Netscape and click on the OK button.

 Perhaps you've noticed a slight switch in terminology here—suddenly in the middle of talking about Windows 95 folders, we're using a dialog box called Choose Directory....This is just a holdover from the past. Nothing to worry about.

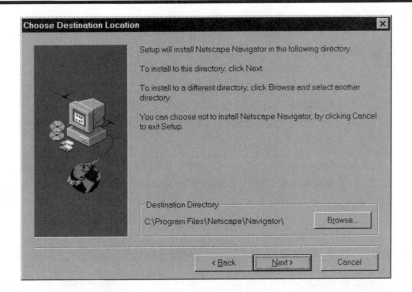

FIGURE 10.1: In the Choose Destination Location dialog box, choose the folder in which you want to store the Netscape files.

Back to business...

5. Click on the Choose Destination Location dialog box's Next button to proceed. At this point, the Setup program will create a new folder in the Windows 95 Program menu named Netscape, which includes an entry for Netscape Navigator. You are not given a choice about where the Setup program places an entry for Netscape. It is always the Netscape folder.

Now Setup will proceed on its own, copying Netscape and all its affiliated files to the folder you chose in Step 3. When all this copying business is over, a dialog box will appear asking if you want to connect Netscape's Setup site. There's no need to do so—click on the No button. Another dialog box will appear, this time saying that installation is complete. Click on the dialog box's OK button to continue. A second dialog box will now appear, giving you the option of reading Netscape's README file. Click on the dialog box's Yes button to read the file. Clicking on the No button ends the installation program and returns you to the Windows Desktop.

The Netscape program archive N32E20.EXE and all its component files are still in your TEMP folder (or wherever you put them). It's always a good idea to have backups in case something unfortunate happens; so copy N32E20.EXE to another folder on your hard disk, just in case. Having done this, you can delete all the files in TEMP and even the folder itself.

You've now got Netscape installed on your machine, but you still have to do a thing or two (or three or four) to set everything up to work properly. Skip to the section titled *Making a Netscape Navigator Connection* to find out about configuring Netscape to work on your machine.

Installing the 16-Bit Version

Until such time as CompuServe and Netcom create 32-bit versions of their Internet connection software, you'll need the 16-bit version of Netscape Navigator to work with CompuServe NetLauncher and Netcom NetCruiser.

The art in this book shows the 32-bit version of Netscape, which was designed for use with Windows 95, but the 16-bit version behaves pretty much identically. You can use this book as a guide to either version.

The installation procedure for the 16-bit Netcscape occurs in two parts, neither of which is very complicated. In the first part, you'll "unpack" and move the file you downloaded in Chapter 9 (N16E20.EXE) to a temporary folder in preparation for installation. In the second part, you'll actually install the software.

Unpacking the Files

The file you downloaded in the last chapter, N16E20.EXE, is what is known as a *self-extracting archive* file. An archive file is one that contains one or more (often *many* more) files that are shrunk to some fraction of their original size. This is much like the *zipping* of files we talked about when we described zipped files and compression technology in Chapter 5. We'll talk more about it in Chapter 11. Archive files and zipped files are a great convenience on the Internet; instead of downloading many large files, you can download one smaller one, which will save you scads of connect time and, therefore, money.

The compressed file that contains Netscape, N16E20.EXE, contains several files, including:

◆ The Netscape program itself

◆ Associated files that are necessary to make it run

◆ Files that contain information about the license you need to use the program

The big difference between this file and the zipped files we've already discussed is that this one is *self-extracting*, which simply means that you don't need any particular unzipping software to restore the file to its original, unpacked state; the file does everything for you.

When you downloaded N16E20.EXE following the earlier steps, it wound up in your C:\ folder. It's a good idea when you unpack any file, however, to do so in a "temporary" folder; this will provide you with an extra measure

of insurance against mixing up the new files with files from another program or with any data you may have lying around. This is a pretty basic procedure—if you have some proficiency in Windows, you'll already know how to do most of this.

Here's how to create a folder called TEMP and move the Netscape archive file there:

1. On the Windows desktop, double-click on the My Computer icon to display the My Computer window.

2. Locate the icon for drive C in the My Computer window, and double-click on it. A window will display the contents of your drive C.

3. From the menu bar in the C:\ window, select File ➤ New ➤ Folder. The New Folder folder will appear in the window.

4. Now type **temp** and press ↵. The name of the new folder will change to what you just typed.

5. We are now ready to move the self-extracting archive file into the folder we just created. Locate N16E20.EXE and click on it to highlight it. It should now appear in reverse video.

6. From the menu bar, select Edit ➤ Cut. The name of the self-extracting archive file will become grayed out.

7. Now double-click on the TEMP folder. A new empty window will appear showing the contents of the folder you've created.

8. Select Edit ➤ Paste from the menu bar to paste the Netscape archive from the clipboard into the folder you created.

Okay, you've got N16E20.EXE in a folder called TEMP. Let's unpack this baby.

9. To unpack the self-extracting archive, double-click on N16E20.EXE.

A DOS window will appear. Because the self-extracting archive is, strictly speaking, a DOS program and not a Windows program, it must unpack itself in a DOS window. Once it is finished unpacking, the title in the title bar of the DOS window will change to Finished. Now, to close the window, click on the close box in the upper-right corner of the DOS window.

When the archive has finished unpacking itself (this should take only a few seconds), all the files that were in the archive will be in your TEMP folder.

If an error message pops up when you're unpacking files you've downloaded, it's probably because something went wrong in the downloading process. No big deal. Simply download the file again, and when you unpack it this time, everything will probably turn out just fine.

Now, with all those files on your machine and unpacked, you're ready to install Netscape.

Installing the Program

With Netscape neatly extracted, you're ready to install the program.

Here's what you do:

1. Click on the Windows 95 Start button to display the Start menu. From the menu, select Run. The Run dialog box will appear.

2. In the Open field of the Run dialog, type **c:\temp\setup** and press ↵. After a brief Please Wait message, you'll see the blue background common to all Windows setup programs; then a dialog box will welcome you to Netscape's own Setup program.

3. Click on the Next button to proceed. The Netscape Navigator Destination Path dialog box will appear, as shown in Figure 10.2. Netscape's Setup program will put Netscape in a folder called \NETSCAPE unless you tell it to do otherwise. It's best to let this happen, but if you really, really want to, you can type another folder name in the Location text box, and Netscape will wind up there.

4. Click on the Next button to proceed. The Select Folder dialog box will appear next, as shown in Figure 10.3. Here you get to choose the program group into which you'd like to place Netscape's icon. By default, Setup will create a group called Netscape 2.0 (makes sense, doesn't it?), and again it's best to just let this happen. If you have some compelling reason to do so, you can create a new group with a different name and make it Netscape's home simply by typing the new name in the Program Folder text box. If instead of either of

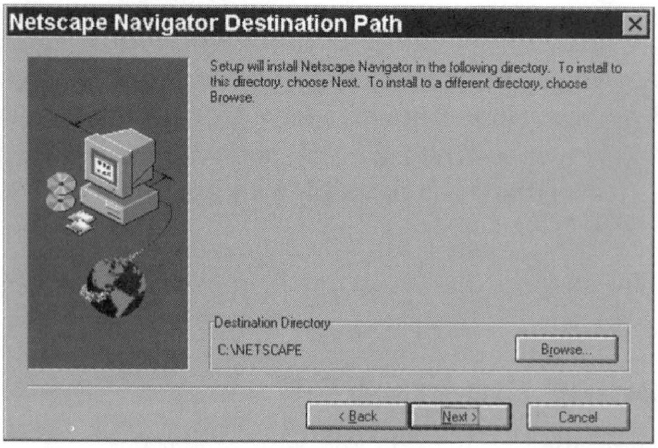

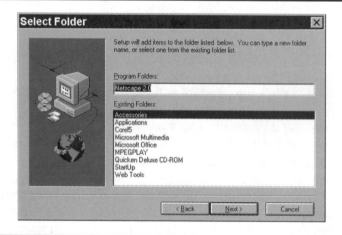

FIGURE 10.2: In the Netscape Navigator Destination Path dialog box, you should accept the default location for the Netscape files unless you have good reason to do otherwise.

FIGURE 10.3: The Select Folder dialog box

these options you want Netscape to reside in a program group that already exists on your system, click once on that group's name in the Existing Folders list. Whatever your choice, click on the Next button to go on when you've made your decision.

From this point, Setup will proceed on its own, copying Netscape and all its affiliated files to the folder you chose in Step 3. When all this copying business is over, installation is complete. One final dialog box will appear, confirming that Netscape was installed correctly and giving you the option of reading Netscape's README.TXT file. Select the dialog box's Yes checkbox and click the Finish button to read the file. Remove any mark from the Yes checkbox by clicking on it, then click on the Finish button to end the installation program and return to the Windows Desktop. The README.TXT file contains important information about using Netscape; so we recommend that you read it. (The file will open in the Windows Notepad. When you're done reading it, select File ➤ Exit from Notepad's menu bar to close Notepad.)

The Netscape program archive N16E20.EXE and all its component files are still in your TEMP folder (or wherever you put them). It's always a good idea to have backups—copy N16E20.EXE to a directory on your hard disk, just in case. Having done this, you can delete all the files in TEMP and the folder itself.

Netscape is installed on your machine, just as we promised, but you still have to set everything up to work together properly. The next section, titled *Making a Netscape Navigator Connection*, shows you how to configure Netscape to work on your machine.

Making a Netscape Navigator Connection

Because Netscape Navigator is an Internet program, you need to start up your Internet connection before you can actually run Netscape. But most of what we're going to do now doesn't require you to be connected to the Internet. These sections are about *creating* the connection, not *using* the connection. First, we're going to start Netscape.

When you use Netscape to access the Internet, you have to engage in a two-step process that involves first starting up your Internet connection and then starting Netscape. In the procedure that follows, we're starting Netscape without first getting connected.

Starting Netscape Navigator

You can start Netscape Navigator in any of several ways:

◆ Double-click on the Netscape Navigator icon on your desktop.

◆ From the Windows 95 Start menu, select Programs ➤ Netscape ➤ Netscape.

◆ Double-click on any Internet shortcut. Once Netscape is installed on your computer, Internet shortcuts may appear as Navigator icons on the Desktop, in other folders, in e-mail messages, or even in other applications' files. You can find out more about Internet shortcuts in Chapter 3.

What's Out There

With your Internet connection going and Netscape up and running, you can find out more about Netscape by choosing Help ➤ Handbook, Help ➤ Release Notes, and Help ➤ Frequently Asked Questions from Netscape's menu bar. Each choice leads to a different page on the Netscape Web server; all these pages are terrifically worthwhile.

Remember—to get connected and use Netscape to surf the Net, you have to start your Internet connection software and *then* start Netscape. But getting connected is not necessary for configuring the software, as we're about to do....

Enhancing the Program's Look and Performance

Okay, we told you in the preceding sections that all you had to do was unpack the files and start up Netscape, and that's true. This is not to say you can't or don't have to configure Netscape; it's just that Netscape can start up and do some useful things before it is configured. You can configure Netscape (if you like) to make it work the way you want it to work.

Configuring Netscape is quick and easy. We've already done a little configuring earlier in the book, but we didn't make a big deal of it. In Chapter 3, we told you how to change the base font to make Netscape display text in a size and color that you like, and then we told you how to get Netscape to load inline images only on demand, speeding up Netscape's performance noticeably. In Chapter 11, we'll tell you how to configure Netscape to use external viewers and players for viewing video and playing sound. Here we're going to make some changes to enhance the cosmetics and performance of the program.

Making the Viewing Area Bigger

Controlling the look of the program is not just a matter of cosmetics; it can be a matter of making the viewing area larger and easier to work with. Above the document-viewing window and below the menu bar, you'll usually see a row of icons representing tools and features, a box showing the URL of the page you are currently viewing, and a row of directory buttons that take you to various Netscape Communications' home pages.

These are handy things to have around. If you want to see the Welcome to Netscape home page, you can simply click on the Welcome button on the row of directory buttons. If you want to view the document you were looking at just a second ago, you can click on the Back button on the tool bar, and so on.

If, however, you'd rather give the Web document you're viewing more room to breathe, you can turn off the tool bar, the Location box, and the directory buttons, in any combination, including all three (see Figure 10.4). Get this: You don't lose anything by turning them off; all their functions are still available on Netscape's menu bar.

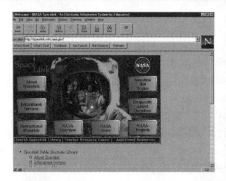

FIGURE 10.4: The Netscape window on the left has the tool bar, the Location box, and directory buttons turned on. The window on the right has all three turned off, making the viewing area a lot bigger.

The tool bar, Location box, and directory buttons are all controlled by a "toggle switch" on Netscape's Options menu. That is, the same option on the menu turns each item both on and off; you can simply select the option once to turn an item off, and then select it again to turn it back on. Fiddle around with these options as you like to see what works for you.

When you've got Netscape's "face" configured to reflect your preferences, you can save your changes by selecting Options ➤ Save Options from Netscape's menu bar. If you don't save your choices, Netscape will go back to its usual configuration (with everything turned on the next time you start the program).

Getting Set Up for Mail and News

Looking past the surface, you might want to tweak a few things in the way Netscape works with mail and news servers. One of the nifty things you can do with Netscape, for example, is to e-mail a page that's caught your eye to a friend or a colleague. To do this, and to read and write articles to Usenet newsgroups, the program has to "know" where to find your Internet service provider's mail and news servers—the computers your provider uses to store and dish up mail and news.

What's Out There

You can learn all the ins and outs of using e-mail from *A Beginner's Guide to Effective E-Mail*, accessible via the URL `http://www.webfoot.com/advice/email.top.html`.

 To find out more about sending a page via e-mail and reading and writing Usenet news, turn to Chapters 2, 3, 4 and 7.

The Mail Server

Specifying the location of your Internet service provider's mail server is an important detail in setting up Netscape, because this is how the program "knows" where to send mail. This is yet another quick and simple Netscape operation. Just follow these steps:

1. From Netscape's menu bar, select Options ➤ Mail and News Preferences. The Mail and News Preferences dialog box will appear.
2. Along the top of the Mail and News Preferences dialog box, select the Servers tab. The contents of the dialog box will change to reflect this choice (see Figure 10.5).

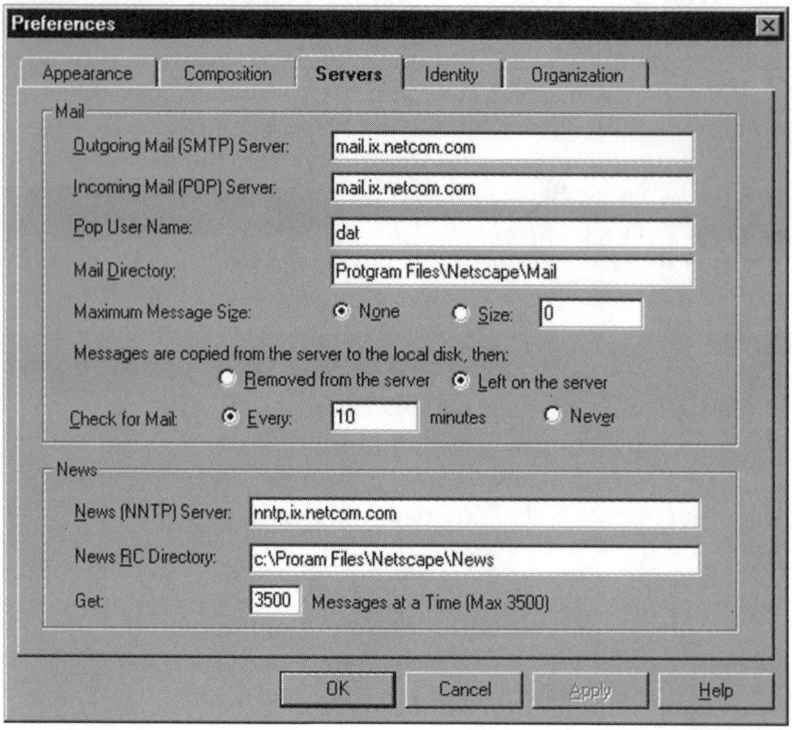

FIGURE 10.5:   The Mail and News Preferences dialog box after it's been filled with e-mail information

3. In the Outgoing Mail (SMTP) Server text box, the presumed name of your provider's mail server appears as *mail.* (SMTP stands for *Simple Mail Transfer Protocol*.) Choose the appropriate address to enter from Table 10.1.

4. In the Incoming Mail (POP) Server text box, the presumed name of your provider's mail POP server appears also as *mail.* (POP stands for *Post Office Protocol*.) Choose the appropriate address to enter from Table 10.1.

TABLE 10.1: Server names for the most common kinds of connections

Connection	Outgoing Mail (SMTP) Server	Incoming Mail (POP) Server	News (NNTP) Server
Microsoft Network	mail.msn.com	mail.msn.com	news.msn.com
CompuServe NetLauncher	mail.compuserve.com	mail.compuserve.com	news.compuserve.com
Netcom NetCruiser	mail.ix.netcom.com	mail.ix.netcom.com	nntp.ix.netcom.com

If you are accessing the Net via a provider other than those shown in Table 10.1, you'll have to find out the server names your provider uses.

5. Now click on the Identity tab along the top of the Preferences dialog box. The contents of the dialog box change to reflect your action.

6. In the Your Name text box, type your name—not your user name, but your real, true, human name.

7. In the Your E-mail text box, type your complete e-mail address.

8. If you want replies to messages that you send to go to an address other than the one you entered in the Your Email field in Step 7, you can enter that address in the Reply-to Address field. If you want replies to your e-mail messages to go to your e-mail address, you can leave this field blank.

9. If you like, you can type the name of your organization (your company or school, perhaps) into the Your Organization text box.

10. You can also arrange matters so that the contents of a short file will be appended to every e-mail message you send. This file is called a *signature* because it appears (like the signature on a letter) at the bottom of every message you send. A signature file can contain your name and e-mail address and maybe a little bit of information about yourself.

It is considered very bad form on the Internet to create a signature file more than four lines in length. To make a "signature" appear at the bottom of your messages, create a file in your word-processing program, save it as a text file with an appropriate filename, and then type that filename along with its path in the Signature File text box.

The Your Name and Your E-mail text boxes must be filled in for you to be able to use either Netscape Mail or Netscape News, the e-mail and Usenet news features in Netscape. This is because your name and e-mail address will appear in the subject headers of messages you send using Netscape.

Once you've got this mail business set up correctly, you won't have to change it (unless you change Internet service providers). The same is true for news, which we'll cover next. You'll be using the same Mail and News Preferences dialog box that we just used to set up mail when you set up news in the next section; so leave the dialog box open.

The News Server

Usenet news looks like it's fully integrated into the Web when you use Netscape to access it, but it's actually delivered to your machine in an interesting way. Unlike the rest of the stuff on the Web, which is delivered to your machine from servers all over the world, Usenet comes to you from a news server machine that is maintained by your Internet service provider. On this machine are copies of Usenet news articles, which the service provider stores and forwards to you. Because of this structure, it's necessary to indicate on which machine your service provider is storing the stuff.

Follow these simple steps to tell Netscape which Usenet news server it can access and exactly where to find that server.

1. With the Mail and News Preferences dialog box still open (you were just using it to set up mail, right?), click on the Directories tab along the top. The contents of the dialog box will update to reflect your choice.

2. Now locate the News section at the bottom of the dialog box. In the News section's News (NNTP) Server text box, the presumed news server name appears as *news*. As you did when configuring mail, you should now look up the name of your news server in Table 10.1 and enter the appropriate name.

Just FYI: NNTP stands for Network News Transfer Protocol. This is the protocol for transferring news on the Internet, just as HTTP is the protocol for transferring hypertext documents on the Internet.

3. Click on the OK button, and the Mail and News Preferences dialog box will close. The Netscape window will reappear.

You're all set. You've got Netscape installed and ready to use. For the sake of form, though, let's look briefly at how to quit the program.

Quitting Netscape Navigator

This is a handy piece of information that we don't want to neglect. When you're done with your travels for the day, simply do the following:

1. From Netscape's menu bar, select File ➤ Exit. This will quit Netscape, but if you happen to have your connection going, it will leave you connected to your Internet service provider, so, in that case...

2. Switch to your connection software—Windows 95 Dial-Up Networking or NetLauncher, for example—and disconnect from the Internet. The way you sever your Internet connection depends on the method and software you use to connect.

You'll be disconnected from your Internet service provider and free now to play with the kids, go to the gym, practice guitar, or whatever.

You're Set to Go

Bingo. You're all set up. You've installed your Internet connection software and Netscape, you know how to start Netscape and make it look the way you want it to, and you can access mail and news servers. If you like, you can turn to Chapter 1 for useful background information or to Chapter 3 to get started navigating with Netscape.

In the next and final chapter, we'll get Netscape to work with video viewers and sound players. This is an option that will enhance the interactivity of your Netscape adventure.

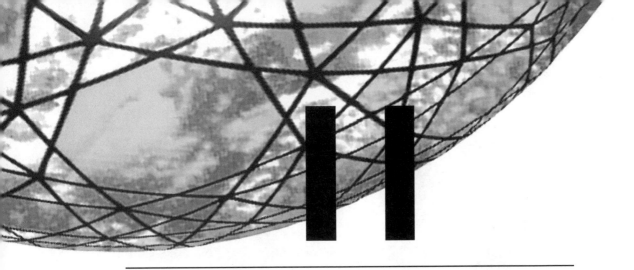

Getting and Installing Video Viewers and Sound Players

In your Web travels, you've probably come across pages that include links to video and sound clips. You can click on these links to view little movies (see Figure 11.1) or play sounds. We've been warning you throughout this book that the files for video and sound can be really big and that, to experience the video or sound, you need external *viewers* or *players*. Viewers and players are special "helper" programs that enable Netscape to handle the video or sound files—really, they're just Windows programs that Netscape calls upon to display or play files it cannot display or play itself.

In this chapter we're going to cover downloading (getting), installing, and using the most useful viewers and players. With these programs and Netscape in your tool kit, you'll be ready to handle video and sound when you encounter it on the Web.

FIGURE 11.1: Stars are interviewed and trailers are shown in an online premiere of a Hollywood movie.

Netscape includes a sound player that can play many of the sound files commonly found on the Web. As long as you have sound hardware (such as a Sound Blaster card) and all the proper Windows sound drivers installed, you can simply click on a link to a sound file, and it will play.

What's Out There

This has nothing to do with viewers and players, really, but you can find a giant archive of Windows programs and other files at the Center for Innovative Computer Applications' FTP server at `ftp://ftp.cica.indiana.edu/pub/pc/win3`. Some really useful stuff is here, so check it out.

What's Available

A number of viewers and players are available to use with Netscape; to pump Netscape up to its best capacity, you might want a video viewer that can handle movies in QuickTime format (with the extension MOV) and in Video for Windows format (AVI) and the sound player RealAudio.

Video and Netscape

The two most popular formats for video on the Web are QuickTime, developed by Apple Computer, and Video for Windows, developed by Microsoft. Although QuickTime was developed by Apple, any video that has the QuickTime extension MOV can be played by any machine that has the correct viewer (the one that works for that machine). In other words, you can play a QuickTime video clip on your PC, even if it was developed on a Mac, as long as you have a QuickTime viewer on your PC.

Functionally, Video for Windows is similar to QuickTime—however, Video for Windows was developed by Microsoft. Windows 95 includes a program that will play Video for Windows files on your computer. All you need to do is configure Netscape to call on this program when it encounters a Video for Windows file. Don't worry—we'll cover this process in this chapter.

Getting and Setting Up the QuickTime Viewer

To view QuickTime video (files that have the extension MOV), you need a QuickTime viewer that works with Netscape. Let's look at how to get such a viewer, how to install it, and how to set it up to work neatly with Netscape.

Downloading the QuickTime Viewer

Before you can view QuickTime video with Netscape, you must *download* (transfer to your system) the correct software. Here's how:

1. With your Internet connection and Netscape both running, select File ➤ Open Location from the menu bar. The Open Location dialog box will appear.

2. In the dialog box, type **http://quicktime.apple.com/form-qt2win.html**. Click on Open. In a few seconds, the QuickTime for Windows page will appear (see Figure 11.2).

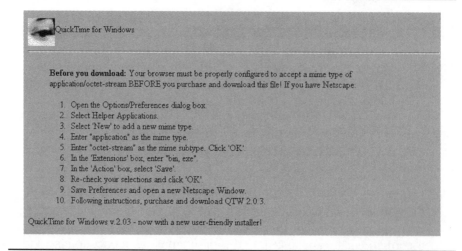

FIGURE 11.2: The QuickTime for Windows page is your key to getting Apple's QuickTime viewer for your PC.

3. Use the scroll bar to scroll down the QuickTime for Windows page until you see the <u>Alright, already! I want it!</u> link. Click on the link, and Netscape will display a page detailing Apple's license agreement.

4. Read the license agreement. If you choose to accept the terms (which you have to if you want to use QuickTime), click on the <u>Yes, I agree to these terms</u> link at the bottom of the page. The Unknown File Type dialog box will appear.

5. In the Unknown File Type dialog box, click on the Save to Disk button. The Unknown File Type dialog box will be replaced by the Save As dialog box.

6. In the Save As dialog box's File name field, type **c:\qtinstal.exe** and click on the Save button. The Save As dialog box will close, and the Saving Location dialog box will appear in its place.

7. When the Saving Location dialog box goes away, the transfer is done. Close Netscape by selecting File ➤ Exit from the menu bar. The Windows 95 Desktop will reappear.

 Transferring a file is not the same as installing the software contained in the file. When you transfer the file, you are simply moving the (presumably) zipped file from its location elsewhere to your machine, where it is simply stored until you unzip it and actually install the software. Installing software these days is usually a pretty simple process—a lot of software installs itself by checking out your machine and what's already on it, then fitting itself in, and making necessary adjustments along the way.

Installing the QuickTime Viewer

Now, with the QuickTime viewer file transferred to your machine, it's time to install the software on your hard disk. Here's how:

1. From the Windows 95 Start menu, select Run. The Run dialog box will appear.

2. In the Run dialog box's Open text box, type **c:\qtinstal.exe** ↵. The Begin Install dialog box will appear, as shown in Figure 11.3.

3. Click on the Begin Install dialog box's Install button. The installation program will start searching your computer to see if you already have a version of QuickTime installed. Once the check is finished, the Complete Install dialog box will appear.

4. In the Complete Install dialog box, click on the Install button. Files will now be copied into your Windows folder.

5. Now click on the OK button to return to the desktop, which now has a QuickTime for Windows window visible.

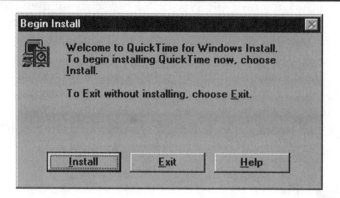

FIGURE 11.3: The Begin Install dialog box is where you begin installing the QuickTime viewer.

You can see a sample of QuickTime video by double-clicking on the QuickTime for Windows window's It's QuickTime icon.

Now let's set up Netscape so that it will automatically call on the viewer you've installed whenever it encounters QuickTime files.

Configuring Netscape to Use the QuickTime Viewer

Actually configuring Netscape to use the QuickTime viewer you've installed is quite simple. (Configuring Netscape is strictly a local operation—it affects only your copy of the program, so there is no need to do this while you are connected to the Net.)

1. Start Netscape (if you happened to end your Net connection at the end of the last procedure, don't bother to connect now). From Netscape's menu bar, select Options ➤ General Preferences. The Preferences dialog box will appear.

2. Click on the Helpers tab, which is along the top of the Preferences dialog box. The Preferences dialog box will update to reflect your choice; it should now look similar to Figure 11.4.

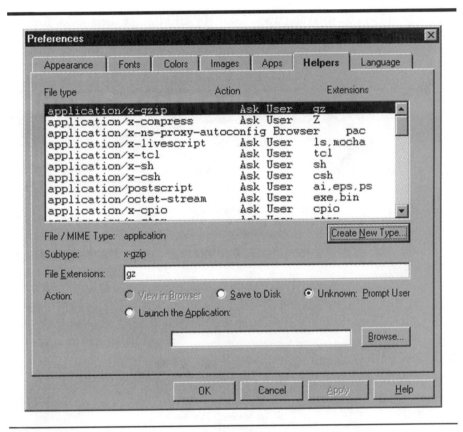

FIGURE 11.4: The Preferences dialog box as it appears after you choose Help Apps

3. In the File type list (shown in Figure 11.5), locate the entry for `video/quicktime`. Click once on this entry.

4. In the Action section near the bottom of the window, click on the radio button for the Launch the Application option. Then, in the text box below the button, type **c:\windows\player.exe**. (Note that you don't type the period at the end. See Figure 11.5 for an example.)

5. Click on OK to close the Preferences dialog box. The Netscape window will reappear.

Now you're set—but you're not connected to the Internet at the moment. You'll have to get connected to actually view anything. Start up your Internet connection and launch Netscape, and then you can view QuickTime movies that are linked to Web pages simply by clicking on their links. Just remember when you do this that QuickTime movies can be big—many megabytes—and can take lots of time to transfer to your computer.

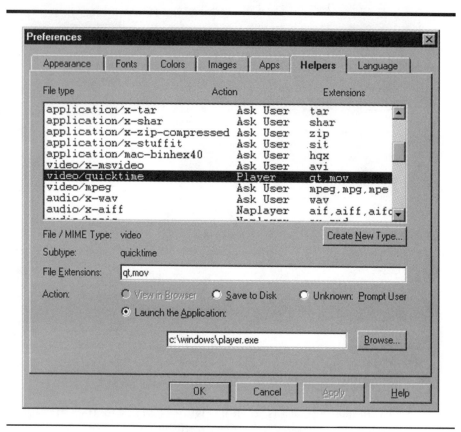

FIGURE 11.5: Type c:\windows\player.exe in the text box, as shown here.

Setting Up the Video for Windows Player

Windows 95 actually comes with all the software you need to play Video for Windows files (AVI files) on your computer. There is nothing that you need to download or install to make it work—all the work has been done for you. You do, however, have to fiddle around with Netscape a little to make the Netscape browser work with Video for Windows files.

Configuring Netscape to Use the Video for Windows Player

Windows 95 comes with the software you need to play Video for Windows files, but Netscape doesn't come "knowing" about that software—you have to configure Netscape to recognize and work with Video for Windows files. This is a straightforward process that we can easily detail.

1. Start Netscape. (No need to get connected to the Internet for this process.) From Netscape's menu bar, select Options ➤ General Preferences. The Preferences dialog box will appear.

2. Click on the Help Apps tab, which is along the top of the Preferences dialog box. The Preferences dialog box will update to reflect your choice (see Figure 11.4).

3. In the Preferences dialog box's File type list, locate the entry for `video/x-msvideo` and click once on it.

4. In the Action section, which is near the bottom of the window, click on the Launch the Application radio button. Then, in the text box below the button, type **c:\windows\mplayer.exe**.

5. Click on OK to close the Preferences dialog box, leaving you with the familiar Netscape window visible.

That's all there is to it. Netscape is ready to play Video for Windows files as you cruise the Web, and you're set for total film enjoyment. Now whenever you click on a link that goes to an AVI file, Netscape will transfer that file to your computer, and in an automatic process, the Video for Windows player will show the movie.

Sound and Netscape

Netscape comes all set up to play the heretofore most common types of sound files—Sun Audio (with the extension AU), Microsoft Windows (WAV), and Macintosh (SND)—but you may wonder what (if any) additional sound program you can use. ...Well, in addition to the commonly experienced sound files mentioned, more and more Web sites are including RealAudio links.

RealAudio files have the extension RA or RAM. Unlike AU and SND files, RA and RAM files don't actually contain sound. Instead they contain just enough data to "point" the RealAudio player on your machine to a RealAudio server, which then will feed the actual sound to your machine. The advantage to this is that with RealAudio you can hear sound as soon as you click on the link, whereas with other sound formats, you must wait for the entire sound file to download before you can hear anything. RealAudio opens up lots of cool possibilities for sound on the Web. For example, radio can be broadcast over the Internet in *netcasts*. National Public Radio now netcasts its programming; so does ABC News. In fact, the advent of live radio broadcasting via the Net is not far off, if it hasn't already occurred by the time you read this book.

What's Out There

For a quick intro to what's happening in sound on the Web, check out National Public Radio at http://www.npr.org and ABC news at http://www.realaudio.com/contentp/abc.html. Then drop by the Internet Underground Music Archive (IUMA). IUMA includes digitized sound from many alternative bands at the URL http://www.iuma.com.

Downloading RealAudio

Before you can use RealAudio, you have to download it from the RealAudio Web site. Sometimes you'll encounter a Web page that includes RealAudio links and provides a convenient button for getting RealAudio so that you can get the full, rich audio impact of those links. That's all well and good, but if you don't want to wait for such an occasion, follow these instructions to get the RealAudio player:

1. From Netscape's menu bar, select File ➤ Open Location. The Open Location dialog box will appear.

2. In the Open Location dialog box, type `http://www.realaudio.com/release/download.html`. Click on Open. The RealAudio Player Download page will appear, as shown in Figure 11.6.

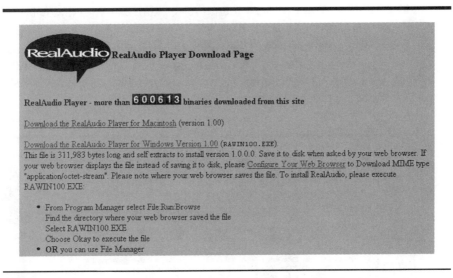

FIGURE 11.6: You can download the Windows version of the RealAudio player (that's the one you need) from the RealAudio Player Download page.

3. Click on the <u>Download the RealAudio Player for Windows</u> link. The Unknown File Type dialog box will appear.

4. Click on the Unknown File Type dialog box's Save to disk button. The Save As dialog box will appear.

5. In the Save As dialog box's File Name text box, type **c:\rawin.exe** and click on the OK button. The Saving Location dialog box will appear.

6. The Saving Location dialog box's progress meter will show the progress of downloading the RealAudio player. When the transfer is done, the dialog box will close, and the Netscape window will be visible.

7. Quit Netscape by selecting File ➤ Exit from the Netscape menu bar. The familiar Windows desktop will become visible.

Now you've got the RealAudio installation program on your computer, and you're ready to install the RealAudio player.

Installing the RealAudio Player

Getting RealAudio working with Netscape is a breeze. In this section you'll run the program that you just downloaded from the RealAudio Web site. That program will install the RealAudio player on your computer and configure Netscape to call on it.

1. From the Windows Start menu, select Run. The Run dialog box will appear.

2. In the Run dialog box's Open text box, type **c:\rawin.exe** (the name you gave the file in the procedure before this one) and press ↵. After a few seconds, the RealAudio Setup program will start. Figure 11.7 shows the Setup program's opening screen for RealAudio 1.0.

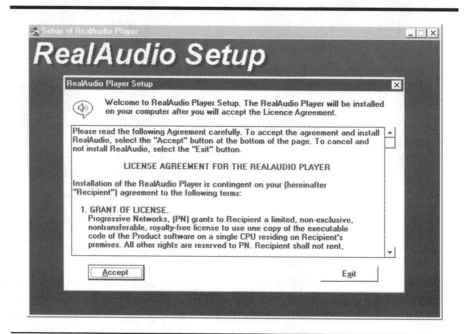

FIGURE 11.7: The RealAudio Setup program very conveniently installs the RealAudio player and even configures Netscape to work with it. Be sure to read the license agreement.

3. Read the RealAudio license agreement and click on the Accept button. The dialog box displaying the license agreement will close and a dialog box asking for your name will appear.

4. In the Setup dialog box's Name text box, type your name. If you like, you can also enter your company's name in the Company text box. Once you have entered this information, click on the Continue button.

5. A dialog box will appear confirming your name. If your name looks right and your company's name is correct (if you entered your company's name), click on the OK button to continue. If you see a typo in your name, click on the Change button and go back to Step 4 to fix it. Once you click on the Continue button, a dialog box will appear in which you can choose between two setup methods.

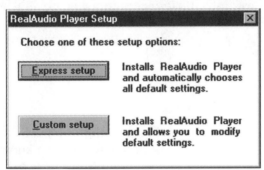

◆ Express setup does everything for you—even determining which Web browser you're using

◆ Custom setup lets you specify where (on which disk and in which folder) RealAudio files will be stored and which Web browser(s) you're using

Express setup is so convenient and generally on the mark that we recommend you simply go with it unless you have some compelling reason (and the skills) to do otherwise.

6. Click on the Express setup button. The RealAudio Setup program will start—files will be copied to your computer, as evidenced by a dialog box showing a progress meter.

7. Some dialog boxes may appear asking questions about which Web browser you have. In any dialog box that asks about Netscape, click on the Yes button.

When RealAudio is fully installed on your computer, you will *hear* a message from the RealAudio people telling you that the software is installed.

RealAudio is installed on your computer and all set to act as a nifty conduit for streams of sound from audio servers around the Internet universe.

What's Out There

News, sports events, talk shows, and other radio netcast events can be heard via Audionet at `http://www.audionet.com`. We the People, a progressive netcast talkshow hosted by former presidential hopeful and ex-California Governor Jerry Brown, is at `http://www.realaudio.com/contentp/rabest/wethepeople.html`.

You're All Set

So—you're a master Web navigator and burgeoning Web publisher after reading the earlier chapters in this book, and now you even know how to get and use viewers and players to augment your Netscape experience. You're ready to proceed full steam ahead into your World Wide Web travels using Netscape.

Bon voyage!

Get Smart with SmartMarks

Netscape's bookmarks feature is great for tracking a handful of your favorite Web sites, but it isn't as well suited for tracking *lots* of Web sites. And, at the rate the Web grows, your Bookmarks menu is highly likely to grow much too large for you to manage effectively very soon. Not to worry—SmartMarks is here.

This Netscape add-on is designed especially to help you manage the hundreds—if not tens of thousands—of Web sites you'll find filled with information that interests you. SmartMarks (once it's installed on your computer) takes over Netscape's Bookmarks menu, letting you make the most of many new options for organizing and searching your bookmarks, and even monitoring your favorite sites for updates. SmartMarks also offers you a wonderful way to search the Web and find those fascinating sites, via an easy-to-use interface to four popular Web searching resources: Yahoo, Lycos, InfoSeek, and WebCrawler. (More are sure to follow.) All the handy features you find in SmartMarks will convince you quickly that this program is a necessity for any serious Web surfer.

You can get SmartMarks from the Netscape site via downloading. The process is much like the one you probably went through to get Netscape Navigator.

In this chapter we'll show you how to:

◆ Download SmartMarks from the Netscape Web site

◆ Install SmartMarks on your computer

◆ Use SmartMarks to organize your bookmarks

◆ Set up SmartMarks to notify you when any of your favorite Web sites changes

First, let's go out on the Net and get the software. This is going to be an easy downloading process.

Getting SmartMarks from the Internet

SmartMarks isn't automatically a part of Netscape—this convenient program is a separate animal, which you must download from Netscape's Internet site, just as you downloaded Netscape itself earlier (in Chapter 9). There is one big difference, however, and that is that now you have Netscape, so you can use it to download SmartMarks from the Netscape site. In the Netscape site (on the home page, actually), you'll find a link to the Netscape Now! pages, which make downloading Netscape software as easy as 1-2-3.

What's Out There

The Netscape Now! page at http://home.netscape.com/comprod/mirror gives you quick access to the latest version of all Netscape software, including SmartMarks.

To download SmartMarks from the Netscape Now! pages, follow these steps:

1. From the Netscape menu bar, choose File ➤ Open Location. The Open Location dialog box will appear.

2. In the Open Location dialog box's text box, type `http://home.netscape.com/comprod/mirror`, and then click on Open. The first Netscape Now! page will appear, as shown in Figure A.1. This page asks the first question of three questions you'll answer in order to download SmartMarks.

3. The first question is: Which operating system are you using?

   ◆ If you're running the 16-bit version of Netscape, you're almost certainly using Windows 3.1; so click on the <u>Windows 3.1</u> link.

   ◆ If you're running the 32-bit version of Netscape, you're using either Windows 95 or Windows NT; so click on the <u>Windows 95 or NT</u> link.

There are also choices available for the Mac and Unix operating systems, but this is a Windows book—so forget them. The second Netscape Now! page will appear. What it looks like will depend on which choice you

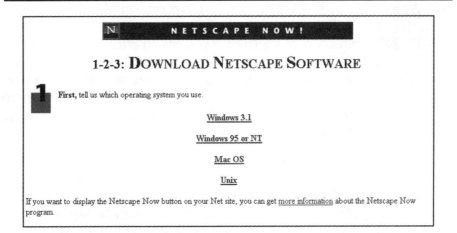

FIGURE A.1: This is the first of three successive Netscape Now! pages that give you quick, easy access to Netscape software, including SmartMarks.

made in answering the operating system question. Here, the question is: Which of the products available for this operating system do you want? When we selected the <u>Windows 95 or NT</u> link, we were offered downloading links for:

◆ Netscape Navigator 2

◆ Netscape Navigator 1.22

◆ Netscape SmartMarks

◆ Netscape Chat

4. You can download any program listed on the page by clicking on its link. You want SmartMarks at the moment; so click on the <u>Netscape SmartMarks</u> link. The third Netscape Now! page will appear.

5. The third Netscape Now! page (shown in Figure A.2) lists the servers—along with their locations—from which you can download Smart-Marks. Look through the list, and choose the server that's geographically closest to you—remember, nearby servers are always faster to respond than those far away. Click on the <u>Download</u> link next to the server you want. The Unknown File Type dialog box will appear.

Following the release of a new version of Netscape, the servers from which you download Netscape's software are often terribly overwhelmed. If you get an error message saying all the servers are busy—or if nothing happens when you click on a server link—try a different server. If that doesn't work, try again later. In general, you'll have the best luck accessing Netscape's servers at odd times of the day, and the worst luck at lunchtime.

6. In the Unknown File Type dialog box, click on the Save to Disk button. The Save As dialog box will appear.

7. In the Save As dialog box's text box, a filename will appear. *Make a note of this filename; you're going to need to know it in a little while.* Type **c:** before the filename in the text box. This will plunk the Smart-Marks file as it's downloaded into a location that will be easy to find when you perform the installation process later in this appendix.

Download	Netscape Communications Corp., Mountain View, California, USA
Download	Netscape Communications Corp., Mountain View, California, USA
Download	Netscape Communications Corp., Mountain View, California, USA
Download	Netscape Communications Corp., Mountain View, California, USA
Download	Netscape Communications Corp., Mountain View, California, USA
Download	Netscape Communications Corp., Mountain View, California, USA
Download	Netscape Communications Corp., Mountain View, California, USA
Download	Netscape Communications Corp., Mountain View, California, USA

ASIA

Download	Keio University, Japan
Download	Institute of Physical and Chemical Research (RIKEN), Saitama, Japan
Download	Radiation Lab/Accelerator Research Facility, Japan
Download	Hebrew University of Jerusalem, Israel

AUSTRALIA

Download	University of Adelaide

NORTH AMERICA

Download	University of Illinois School of Life Sciences, Illinois
Download	Massachusetts Institute of Technology, Cambridge Massachusetts
Download	New York University, New York
Download	Washington University, St. Louis, Missouri
Download	University of Nebraska, Omaha, Nebraska
Download	University of North Carolina

FIGURE A.2: In the third Netscape Now! page, you choose the server from which you'll download software. Select one that's geographically near you.

8. Click on the Save button to start the transfer. The Saving Location dialog box will appear. Its progress meter will indicate the transfer's progress.

When the Saving Location dialog box closes, the transfer is done. Now you have a copy of Netscape's SmartMarks program on your machine, and you're ready to install the software.

Installing SmartMarks

Let's get this software installed and running. Installing SmartMarks couldn't be easier—you'll probably even recall some of this procedure from installing Netscape itself.

To install SmartMarks, follow these steps:

1. From the Windows Start menu, select Programs ➤ MS-DOS Prompt. (The software you downloaded from Netscape is a Windows product, but it comes compressed as a self-extracting DOS file, which is not as weird as it might seem.) The MS-DOS Prompt window will appear, with a DOS prompt (which may have something such as C:\WINDOWS in it).

2. Remember how cleverly we put the SmartMarks files in a location that would be easy to find? To be sure we're in that location, type **cd** and press *f*. The DOS prompt will change to show the directory you're in (it should be C:\).

3. Now we need to create a temporary directory to hold the files used to install SmartMarks. Type **mkdir sm** and press *f*. Nothing's going to appear to show you that the directory has been created—but it has. The DOS prompt (C:\) will reappear.

4. To go to the directory you just created, type **cd sm** and press *f*. The prompt will change to show the current directory, C:\SM.

5. Now, to unpack the SmartMarks files, type a \ followed *immediately* by the filename you jotted down earlier (no space between the \ and the filename) and press *f*. As the files are unpacked, a list of them will appear. When the whole shebang is done, the C:\SM prompt will reappear.

6. Type **exit** and press *f* to close the MS-DOS Prompt window and return to Windows.

Okey dokey. You've got the SmartMarks files unpacked and in the C:\SM directory. Next, you'll run the SmartMarks set-up program to get everything all set up.

1. From the Windows Start menu, select Run. The Run dialog box will appear.

2. In the Run dialog box's text box, type **c:\ns\setup**, as shown in Figure A.3.

3. Click on the OK button. In a few seconds, the SmartMarks Setup dialog box will appear (see Figure A.4).

4. In this dialog box, a suggested location (C:\SMRTMRKS) for Smart-Marks to make its permanent home will appear. You can, if you have some compelling reason to, indicate some other location, but why? Click on the Continue button to go on. The Product Registration dialog box will appear.

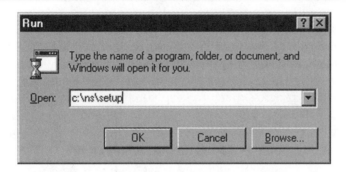

FIGURE A.3: The Run dialog box will get the SmartMarks installation program started.

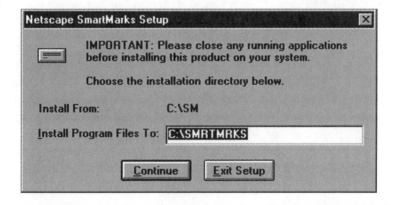

FIGURE A.4: In the SmartMarks Setup dialog box, you'll indicate just where you want SmartMarks to reside.

5. In the Product Registration dialog box's Name text box, type your name. You may also enter your company name in the Company name text box if you like. And, if your time zone does not appear in the Timezone field, click on the down-arrow and select the correct one from the list that appears. The other fields in the dialog box will be all filled in. Just leave them alone.

6. Click on the Continue button. A slightly modified Product Registration dialog box will appear, displaying all the information you just entered and asking you to verify its correctness. If everything's a-okay, click on the Yes button to continue. (If something's wrong, click on the No button and return to Step 5 to fix the problem; then click on Yes to go on.) The Installing Netscape SmartMarks dialog box will appear, with a progress meter to keep you informed of the highly automated installation's progress.

7. When installation is complete, a dialog box will appear informing you so. Click on the dialog box's OK button.

8. Now a dialog box will appear asking if you want to see the README file. Click on the Yes button, and the Setup program will close. Netscape will start, and the README file will be in view so you can read it—this file's filled with important information about Smart-Marks, so don't skip it.

9. To exit Netscape, from the Netscape menu bar, select File ➤ Exit. The familiar Windows desktop will appear.

Installation is complete—easy, eh? From now on, whenever you start Netscape, SmartMarks will start along with it. You'll know SmartMarks is there because you'll see a button for it on the Windows task bar. You'll also notice in the Bookmarks menu on the Netscape menu bar that Smart-Marks appears as a couple of menu items and that your bookmarks are "gone." (Don't worry—we'll show you how to import your old bookmarks into a SmartMarks folder so that you don't have to rebuild your Bookmarks list. See *Adding Your Existing Bookmarks to SmartMarks* later in this appendix.)

 As one of its nifty organizational features, SmartMarks lets you put bookmarks into different folders. It even starts out its existence in your life with some folders in place that already have bookmarks in them.

Using SmartMarks

So now that you have SmartMarks installed, what do you do with it? As mentioned, SmartMarks is designed to help you navigate the Web quickly and efficiently. Here's how.

Starting SmartMarks

You can start SmartMarks simply by starting Netscape—SmartMarks will also start automatically. Many SmartMarks features can be accessed directly from the Bookmarks menu; because SmartMarks is running whenever you start Netscape, all you'll have to do is pull down the Bookmarks menu to use SmartMarks for those features. For example, you can add bookmarks this way. More on this as we go along....

Some SmartMarks features, however, can be accessed only through the SmartMarks window. To open the SmartMarks window, from the Netscape menu bar, select Bookmarks ➤ View SmartMarks. The SmartMarks window will appear. Let's go over some of what you see in this window and the things you can do with it.

Looking into the SmartMarks Window

Looking into the SmartMarks window (see Figure A.5), you'll see that it's divided into three sections. The upper-left portion contains a list of folders—with SmartMarks you can organize your bookmarks into folders just as you did with Netscape's bookmarks. The upper-right portion contains a list of those bookmarks that are contained in the currently open folder. Along the bottom of the Window is the Web Monitor, the tool that automatically monitors specified Web pages for changes. We'll go over all these features as we go along.

To open a SmartMarks folder, click on the folder name. To load any page into Netscape, double-click on the bookmark for that page.

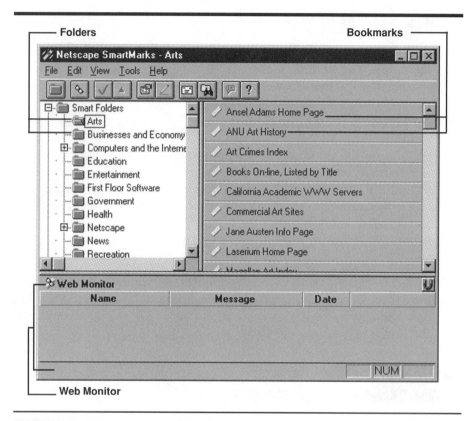

FIGURE A.5: The SmartMarks window

Adding Bookmarks to SmartMarks Folders

When you come across a page that you like so much you want to keep track of it, add a bookmark for it to a SmartMarks folder. This is very similar to what you did before when you used Netscape's Bookmarks menu.

To add a bookmark to a SmartMarks folder, you have two options. You can:

◆ Add the bookmark to the special SmartMarks folder named Bookmark Menu, whose contents then appear on Netscape's Bookmarks menu

or

◆ Add the bookmark to any SmartMarks folder

The advantage of the first option is that you can use the Bookmarks menu as a direct route to the page without having to get into the SmartMarks window. The disadvantage is that if you add lots of bookmarks this way your Bookmarks menu will become unwieldy. The advantage of the second option is that you can then group similar bookmarks in a single folder, providing for better organization; the disadvantage is that to access those nicely organized bookmarks you first have to open the SmartMarks window. Which is better is your call.

Adding a Bookmark to the Bookmark Menu Folder

To add a bookmark to the Bookmark Menu folder, which is a special folder whose contents appear on the Bookmarks menu, first open the page you want to bookmark in Netscape. Now, from the Netscape menu bar, select Bookmarks ➤ Add SmartMark. You won't see anything change or appear, but rest assured, the pages will be added to SmartMarks' Bookmark Menu folder. Next time you open the Bookmarks menu, the bookmark you just added will appear there.

Adding a Bookmark to a SmartMarks Folder

The Bookmark Menu folder is just one folder—albeit a special one. If you were to add all your bookmarks to this one folder, you'd end up with the same problem you might have had with Netscape's regular old bookmarks—too many bookmarks all mixed up together. To remedy this, you can add bookmarks to any SmartMarks folder. (You can even create your own folders to hold bookmarks, and you can name these folders so you know which ones contain what stuff. We'll show you how later in this appendix.) This will keep them organized as neatly as your filing cabinet.

To add a new bookmark to a SmartMarks folder, follow these steps:

1. With Netscape running and the page you want to add to a SmartMarks folder in view, from the menu bar, select Bookmarks ➤ File SmartMark. The Add SmartMark dialog box will appear (see Figure A.6).

2. In the Add SmartMark dialog box's File Into Folder list, highlight the folder into which you want to place the bookmark.

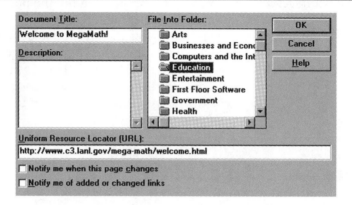

Document Title:
Welcome to MegaMath!

Description:

File Into Folder:
- Arts
- Businesses and Econc
- Computers and the Int
- **Education**
- Entertainment
- First Floor Software
- Government
- Health

OK
Cancel
Help

Uniform Resource Locator (URL):
http://www.c3.lanl.gov/mega-math/welcome.html

☐ Notify me when this page changes
☐ Notify me of added or changed links

FIGURE A.6: The Add SmartMark dialog box allows you to add a new bookmark to any SmartMarks folder.

3. In the dialog box's Description text box, type a description of the bookmark you are going to place in the folder. You can use this description later to help you locate SmartMarks folders and bookmarks; so describe the content clearly.

You can have SmartMarks automatically monitor this bookmark for changes by selecting either the Notify Me When This Page Changes or the Notify Me of Added or Changed Links checkbox. (We discuss using SmartMarks to monitor specified Web pages for changes in <u>Monitoring Pages for Changes</u>, later in this appendix.)

4. Once you've entered all the appropriate information in the Add SmartMark dialog box, click on the OK button. The dialog box will close, and the SmartMarks window will reappear. It will be more or less covering the Netscape window.

Now you undoubtedly want to get surfing with Netscape (and maybe use your newly ensconced bookmark). To get the SmartMarks window out of the way and switch back to Netscape, simply click on any scrap of the Netscape window that's showing.

There's nothing except your own good sense of organizational aesthetics stopping you from placing one bookmark in a bunch of folders.

Getting Rid of a Bookmark

When you get tired of a page or a site and you want to clean up your folders to wipe that old junk out of your way, you can get rid of a bookmark listed in a SmartMarks folder. To do this, either

♦ Remove the bookmark from a single folder, leaving it in any other folders in which it may appear

or

♦ Delete the bookmark altogether from SmartMarks, removing it from any and all folders in which it may appear

Let's look at both of these techniques.

Removing a Bookmark from a SmartMarks Folder

It's old, it's useless, it's boring, it's out of here. To remove a bookmark from a single folder, follow these steps:

1. Open the SmartMarks window if it's not already open. Along the left portion of the SmartMarks window, click on the folder that contains the bookmark you want to remove. The right section of the window will update to show the bookmarks in that particular folder.

2. Locate the bookmark of disinterest in the area along the right side of the window, and right-click on it. A menu will appear.

3. From the menu, choose Remove From Folder. The bookmark you no longer want will disappear from the folder.

That, friends, is all there is to removing a bookmark from a single folder. If that was the only folder that contained the deleted bookmark, all is said and done. If the bookmark was also contained in other folders, however, it will still appear in those other folders.

Adding Your Existing Bookmarks to SmartMarks

When you start Netscape for the first time after installing SmartMarks, you may notice that all your old, carefully compiled bookmarks seem to have vanished. Your Bookmarks menu now contains only a few entries, all having to do with SmartMarks. Not to worry. You can easily import your existing bookmark file into SmartMarks bookmarks so that it appears as another SmartMarks folder.

1. From the Netscape menu bar, select Bookmarks ➤ View SmartMarks. The SmartMarks window will appear (over the Netscape window).

2. From the SmartMarks menu bar, select Tools ➤ Import. The Select a File to Import dialog box will appear.

3. Navigate to your Netscape directory—it is most likely C:\PROGRA~1\ NETSCAPE\NAVIGA~1—and highlight the file BOOKMARK.HTM. (Note that SmartMarks does not support Windows 95 long filenames. All those long filenames that Windows 95 would allow are munged down to old-style DOS filenames.) Click on OK. The Import dialog box will close, and the SmartMarks window will include a new folder.

SmartMarks has imported the contents of your BOOKMARKS file into a SmartMarks folder named automatically—and appropriately enough—after you. For example, DANIEL A. TAUBER'S BOOKMARKS. To move all your old bookmarks to this folder, follow these steps:

1. Click on the folder to open it. The bookmarks in it will appear in a list along the right side of the window.

2. Highlight all the bookmarks in the list, and then drag them to the Bookmark Menu folder. (If you click on the folder to open it, you'll see them there; but there's no need to do so.)

The SmartMarks window is over the Netscape window; you can switch to Netscape by clicking on any corner or piece of its window. Now if you pull down the Bookmarks menu, all your bookmarks will appear there, waiting for you to use them.

Deleting a Bookmark Altogether from SmartMarks

Removing a bookmark from a single folder is fine for simple housekeeping, but sometimes you want a major overhaul that involves purging a single file from many locations. What do you do when you want to remove a bookmark from all SmartMarks folders? Maybe the page it points to no longer exists, or maybe it just doesn't hold your interest any more. For this process, you'll use the Delete option. To remove a bookmark from every single folder in which it appears, follow these steps:

1. Open the SmartMarks window if it's not already open. Along the left portion of the window, click on the folder that contains the bookmark you want to delete. The right section of the window will update to show the bookmarks in that particular folder.

2. Locate the bookmark of disinterest in the area along the right side of the window, and right-click on it. A menu will appear.

3. From the menu, choose Delete. The Deleting dialog box will appear.

4. The Deleting dialog box (see Figure A.7) will list all the folders that contain this particular bookmark. Click on the Yes button to delete the bookmark from all the folders listed. (If you highlighted more than one bookmark in Step 2, selecting Yes to All will delete all the highlighted bookmarks without further questions or ado.)

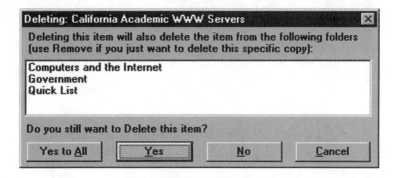

FIGURE A.7: The Deleting dialog box

The bookmark is now gone both from the folder that's open and obvious and from all the SmartMarks folders it once called home.

Creating Your Own SmartMarks Folders

Not only can you add bookmarks to SmartMarks, you can also create your own folders. For example, you might want to create a folder for related sites (all the food and beverage sites, all the travel sites, all the home office sites). You might even want to reorganize by moving some things from the existing SmartMarks folders into your own. To do any of this, you must first create an appropriately named and designated folder. Follow these steps:

1. From the Netscape menu, select Bookmarks ➤ View SmartMarks. The SmartMarks window will appear.

2. From the SmartMarks menu, select File ➤ New Folder. The Assistant dialog box will appear, as shown in Figure A.8.

FIGURE A.8: The Smart Folder Assistant will help you create new folders to hold SmartMarks bookmarks.

3. In the dialog box's Folder Name text box, type a descriptive name for the new folder.

4. In the dialog box's Description text box, type a description of the bookmarks you plan to place in the folder. You can use this description later to help you locate folders and bookmarks; so enter something that identifies the content.

5. Click on the Next button. The next Assistant dialog box will appear (see Figure A.9).

6. In the dialog box's Keywords text box, type some words that describe the folder. Although you were able to enter entire sentences (such as *A great site for finding out about weather in Sausalito*) in the Description text box in Step 4, here you can enter only a series of distinct words that describe the bookmark (for example, *weather, Sausalito*). Once you are done, click on Finish. The dialog box will close, and the SmartMarks window will reappear with the new folder in view in the left portion of the window.

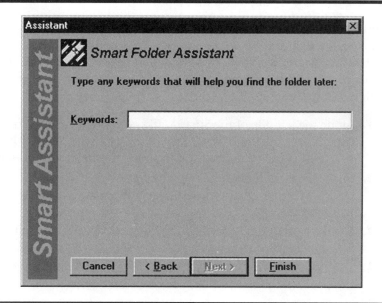

FIGURE A.9: In this Assistant dialog box, you'll specify keywords that describe the folder.

You now have a new SmartMarks folder into which you can place all the bookmarks you know and love.

Automatically Monitoring Pages for Changes

How much time have you and I and many other Netsurfers wasted accessing Web pages to see if they have changed recently, only to find them exactly the same as the last time you viewed them? And how about the time you were the *last* person to know about an important change to a waycool site? SmartMarks solves these among other pressing problems. You can tell SmartMarks to monitor specific pages for any changes that occur, and then the program will notify you when it's time to have a look because something new has been posted. This feature alone—the ability to monitor pages—makes SmartMarks a worthy addition to any Netsurfer's tool kit.

Setting SmartMarks to Track Page Changes

SmartMarks can monitor any bookmark that is in any SmartMarks folder. Once you tell SmartMarks to monitor a bookmark, that bookmark appears in the Web Monitor folder—as well as in any other folders it already occupied. To monitor a bookmark that is in one of your SmartMarks folders, follow these steps:

1. Along the left side of the SmartMarks window, locate the folder that contains the bookmark you want to monitor, and click on it. The right side of the window will update to show the bookmarks in that folder.

2. In the list of bookmarks along the right side of the window, right-click on the bookmark for the page you want to monitor. A menu will appear.

3. From the menu, select Monitor Changes. The Monitor dialog box will appear (see Figure A.10).

4. You now have two choices for how you want SmartMarks to monitor the page. In the dialog box, you can select either

   ◆ Notify me when this page changes

   or

   ◆ Notify me of added or changed links

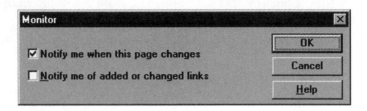

FIGURE A.10: In the Monitor dialog box, you can specify that a given Web page be monitored for changes.

If you select the first option, SmartMarks notifies you whenever the contents of a single page change—when some new text is added or when an image changes, for example. Selecting the second option vastly expands the number of pages SmartMarks monitors. If you select Notify Me of Added or Changed Links, SmartMarks lets you know whenever *a page that is linked to that page* changes. If you select this option for an index of Web resources, such as Yahoo, for example, you can imagine how many pages SmartMarks will monitor.

Select one of the two options by clicking on its checkbox.

5. Click on the OK button to continue. SmartMarks will check the current status of the page (it has to identify what is there now so that it can know when it changes). The page will appear now in the Monitored Items folder as well as in its original folder.

Forever after, until your machine dies or you modify things, SmartMarks will monitor the page and tell you if and when it changes. If you no longer want the page to be monitored, you can remove its bookmark from the Monitored Items folder—this folder behaves just like any other folder—and it will no longer be monitored.

Checking for Changes

Once you have placed bookmarks in the Monitored Items folder, you can specify just when and how SmartMarks will check to see if the pages have changed. You can arrange for either automatic or manual checks to occur.

Setting the Update Frequency You can specify how frequently pages are checked for updates using SmartMarks' Preferences dialog box.

1. With the SmartMarks window open, from the menu bar, select Tools ➤ Preferences. The Preferences dialog box will appear.

2. From the tabs along the top of the Preferences dialog box, click on Internet. The Preferences dialog box will be updated to reflect your choice (see Figure A.11).

3. In the Update Monitored Items area, select one of these options:

Manually	To check for updated links only when you tell it to
At Program Start-up	To check the monitored items when SmartMarks starts
Every	At the specified time interval

If you select the Every option, you can specify the interval at which the checks will occur.

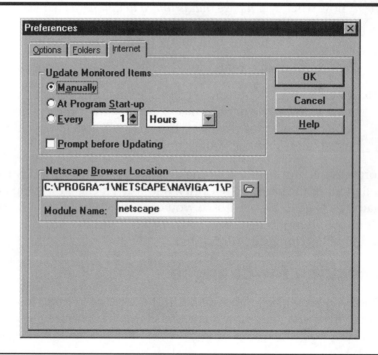

FIGURE A.11: The Internet area of the Preferences dialog box is where you control how SmartMarks checks for updated pages.

4. Click on OK to close the dialog box. The SmartMarks window will reappear, and your references will be implemented.

Checking Now Sometimes you may want to force SmartMarks in the moment to see if any of the pages you are monitoring has changed. You might want to do this because you don't want all that automatic monitoring going on all the time, taking up valuable bandwidth, memory, and storage. You can cause a check to take place right now by using the View menu.

1. In the SmartMarks window, click on the Monitored Items folder or in the Web Monitor area.

2. From the menu bar, choose View ➤ Refresh. All the pages in your Monitored Items folder will be checked.

Retrieving an Updated Page

If one of the pages you are monitoring has been updated, a checkmark will appear to the right of its bookmark in any folder that contains it—including the Monitored Items folder. Its bookmark will also appear in the Web Monitor area of the SmartMarks window. You can load a newly modified page just as you would any other page that appears in a SmartMarks folder—simply double-click on its bookmark in any folder. A new Netscape window will appear, and your Web page will be loaded into it.

Clearing the Flags Once you have loaded the updated page into Netscape, you have to indicate to SmartMarks that you have seen the page and that it should no longer consider the page newly modified.

This is a little weird. You'd think that marking a page as having been read would be as automatic in SmartMarks as it is in e-mail, but them's the breaks.

To do this, follow these steps:

1. Locate the bookmark in any SmartMarks folder or in the Web Monitor area, and right-click on it. A menu will appear.

2. From the menu, select Clear Flags. The checkmark next to the SmartMark will be removed.

That's it. A small but necessary housekeeping task, this one. Now the checkmark will reappear the next time the page is modified, showing that you've looked at the modified page. Until then, it will appear just like all your other bookmarks in SmartMarks—without a checkmark.

It is important to clear the flag after you visit one of your monitored pages. If you don't, it will continue to appear listed as a newly modified page indefinitely.

Searching with SmartMarks

In addition to allowing you to organize and monitor bookmarks, Smart-Marks also offers a powerful search feature. With SmartMarks you can search:

◆ Online catalogs, which we discussed in Chapter 6

◆ Bookmarks you've put into SmartMarks

In this section, we'll look at how to search these two types of resources.

Searching the Internet via SmartMarks

SmartMarks gives you an easy-to-use front-end to four popular search tools on the Web. In particular, you can use the Smart Finder dialog box to search:

◆ Yahoo

◆ Lycos

◆ Web Crawler

◆ InfoSeek

You may wonder why you'd ever want to use SmartMarks to search these resources—they're all available on the Web and are even accessible directly from Netscape. But with SmartMarks you get some additional power:

◆ You don't have to know the resource's URL.

◆ You can use the same dialog box to search any resource—no learning different user interfaces for each search tool.

◆ You can save your searches and have SmartMarks repeat them regularly and inform you of any changes in the results (because, for example, a page is updated).

To use SmartMarks to search the Internet, follow these steps:

1. From the Netscape menu, select Bookmarks ➤ View SmartMarks. The SmartMarks window will appear.

2. From the SmartMarks menu bar, select Tools ➤ Find, or click on the Smart Finder icon on the tool bar.

The Smart Finder dialog box will appear as shown in Figure A.12.

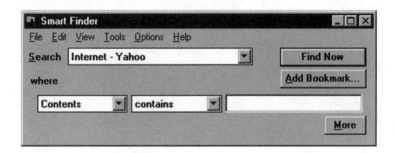

FIGURE A.12: You can use the Smart Finder dialog box to search the bookmarks you have categorized on your computer as well as a number of powerful Internet indexes and databases.

3. In the dialog box's Search drop-down list, select the resource you want to search. Your options are:

◆ Internet–Yahoo

◆ Internet–Lycos

◆ Internet–Web Crawler

◆ Internet–InfoSeek

 Each of these resources indexes its own selection of Web pages. If searching one resource doesn't produce results that interest you, repeat your search using another. For tips on search strategies and tools, see Chapter 7.

4. In the text box of the Where area, type some text that describes what you want to find. In the first drop-down list, specify what you want to search—the Contents or Title, for example. The options you have here depend on what you are searching. For example, the options for searching Yahoo are different from the options for searching Smart-Marks on your machine.

5. In the next drop-down list, specify the type of comparison you want to make. Again, the options you have here depend on what you are searching. In all cases, however, if you select Contains, SmartMarks will search for Web pages whose description contains what you are looking for.

6. Now click on the Find Now button. In a few seconds, the results of your search will appear in the Netscape window. The SmartMarks window will still be on top of the Netscape window, however.

7. Switch to the Netscape window by clicking anywhere within it, and take a look at your search results.

Now you know how to search the Internet using SmartMarks' Smart Finder feature. In the next section, you'll learn how to use Smart Finder to locate pages in the folders you've created to hold your bookmarks.

Searching Your Bookmarks via SmartMarks

Can't quite find that whoop-de-do page you bookmarked just last month? You can use the Smart Finder dialog box, a special feature of SmartMarks, to search the bookmarks you've added to SmartMarks just as you used it to search the entire Internet in the preceding section. When you search your bookmarks for information, you are searching a much smaller—and presumably more focused—set of pages than when you search the entire Internet.

To search through all your SmartMarks bookmarks, follow these steps:

1. From the Netscape menu bar, select Bookmarks ➤ View SmartMarks. The SmartMarks window will appear.

2. From the SmartMarks menu bar, select Tools ➤ Find, or click on the Smart Finder icon on the tool bar.

The Smart Finder dialog box will appear.

3. In the Search drop-down list in the Smart Finder dialog box, you can select what you want to search. Your options are:

◆ All Folders

◆ Folders

 These are the last two options in the Search drop-down list. The first four options are used to access Internet search tools, as described in the previous section.

4. In the text box of the Where area, describe what you want to find. For example, to find all the bookmarks about Netscape, type **Netscape**.

5. In the first drop-down list, specify where you want to search. Your options are:

- ◆ Name
- ◆ Description
- ◆ Comments
- ◆ Keywords

6. In the next drop-down list, specify the type of comparison you want to make. The type of comparison available depends on what you chose to search in Step 5. Your options are:

- ◆ Contains
- ◆ Does not contain
- ◆ Starts with
- ◆ Ends with

7. Now click on the Find Now button. In a few seconds, the results of your search will appear in the lower portion of the Smart Finder window.

8. You can now load any page that Smart Finder found by double-clicking on its bookmark in the bottom part of the Smart Finder window. The SmartMarks window will close, and the page you chose will appear in the Netscape window.

Now you can seek and find whatever interests you via Netscape SmartMarks.

Feature Complete

In this book, we've covered a lot of useful Netscape features, including the very hardworking SmartMarks add-on. Netscape offers other add-ons via the Net. Perhaps you'd like to check out the glamorous chat program. Whatever your fancy, after reading this book you're now armed with all the essential Netscape skills and even a few that are more for fun than anything else.

Internet Service Providers

If you need to set up an account with an Internet service provider so that you can get started with Netscape, this is the place for you. This appendix lists providers that supply the type of service you need to use Netscape.

This list is by no means comprehensive. We concentrate on service providers in the United States, Canada, the United Kingdom, and Australia/New Zealand that offer national or nearly national Internet service. There are also thousands of smaller, regional service providers that offer access to specific geographical areas. Whichever you choose, it is important to find a service provider that offers a local or toll-free access number to minimize your phone bill.

When you inquire into establishing an account with a service provider, tell the service representative that you want a SLIP or a PPP account and that you plan to run Netscape. Make these points very clearly—some providers also offer *shell* accounts, which is not what you want, because you must know Unix commands to use a shell account and (far more important) you cannot run Netscape with a shell account.

What's Out There

Two good sources of information about Internet service providers are available on the Internet itself:

◆ The List is a comprehensive directory of Internet service providers worldwide, searchable by country, area code, and name. You'll find The List at `http://thelist.com`.

◆ Yahoo's list of Internet service providers is also extensive and easy to use. It's at `http://www.yahoo.com/Business_and_Economy/Companies/Internet_Access_Providers/`.

 When you're shopping around for an Internet service provider, the most important questions to ask are (a) Is this a SLIP or a PPP account? (either is fine, although PPP is somewhat better) (b) What is the nearest local access number? (c) What are the monthly service charges? and (d) Are there setup and/or hourly usage fees?

In the United States

In this section we list Internet service providers that have local access phone numbers in most major American cities. These are the big, national companies. Many areas also have smaller regional Internet providers, which may offer better local access if you're not in a big city. You can find out about these smaller companies in two ways:

◆ By looking in local computer papers such as *MicroTimes* or *Computer Currents* or

◆ By getting on the Internet via one of these big companies and checking out The List and Yahoo's service provider listings.

Big and Small Internet Service Providers

In this appendix we focus on the big, national service providers, but smaller, more local providers are also an important option to consider. Both the big guys and the little guys have advantages, which parallel the advantages you might find in, say, a national retail chain and a small local shop. For example, a big service provider offers POPs (points of presence, or local phone numbers to dial in to) all over the place. So if you travel a lot and want to have local Internet access across the country (or across the world), a national provider may be for you. However, lots of other people are also dialing in—the sheer volume of usage may mean you have difficulty connecting sometimes. With all those people to attend to, the big service providers sometimes have trouble getting around to customer service. Local providers, on the other hand, offer access to a smaller geographical area but can be easier to dial into; often they can also give you more personal attention than the big guys can. Often, a local Internet service provider makes special services available to attract and keep its users. For example, DNAI, a small but mighty service provider in the San Francisco Bay Aarea, offers Instant ISDN—it sets up your ISDN account (providing a higher-speed connection that takes special phone lines) and gets it going for you. The folks at DNAI do this at a very reasonable cost; this is just the sort of thing that's a major convenience but that a bigger service provider might not want to get into.

Opening an account with any of the providers listed here will get you full access to the World Wide Web along with full-fledged e-mail service (which allows you to send and receive e-mail). You'll also be able to read and post articles to Usenet newsgroups.

Netcom Netcom Online Communications Services is a national Internet service provider with local access numbers in most major cities. (As of this writing, Netcom has 200 local access numbers in the United States.) Netcom's NetCruiser software gives you point-and-click access to the Internet.

(Netcom also provides a shell account, but stay away from it if you want to run Netscape.) Especially for beginning users who want a point-and-click interface and easy Netscape setup, this may be a good choice.

NetCruiser software is available on disk for free but without documentation at many trade shows and bookstores. It is also available with a very good book (*Access the Internet*, by David Peal, Sybex, 1996) that shows you how to use the software. To contact Netcom directly, phone (800) 353-6600.

Performance Systems International Performance Systems International (PSI) is a national Internet service provider with local access numbers in many U.S. cities and an expanding international presence.

To contact PSI directly, phone (800) 82P-SI82.

UUNet/AlterNet UUNet Technologies and AlterNet offer Internet service throughout the United States. They run their own national network.

To contact UUNet and AlterNet directly, phone (800) 900-0241.

Portal Portal Communications, Inc., an Internet service provider in the San Francisco Bay Area, lets you get connected either by dialing one of its San Francisco Bay Area phone numbers or via the CompuServe or Sprint-Net networks. (This is not CompuServe Information Services, but rather the network on which CompuServe runs.) The CompuServe network, with more than 400 access phone numbers, and SprintNet, with more than 700 local access numbers, are a local call from almost anywhere in the United States.

To contact Portal directly, phone (408) 973-9111.

In Canada

Listed here are providers that offer access to Internet service in the areas around large Canadian cities. For information about local access in less-populated regions, get connected and check out The List and Yahoo resources described earlier in this appendix.

Many Internet service providers in the United States also offer service in Canada and in border towns near Canada. If you're interested and you're in Canada, ask some of the big American service providers whether they have a local number near you.

UUNet Canada UUNet Canada is the Canadian division of the U.S. service provider UUNet/AlterNet, which we described earlier in this appendix. UUNet Canada offers Internet service to large portions of Canada.

To contact UUNet Canada directly, phone (416) 368-6621.

Internet Direct Internet Direct offers access to folks in the Toronto and Vancouver areas.

To contact Internet Direct directly, phone (604) 691-1600.

In the United Kingdom and Ireland

The Internet is, after all, international. Here are some service providers located and offering service in the United Kingdom and Ireland.

EUNet GB Ltd. Located in the northwest part of England, with more locations promised, EUNet offers access across the United Kingdom and has various Internet tools for your use.

To contact EUNet directly, phone 44 1227 266 466.

Easynet London-based Easynet provides Internet service to the majority of the United Kingdom along with a host of Internet tools.

To contact Easynet directly, phone 44 171 209 0990.

Ireland On-Line Serving most (if not all) of Ireland, including Belfast, Ireland On-Line offers complete Internet service, including ISDN and leased-line connections.

To contact Ireland On-Line directly, phone 353 1 855 1739.

In Australia and New Zealand

Down under in Australia and New Zealand the Internet is as happening as it is in the Northern hemisphere; many terrific sites are located in Australia especially. Here are a couple of service providers for that part of the world.

Connect.com.au In wild and woolly Australia, Internet service (SLIP/PPP) is available from Connect.com.au Pty Ltd.

To contact Connect.com.au directly, phone 61 3 528 2239.

Actrix Actrix Networks Limited offers Internet service (PPP accounts) in the Wellington, New Zealand, area.

To contact Actrix directly, phone 64 4 499 1122.

Get Connected, Get Set, GO!

Selecting an Internet service provider is a matter of personal preference and local access. Shop around, and remember—if you aren't satisfied at any point, change providers.

What's on the Disk

Inside the back cover of this book you'll find a disk, and on that disk is a customized home page. All the many, many Internet sites discussed in this book (and then some) are linked to that page. We call it the What's Out There disk, because, obviously, it links you to all the great stuff we've pointed out in the What's Out There boxes throughout this book. You can make the What's Out There page the start-up home page you'll see when you start Netscape, or you can keep it nearby for convenient reference. In either case, you'll get quick access to a wide array of Internet resources, including:

◆ Directories and meta-indexes—such as Magellan, GNN, and Yahoo—that will be your entry point to literally millions of Web pages

◆ Search tools such as Lycos, Inktomi, and InfoSeek that will enable you to find what you seek on the Internet in a jiffy

◆ Sources of free and inexpensive software that will enhance your Internet capabilities

◆ Publishing tools and resources that will get you started and help you to refine and even publicize your own Web publications

◆ Various Best of the Web award givers and winners

What's on the Disk

◆ Hand-selected sites on topics such as Arts and Entertainment, Computers and the Net, Education, Food and Beverages, Government and Politics, Health and Wellness, News and Weather, People Everywhere, Personal Finance, Publishing and Literature, Science and Technology, Sports, Travel, World Wide Weirdness, and Zines

The What's Out There home page takes advantage of the new design features offered in Netscape version 2, providing easy navigation and a lot of information packed into a comprehensive layout (see Figure C.1).

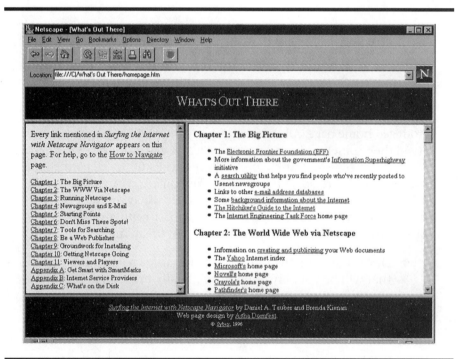

FIGURE C.1: The What's Out There home page you've gotten with this book makes exploring the Internet easy.

The What's Out There page actually (and technically) consists of seven interlinked HTML and graphic files that are stored in a single folder on the disk. All you have to do is copy the folder to your hard drive (a simple task with Windows 95) and launch Netscape, and then you can view the page. Read on for easy instructions.

Copying the Home Page onto Your Hard Drive

The first part of this process is to copy the home page folder to your hard drive.

1. Insert the disk into your floppy disk drive. (We'll assume you're using drive A: here, but if you use drive B:, just change A: to B: in the instructions that follow.)

2. From your desktop, double-click on the My Computer icon to display your computer's hard disk and floppy drives.

3. Double-click on the 3½ Floppy A: drive icon to display the contents of the What's Out There disk. You'll see one folder named WHAT'S OUT THERE.

4. Copy the WHAT'S OUT THERE folder to your hard drive by clicking on it and dragging it to the drive C: icon.

That's all there is to it. Now let's take a look at your new home page.

Launching Netscape and Looking at the Page

Now that the files are stored on your hard drive, you can use Netscape to view the What's Out There home page.

 Although you don't have to be connected to the Internet to view the page, you do need to be connected to follow many of its hyperlinks, because they point to sites all over the Net.

1. Launch Netscape. (See Chapter 3 if you need more details.)

2. From the menu bar, select File ➤ Open File. The Open dialog box will appear.

3. Click on the Look In pull-down list and select your hard drive (in our case, it's drive C:) to make its contents visible in the dialog box's big text area. (See Figure C.2.)

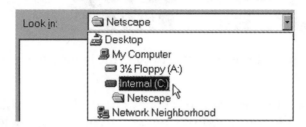

FIGURE C.2: Select your hard drive from the pull-down list.

4. Double-click on the WHAT'S OUT THERE folder to open it.

5. Double-click on HOMEPAGE.HTM (see Figure C.3). The Netscape N icon will become animated, and the What's Out There page will appear on your screen.

The What's Out There page has been created especially for users of Netscape version 2. (You're one of those folks, right?) If you open the page using another browser (or a version of Netscape earlier than 2.0), you won't be able to see the thing. Instead, a message will appear saying that the page is viewable only using Netscape version 2.0 or later.

Navigating the Page

The What's Out There page takes advantage of *frames*, a terrific design effect new in Netscape version 2. Each frame is actually the result of a distinct HTML file; all the frames are displayed in one viewing window—it's as if several Web pages were combined into one screen. In fact, it isn't *like* that—it is that. Pages that use frames present new options for navigating around. For helpful information about how to get around this particular page, click on the How to Navigate link in the page's left frame.

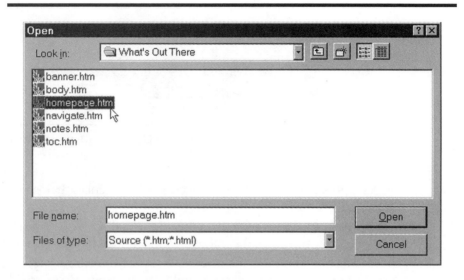

FIGURE C.3: Double-click on the file named HOMEPAGE.HTM to open it.

Making the What's Out There Page Your Home Page

You can keep the What's Out There page on your hard disk and open it whenever you like to use as a reference source, while retaining some other page as your start-up home page. Or you can make the What's Out There page your start-up home page—that is, the page that automatically appears each and every time you launch Netscape. We went over this in Chapter 3, but let's take a quick look at the process again.

1. Launch Netscape.

2. Open the What's Out There page using the instructions in the *Launching Netscape and Looking at the Page* section earlier in this appendix.

3. A URL beginning with the phrase `file:///` will be visible in the Location text box near the top of the Netscape viewing window. Click on the URL to highlight it. (See Figure C.4.)

4. From the menu bar, select Edit ➤ Copy (or press Ctrl+X) to copy the page's location to the Clipboard (the page location will remain stored there until you are ready to use it in a moment in Step 7).

What's on the Disk

FIGURE C.4: Here you can see the location of the file for the What's Out There page, appearing in the familiar format of a URL.

5. Select Options ➤ General Preferences. The Preferences dialog box will appear.

6. Click on the Appearance tab at the top of the dialog box. The dialog box will change to make that set of preferences visible (see Figure C.5).

7. In the Startup section of the dialog box, select the Home Page Location button, click in the text box under it, and then press Ctrl+V to paste in the location of the What's Out There page (you copied it to the Clipboard in Step 4, remember?). It'll look like Figure C.6 when you're done.

9. Click on the OK button at the bottom of the Preferences dialog box.

10. From Netscape's menu bar, select Options ➤ Save Options to save the change you just made.

Now, each and every time you start Netscape, the What's Out There page will be your launch point.

You can add your favorite links to the What's Out There page using the HTML skills you learned in Chapter 8. Read on to find out more.

● Adding Your Own Links to the Page

As your Web exploration expands, you may want to add your own newly discovered hyperlinks to the What's Out There page. You can keep adding stuff and expanding the page all you like, customizing it for your own

Preferences ☒

| Appearance | Fonts | Colors | Images | Apps | Helpers | Language |

Toolbars

Show Toolbar as: ⊙ Pictures   ○ Text   ○ Pictures and Text

Startup

On Startup Launch:

☐ Netscape Browser   ☐ Netscape Mail   ☐ Netscape News

Start With: ○ Blank Page   ⊙ Home Page Location:

    http://home.netscape.com

Link Styles

Links are: ☑ Underlined

Followed Links: ○ Never Expire   ⊙ Expire After: 30 Days   [Expire Now]

[OK]   [Cancel]   [Apply]   [Help]

FIGURE C.5: The Preferences dialog box

Startup

On Startup Launch:

☐ Netscape Browser   ☐ Netscape Mail   ☐ Netscape News

Start With: ○ Blank Page   ⊙ Home Page Location:

    file:///C|/What's Out There/homepage.htm

FIGURE C.6: Paste in the location of the What's Out There page.

purposes. All you need is some basic HTML know-how (which you have if you've gone through the exercises in Chapter 8 of this book). The home page files are fully customizable, and you can make any changes to them you want.

The What's Out There home page is a document whose copyright is held by Sybex. You can copy and customize the document for your own use, but you may not copy or distribute the document for the use of others.

It's always a good idea to make changes to your important files on copies, not on the original files.

The HTML file that contains the hyperlinks to Internet sites is called BODY.HTM. It is stored on your hard drive in the WHAT'S OUT THERE folder. To add your own links, simply open BODY.HTM using your word processor, add hyperlinks where you would like them to appear in the page (see Chapter 8 for details), and then save and close the document. The next time you open the What's Out There page using Netscape, your links will appear.

Of course, making more sophisticated changes in the home page requires more HTML expertise—that's the sort of thing you'll want to get into only if you have some serious HTML experience.

What's Out There

Although the HTML processes you need to use to create frames are a bit advanced, they're not very difficult to learn. If you'd like to look into learning how to make frames in your pages, go to http://home.netscape .com/comprod/products/navigator/version_2.0/frames/index.html or click on the Netscape's introduction to the HTML behind frames link in the *Appendix C* section of the What's Out There page.

Surf's Up!

You've got everything you need to surf the Internet with Netscape Navigator. You've got the skills, the software, and now the convenient What's Out There home page. You're on your way....

Glossary

anchors Links, from the other side of the picture—*anchor* is HTML-lingo for a text or image link to any other document.

anonymous FTP A *File Transfer Protocol* that lets *anyone* (regardless of whether he or she has a user name or password) transfer files from the server machine to his or her own.

applet A "small" application or program that, when written in Java and embedded into a Web page, adds extra pizzazz and functionality to Netscape. *See* Java; application.

application A computer program designed to specialize in a specific set of tasks. Word and WordPerfect are word-processing applications; Excel and Quattro Pro are spreadsheet applications.

ARPAnet A now-defunct experimental network of the 1970s on which the theories and systems that became today's Internet were tested. ARPA-net is short for *Advanced Research Project Agency network.*

article A message posted to a Usenet newsgroup and readable with a newsreader.

ASCII The acronym for *American Standard Code for Information Interchange;* a basic text format most computers can read.

authentication A security feature, *authentication* lets users have access to information only if they can provide a user name and password that the security system recognizes.

backbone One of the high-speed networks that form the core, or "backbone," of the Internet.

bandwidth The amount of data that can be sent through a communications channel such as a network or a modem.

baud A measurement of the speed at which signals are sent by a modem (more precisely, a measurement of the number of changes per second that occur during transmission). A baud rate of 2400, for example, indicates that 2400 signal changes occur in one second. Baud rate is often confused with *bps* (bits per second), which is defined below.

BBS An online *bulletin board system;* an electronic place provided by kind strangers or misguided entrepreneurs for people with like interests to post (make public) messages in an ongoing conversation, and to upload and download software and files.

binary transfer A transfer of data between computers in which binary data is preserved; often the best type of transfer for software and graphic images.

bitmap An electronic file that represents an image with a collection of bits. (A bit is smaller than a byte.)

bookmark A method for marking and tracking pages for easy retrieval.

bounced message A message that has been returned is known as one that has *bounced.* Usually this happens because the address was incorrect.

bps A measurement—*bits per second*—of the speed at which data is transferred between modems. Higher bps rates indicate faster transfer. *See* baud.

browser Software that enables the user to look at, interact with, and generally "browse" files on the Internet.

BTW Electronic shorthand for *by the way.*

bye A log-off command that means essentially "quit" or "exit."

CERN *The Conseil Européen pour la Recherche Nucleaire*—the European particle physics laboratory that was the birthplace of the World Wide Web.

client A computer that *receives;* the computer that connects to a *server.* *See* server.

commercial online service A provider of content to subscribers. This content may include access to the Internet, but commercial online services (America Online, CompuServe, and Prodigy, for example) are *not* part of the Internet.

compressed   (a) A term used to describe data that has been *shrunk* or "zipped." This process, performed by utility programs such as PKZip, LHArc, and Zip, makes it possible to conserve storage space and to transfer files more quickly; (b) A process of shrinking motion picture files by leaving out some frames, retaining only as many as are necessary to create the perception of action. QuickTime and MPEG are examples of the use of this process.

configure   To set up or make programs, applications, and computer systems work together.

copyright   The right of ownership to a work (document, art, music, etc.). *See* public domain.

dedicated   A line, server, or other piece of computer-associated equipment that has only one purpose; a *dedicated line,* for example, might be a phone line that leads *only* to your PC (or modem) and *not* also to a phone.

dial-up   A connection to a computer that is accomplished by calling on a phone line with a modem.

Dial-Up Networking   The component of Windows 95 that allows you to dial-up an Internet service provider with very little fuss or muss.

dir   A shorthand version of the commonly used command *directory.* If at a DOS prompt or an FTP site you type dir and press ↵, you will see the contents of the current directory.

distribution   A variation on the original software, usually enhanced, that is being distributed by parties who did not develop the software but who are licensed or permitted to add to and distribute the software. This differs from a *version* in that it does not represent a generation in the development of the software. Air Mosaic is an enhanced distribution of the original Mosaic; Netscape Navigator is not a distribution of Mosaic but rather a whole new product.

domain   A level in an address, as defined in the Domain Name system (see below). In the address, domains are separated by a period, as in ed.sybex.com.

Domain Name system   A system for classifying computers into increasingly large groups with names; for example, in laxness.ed.sybex.com, *laxness* is a specific machine in a group named *ed*itorial in a company called *sybex* that is in the general category of *com*mercial.

download To transfer files to your machine from another machine.

drive A physical device on which you can store files. Each drive is identified by a letter (A:, B:, C:, etc.).

driver A program that tells your computer what to do with something added to your computer—a printer, a mouse, a sound board, and so on.

e-mail The common way to refer to *electronic mail;* messages that are addressed to an individual at a computer and sent electronically.

emoticon *See* smiley.

encryption Disguising a message (by scrambling it) to prevent intruders from reading it.

FAQ Electronic shorthand for *frequently asked question.*

file transfer The movement of a file from one computer to another over a network or via a modem.

firewall A security system that creates an electronic barrier protecting an organization's network and PCs from access by outsiders via the Internet.

flame A very unfriendly, often violent, written attack against someone in an electronic forum such as a newsgroup or a message area. (A *flame war* occurs when both parties engage in and continue such an exchange, perhaps even inspiring others in the newsgroup or message area to take sides.)

form support To *support* is to allow for or to be capable of using; a Web browser that has form support is one that allows for (is capable of using) on-screen *forms,* which are on-screen versions of the types of forms you'd usually see on paper. Netscape includes form support.

frames A new feature in Netscape Navigator version 2 that allows the appearance of several Web pages on screen (in "frames" within one document). Each frame can have its own scroll bars and other navigational features.

Free-net A network in a community providing free access to the Internet; often the Free-net includes the community's own forums and news.

freeware Programs that are distributed free of charge by those who developed them.

front end   The "face" you see on a program, its *interface*, is also often called its *front end*. Sometimes, one program provides a *front end* for other programs or for viewing data or files. Thus, Netscape is a front end for the Internet.

FTP   The abbreviation for *File Transfer Protocol,* a standard, agreed-upon way for electronic interaction to occur in the transferring of files from one computer to another over the Internet. *See* anonymous FTP.

FYI   Electronic shorthand for *for your information.*

gateway   A computer system that transfers data or messages between programs or networks that are normally incompatible.

Gopher   A menu-based system for finding directories on the Internet. Gopher will "go-fer" what you ask it to find.

graphical   Represented by pictures or icons.

GUI   Short for *graphical user interface;* a gui (pronounced *gooey*) provides a way for you to interact with your computer by pointing and clicking or otherwise manipulating pictures and icons on the screen.

hack   To fiddle around "behind the scenes" in a program or a system, presumably to make improvements or to find out how the thing works. (A "hacker" is actually someone who makes furniture with an axe. No kidding.)

header   The information at the *head* or top of a page, as in the message header containing the To:, From:, and Time/Date information in an e-mail message.

hit   A single access of an Internet resource (example: the Enterzone home page gets more than 20,000 *hits* per day).

home page   The main screen in a World Wide Web site; a home page is like a cross between the cover of a book its Table of Contents. But just as you can flip open a book and start reading anywhere within it you don't necessarily have to start at the home page. You can dig anywhere in the web site.

host   *See* server.

HTML   The abbreviation for *HyperText Markup Language,* the language used to make ordinary text into Web documents. HTML + and HTML 3.0 include enhancements to the original HTML.

HTTP   The abbreviation for *HyperText Transfer Protocol;* the agreed-upon standard way for electronic interaction to occur in the transferring of Web documents on the Internet.

hypermedia   Hypertext combined with graphics, sound, and even video.

hypertext   Text that includes links to other documents.

IMHO   Electronic shorthand for *in my humble opinion.*

Infobahn   The hip and cool term for the so-called Information Superhighway.

inline image   A graphic *in* a Web page—a graphic that does not have to be downloaded to be viewed.

interface   The "face" a program shows you, with which you interact.

Internet   A global, interconnected network of networks (and single computers that act as if they were networks).

Internet service provider   The company or organization that provides a connection to the Internet. Internet service providers offer access but not content. *See* commercial online service.

IP   The abbreviation for *Internet Protocol; see* TCP/IP.

ISOC   The abbreviation for *Internet Society,* a group whose purpose is to support and govern the Internet.

Java   A programming language developed by Sun Microsystems and implemented in Netscape Navigator version 2. *See* applet.

knowbot   An information-retrieval tool, still experimental but wonderfully named.

LAN   The acronym for *local area network;* a lot of machines (well, at least *two*) cabled together so they can share resources such as printers and software.

link   A connection between Web documents, sometimes called a *hot link.*

LiveScript   A programming language similar to Java but developed by Netscape Communications. Web-site developers can extend the functionality of Netscape by embedding LiveScript programs in their pages. *See* Java; applet.

local Your local machine is the one on your desk, the one that's nearby. Your local drive is the one on your machine. Local is the opposite of *remote.*

lurker Someone who lurks about on a Usenet newsgroup or other interactive forum without contributing anything to the talk. A silent voyeur. Many people think it best to lurk for a while before you join in; that way you'll get to know the customs and avoid social blunders.

modem The device that connects your computer to a phone line so you can make connections via the phone line to other modems, which are connected to remote machines.

Mosaic Any of a group of programs that lets you browse hypertext pages on the World Wide Web. NCSA was the original. Netscape is a Mosaic-like Web browser, but is not actually a Mosaic.

multimedia The combination and use of *multiple types of media* (graphics, sound, video, and text) in a single document or presentation.

NCSA The abbreviation for *National Center for Supercomputing Applications,* a federally funded research lab run by the University of Illinois that was the birthplace of the original Mosaic.

NetCruiser Internet access software developed by Netcom On-Line Communications

NetLauncher Software provided by CompuServe to allow its members to run Internet programs such as Netscape.

Netsite Commerce server A Web server, developed and sold by Netscape Communications, that allows providers to make secure transactions available.

network A lot of (or even just two) computers linked via cables or phone lines so they can share resources, such as software, printers, and so on.

network administrator The person who organizes, maintains, troubleshoots, and generally watches over a network.

newsgroups Usenet message areas, each of which is focused on a particular topic.

node A machine on the Internet.

online To be ready or electronically connected.

operating system A program that controls the most basic functions of a computer.

packet Data bundled together—a packet may be thought of as similar to an envelope full of data, with some of the data contained in the envelope actually representing the address or destination information. Packets of data traverse the Internet independently of each other because IP, the Internet protocol, is connectionless and orderless.

path The complete description of the location of a file on a specific machine.

player A helper program that lets you hear sound. *See* viewer.

point-and-click access An Internet access account that provides you with a Windows-type graphical user interface—one in which you point and click your way around the Internet. *See* GUI, shell account.

point of presence A phone number that gives you (presumably) local access to a specific Internet service provider. Sometimes, unfortunately, there's quite a distance from the nearest point of presence (POP) to you, in which case you may be charged long-distance fees by your phone company for the time you're online.

port (a) One of a machine's input/output plugs; (b) A number that identifies a particular Internet server.

post To make public, as in *posting a message*.

PPP The abbreviation for *Point-to-Point Protocol,* an agreed-upon way for the interaction to occur on a phone line, which allows packets to be transferred along an Internet connection.

protocol An agreed-upon way for an interaction to occur.

public domain To be in the public domain is to be *not* copyrighted; to be available to the public at large. Information or art is *not* in the public domain simply because it's on the Internet.

real-time The Internet term that means *live,* as in "real-time conversation" (a *chat*).

remote Somewhere else. A *remote machine* is not near you; it is somewhere else.

robot An information-gathering tool; a program that wanders the Web gathering data and building a database of resources. Also known as a *spider,* a *wanderer,* or a *crawler.*

router A machine that transfers packets of data between networks.

RTFM Electronic shorthand for *read the f***ing manual.*

searchable A document or database that can be searched for specific information.

secure transaction An interaction (which may or may not involve money changing hands), over the Internet, that is *encrypted* to protect against prying "eyes." *See* SHTTP; SSL.

self-extracting archive file A compressed file that uncompresses itself. *See* compressed.

server A computer that *serves;* the computer that provides stuff to a *client.* *See* client.

shareware Software that is made available by its developer for people to use on a trial basis and, if they like it, to continue to use in exchange for a one-time fee. *Shareware is not in the public domain.*

shell account A Unix-based Internet access account—one in which you have to type Unix commands to make your way around the Internet. Portal Communications and Netcom offer shell accounts, as do some other service providers and many universities. *See* point-and-click access.

SHTTP A form of HTTP, also known as *Secure HTTP,* that allows secure transactions to take place over the Internet.

SLIP The acronym for *Serial Line Internet Protocol,* an agreed-upon way for the interaction to occur on a phone line allowing packets to be transferred along an Internet connection.

smiley Any of a lot of little pictures drawn with keyboard characters to indicate an emotion or to illustrate a sentence. The first one in common use was meant to indicate a smile. :-)

snail-mail What the U.S. Postal Service carries and delivers.

spider *See* robot.

SSL The abbreviation for *Secure Socket Layer*, which is the protocol developed by Netscape Communications to allow for secure transactions over the Internet.

support To *support* is to allow for the use of; as an example, software that supports hypertext is software that allows you to view or create hypertext.

system administrator *See* network administrator.

TCP/IP The abbreviation for *Transmission Control Protocol/Internet Protocol,* the agreed-upon way machines on the Internet interact with one another by sending packets across multiple networks until they reach their destinations.

Telnet An Internet program with which you can log onto another machine (with permission, of course).

time out What happens when two machines are interacting and one does not respond—the other one *times out.*

Unix The operating system used to develop the Internet.

upload To transfer files from your machine to another machine.

URL The abbreviation for *Universal Resource Locator,* an address or a location of a document on the World Wide Web. URL is pronounced *you-are-ell.*

Usenet An informal, anarchistic network of machines that exchange public messages, also known as *news.* Usenet *newsgroups* tend to focus on specific topics.

version A new form of a program, usually with new features and tools; often indicated by a number tacked onto the end of the program's name.

viewer A helper program that lets you look at video. *See* player.

Wanderer *See* robot.

Web *See* World Wide Web.

Web crawler *See* robot.

workstation   (a) The physical area where you work on your computer; (b) A desktop computer, typically more powerful than a PC, running Unix.

World Wide Web   On the Internet, a loose network of documents of different types, connected through hypertext links embedded in the documents themselves.

Worm   *See* robot.

zip, zipped   *See* compressed.

Index

Note to the Reader: Throughout this index **boldface** page numbers indicate primary discussions of a topic. *Italic* page numbers indicate illustrations.

Surf Savvy with the What's Out There Disk

What's out there on the Net is easy to find with the help of this book and its companion disk. The book shows you how to get and use Netscape, yes, but it also shows you what's out there that will deepen and add dimension to your Internet experience. You can get to that stuff in an instant with this disk.

On the What's Out There disk is a customized home page, easy to use as your own start-up home page, that includes links to:

◆ Directories and meta-indexes such as Magellan, GNN, and Yahoo that will be your entry point to literally millions of Web pages

◆ Search tools such as Lycos, Inktomi, and InfoSeek that will enable you to find what you seek on the Internet in a jiffy

◆ Sources of free and inexpensive software that will enhance your Internet capabilities

◆ Publishing tools and resources that will get you started and help you to refine and even publicize your own Web publications

◆ Various Best of the Web award givers

◆ Hand-selected sites on topics such as Arts and Entertainment, Computers and the Net, Education, Food and Beverages, Government and Politics, Health and Wellness, News and Weather, People Everywhere, Personal Finance, Publishing and Literature, Science and Technology, Sports, Travel, World Wide Weirdness, and Zines

All the many, many Internet sites discussed in this book are linked to the customized home page provided on this disk. You can make it the start-up home page you'll see when you start Netscape, or you can keep it nearby for convenient reference. In either case, you'll get quick access to thousands of Internet resources. See Appendix C for easy installation instructions for the What's Out There disk.